GEORGE Q. CANNON

George Q. Cannon

GEORGE Q. CANNON

POLITICIAN, PUBLISHER, APOSTLE OF POLYGAMY

KENNETH L. CANNON II

SIGNATURE BOOKS | 2023 | SALT LAKE CITY

To Ann

Join our mail list at www.signaturebooks.com for details on events and related titles we think you'll enjoy.

Design by Jason Francis

FIRST EDITION | 2023

LIBRARY OF CONGRESS CONTROL NUMBER: 2023939918

Paperback ISBN: 978-1-56085-459-3
Ebook ISBN: 978-1-56085-438-8

CONTENTS

ABBREVIATIONS

AHCJ — Abraham H. Cannon Journal, USHS

Bitton, *GQC* — Davis Bitton, *George Q. Cannon: A Biography,* Salt Lake City: Deseret Book Co., 1999

BY — Brigham Young

BYUS — *BYU Studies*

CD — Brian H. Stuy, ed., *Collected Discourses,* 5 vols., n.p., B.H.S. Publishing, 1987–92

CFHT — Beatrice Cannon Evans and Janath Russell Cannon, eds., *Cannon Family Historical Treasury*, 1st ed., Salt Lake City: George Q. Cannon Family Association, 1967

CHC — B. H. Roberts, *A Comprehensive History of the Church of Jesus Christ of Latter-day Saints*, 6 vols., Salt Lake City: Deseret News Press, 1930

CHL — Church History Library, Historical Department of the Church of Jesus Christ of Latter-day Saints, Salt Lake City

Dialogue — *Dialogue: A Journal of Mormon Thought*

DN — *Deseret News* (daily edition) or *Deseret Evening News*

DW — *Deseret News* (weekly edition), *Deseret Weekly* or *Deseret News Weekly*

GQC — George Q. Cannon

GQCJ — George Q. Cannon Journal, Historical Department of the Church of Jesus Christ of Latter-day Saints. Available at churchhistorianspress.org

GQCJH	Chad Orton, ed., *The Journals of George Q. Cannon, Hawaiian Mission, 1850–1854*, Salt Lake City: Deseret Book Co., 2014
GQCJ Cal	Michael N. Landon, ed., *The Journals of George Q. Cannon, Volume I, To California in '49*, Salt Lake City: Deseret Book Co., 1999
HJGJ	Heber J. Grant Letterbook Journal, CHL
JD	*Journal of Discourses*, 26 vols., Liverpool: various publishers and publication dates
JH	*Journal History of the Church*, CHL
JI	*Juvenile Instructor*
JMH	*Journal of Mormon History*
KLC	Kenneth L. Cannon II
MS	*Millennial Star*
NYT	*New York Times*
SLH	*Salt Lake Herald*
SLT	*Salt Lake Tribune*
USHS	Utah State Historical Society, Salt Lake City
UHQ	*Utah Historical Quarterly*
WS	*Western Standard*
WWJ	Dan Vogel, ed., *The Wilford Woodruff Journals*, 6 vols., Salt Lake City: Benchmark Books, 2020

PROLOGUE

BROTHER PUKUNIAHI RETURNS TO THE ISLANDS[1]

"These two days have been days of unalloyed happiness and enjoyment."
—George Q. Cannon, Dec. 13, 1900

George Q. Cannon stood along the rails of the steamship and watched as the ship passed the big island of Hawai'i, then Maui, then Moloka'i in the afternoon sun. Finally, as the sun set, the natural entrance to Honolulu harbor appeared. Cannon remembered the first time he sailed into the harbor, almost exactly fifty years before.[2] He had been a green twenty-three-year-old missionary "full of zeal and vigor, freshly sent from the California gold fields" where he and other young Latter-day Saints had panned for gold hoping to improve the dire financial condition of their church.[3] Now, in December 1900, Cannon returned to the Sandwich Islands for the first time to celebrate the golden anniversary of the opening of the church's mission there. He returned to this celebration as the most famous living Latter-day Saint, viewed by admirers as a man of extraordinary talent, character, vision, and inspiration. To detractors, he was the "Mormon premier," "the sweetest, smoothest, and most plausible sophist in all this round earth," and "the most vindictive,

1. The Hawaiian Book of Mormon, *Buke a Moramona*, was largely translated by George Q. Cannon and published under his name in San Francisco in 1855. His name was listed as "Geogi Q. Pukuniahi." "Pukuniahi" is Hawaiian for cannon and is what some called him in the islands. GQCJ, Aug. 27, 1890.

2. GQCJ, Dec. 10, 1900. Ships steamed with the prevailing currents and would circle south of the islands and turn north as they headed to Honolulu.

3. GQCJ, Nov. 29, 1900.

and ... blood-thirsty of all the Mormon Priesthood."[4] As the first counselor in the sect's First Presidency, he was the official emissary of the church, but this trip meant much more to him personally. Because this trip was so important to him, he brought his wife Caroline "Carlie" Young Cannon and three of his youngest sons, Clawson (15), Espey (14), and Georgius (8).[5]

In 1850, the ten young Mormon missionaries originally called to serve in the Sandwich Islands were impoverished and could barely cover their passage aboard the *Imaum of Muscat*.[6] Once they arrived, they were strangers "to the people and to the language and friendless and homeless."[7] Now President Cannon came aboard the venerable *SS Zealandia*, a relatively luxurious steamship that had carried mail across the Pacific Ocean, Chinese workers from China to San Francisco, and American soldiers to and from the Philippines during the Spanish-American War.[8] He, Carlie (his official, though last, wife), and the boys traveled in staterooms, ate formal meals, periodically experienced seasickness, and had a relatively pleasant seven-day voyage from San Francisco to Honolulu.[9]

Cannon had had a remarkably successful three-and-a-half year mission in Hawai'i a half century before, spending most of his time on Maui. While half of the original missionaries decided not to remain in the islands and soon left, Cannon and the others remained. He and his companions quickly realized that they would never be successful in converting the small white population, and they chose to focus their proselyting efforts primarily on the natives. He and the others struggled to find places to live, but most of them were met with extraordinary kindness and generosity.

A Hawaiian woman named Nalimanui gave George, Henry Bigler, and James Keeler her modest home near Lahaina on the island of Maui to live in. As he later recorded in his journal and recounted to

4. C. C. Goodwin, "The Political Attitude of the Mormons," *North American Review*, 132 (Mar. 1881): 282; "The Blood Atoner," *SLT*, Oct. 13, 1874, 4.

5. Clawson and Georgius were George and Carlie's sons, Espey was the son of George and his fourth wife, Martha Telle.

6. *GQCJH*, xxxix, 15–16.

7. GQCJ, Dec. 13, 1900.

8. "Passenger on the Mail Steamer Zealandia Drops a Roll of Greenbacks into the Bay While Taking Off His Hat to His Lady Friend," *San Francisco Call*, Dec. 4, 1900, 13.

9. GQCJ, Dec. 4–10, 1900.

a few carefully chosen audiences, it was in the garden of this humble abode that he had sought "the Lord in secret prayer." In response he had been visited by Jesus Christ and "heard his voice more than once as one man speaks with another and showing me the work which should be done among this people if I would follow the dictates of his spirit."[10] This experience was life-transforming for young Cannon.

Over the next three years, with hard work and faith, he learned the Hawaiians' language, adapted to their food, and fearlessly taught the gospel. Looking back with fifty years of hindsight, his feelings were "indescribable when I see how fully the Lord has full filled his words to me concerning that which should be accomplished."[11] He had baptized hundreds, demonstrated the force of his deep faith and devotion to his church while also displaying the energy, administrative and political talents, speaking skills, and native quick intelligence that soon brought him to the attention of Brigham Young in Great Salt Lake City. He had organized native Latter-day Saints into congregations and ordained male natives as elders to lead those congregations. He had visited and negotiated with government leaders in an attempt to gain official recognition of Mormon missionary work and was rebuffed by almost all. With critical native assistance, George had translated and published the Book of Mormon into Hawaiian.[12]

Now, he returned to Honolulu for a two-day celebration as the official representative of the First Presidency of the Church of Jesus Christ of Latter-day Saints. As the *Zealandia* docked at the wharf, throngs of Hawaiian Saints and missionaries gathered to meet George Q. Cannon and his party with leis and open arms. They all knew the legend of the man—how he had established the church in the islands, had learned their language well enough to translate the Book of Mormon, was called as an apostle in the church at the age

10. GQCJ, Dec. 27, 1900, spelling corrected. Cannon's fifteen-year-old son, Clawson, acted as his amanuensis and his spelling was not perfect. In the 1880s and 1890s, Cannon testified to several groups of his experience in Hawai'i, for example, speaking to a group of young people in Canada in 1889 he said, "I testified that the Lord Jesus lived, for I had seen Him and heard His voice, and I had heard the voice of the Spirit, speaking to me as one man speaketh to another." GQCJ, Nov. 4, 1889.

11. GQCJ, Nov. 4, 1889.

12. GQC, *My First Vision* (Salt Lake City: Juvenile Instructor Office, 1979), 60–62.

of thirty-three, just a few years after leaving the islands, and gone on to become the world's best-known living Mormon after Brigham Young's death. The San Francisco and Honolulu papers covered his trip and the local papers reported all his doings in Hawai'i, usually on their front pages. He was identified as the "brains of the Mormon Church," "the founder of Mormonism in Hawaii," and "the real leader of the great Mormon Church."[13]

While he had initially been homeless in Maui as a missionary, he and Carlie and the boys were hosted in the commodious home, near Honolulu, of Abraham and Minerva Fernandez, affluent Hawaiian Saints who were delighted to have the Cannons stay with them.[14] After a good night's rest, he was ready for the golden jubilee of the Hawaiian Mission, an event the Hawaiian Saints had been planning for months and that he had been anticipating with relish.

The golden anniversary celebrations lasted two full days, beginning Wednesday, December 12. From the 10:00 a.m. start time, music was everywhere—church bands, a city group that was a "very fine band and not excelled by any on the Coast," large choirs, small choirs, sextets, quartets, duets, and solos. Some of the music was distinctly Mormon, some was Hawaiian, some pieces were patriotic American numbers, while others were Protestant hymns. Attendees were mostly Latter-day Saints from all over Hawai'i. Visitors from Utah, government officials, and leaders and members of other churches also attended. The entire community joined in the festivities. Several thousand excited participants filled every seat and open space in the Orpheum auditorium. Many Utah church leaders and Hawaiian Saints addressed the throng.[15]

In the morning session, Cannon was the main speaker. In contemplation of his return to the islands, he dreaded two things, violent seasickness, to which he had been susceptible his entire life, and his

13. "Mormon President Cannon Here for the Big Jubilee," *Hawaiian Gazette*, Dec. 11, 1900, 4; "Mormon Jubilee to Begin Today," *Pacific Commercial Advertiser*, Dec. 12, 1900, 1.

14. Abraham and Minerva Fernandez were both from the traditional nobility of Hawai'i. Abraham had served in the Queen's privy council before the queen was deposed. The Fernandezes were baptized in the mid-1890s and quickly became stalwart members of the Mormon Church and the Mormon community. R. Lanier Britsch, *Moramona, The Mormons in Hawai'i*, 2nd ed. (La'ie, HI: BYU Hawaii, 2018), 213.

15. GQCJ, Dec. 12, 1900; "Music, Feast, and Addresses Abounded, Anniversary Jubilee of Mormon Church Well Attended," *Honolulu Republican*, Dec. 13, 1900, 1.

"inability to talk the native language." "Through the blessing of the Lord upon me, He removed all my causes for dread." The sea voyage was pleasant. Now, he hoped for the Lord's blessings as he filled his role as the main speaker in all the festivities. In the morning he spoke principally in English "with great power." He told stories of the first Mormon missionaries to the islands "in an interesting manner" as the audience listened intently. As he did so, to his surprise and the "delight of the people," the "spirit of the Lord would bring the Native Language back to me," and he gave parts of all his speeches in Hawaiian. He noted that it "was a great cause of wonder to them that I should be able to speak in their language at all after so long an absence from the Islands." The *Honolulu Republican* reported that Cannon's "voice still possesses great clearness and his remarks could be heard throughout the entire auditorium." Cannon grew emotional over the extraordinary "loving affection for me," and he "was honored to my heart's content."[16]

Festivities shifted about 2:00 p.m. to a large luau held in what Cannon referred to as the "Government Armory" and the newspapers called the "Drill Shed." Six tables that accommodated 500 or 600 at a time were "covered with food." A local paper referred to "the bill of fare" as "poi, beef, pork, lipoa, loli, alamihi, limu, alaula, hee, opae, amaama, and awa."[17] George Q. described the food as "oxen, sheep, chicken, and fish and everything that the sea produces, . . . sweet potatoes and other vegetables and poi for the natives and suitable diet for the white people." He also fondly remembered how much he "relished" "squid or hee." Between 1,500 and 2,000 people were fed at the gargantuan luau and George Q. noted the delight of all because "no nation or people enjoy gustatory performances more than the Hawaiians."[18]

The festivities were to have returned to the Orpheum at 7:00 p.m., but long before that, "every available seat" in the auditorium was once again filled. To cap the first day's festivities, a "stereopticon [slide projector] was brought into action" with excellent views of

16. GQCJ, Dec. 12, 1900; "Music, Feast."
17. "Music, Feast."
18. "Music, Feast"; GQCJ, Dec. 12, 1900. "He'e" in Hawaiian is usually translated as octopus.

"Utah, Hawaii, and other island points of interest" as well as many other places of "religious and historical interests." Wonderful music continued to fill the auditorium for several hours.[19] George Q. noted in his diary that the program had "passed off excelently [*sic*] and this ended a day of great enjoyment for me.[20]

If the celebrations were too much for the aging church leader, he made no showing of it. The next day, again at 10:00 a.m., the golden jubilee resumed at the Orpheum with a large choir singing "How Firm a Foundation" and the La'ie choir singing the "Hallelujah Chorus." Charles Bush, a local LDS leader, provided background to visitors from Utah and warmly welcomed them to Hawai'i. The visitors expressed their "pleasure and appreciation for the hospitality with which they were being treated by the churches and people of the Islands."[21]

After more speeches and music, Cannon gave his second keynote speech. While the day before he had reminisced about his mission and the islands, this time he reverted to what he had been preaching about for fifty years—spreading the gospel of Jesus Christ throughout the world.

> I feel today more than ever the ties that bind the people of God together, the spirit of the Lord that makes us all love each other, irrespective of race and condition, bound together with the blessed ties of a common religion. It must be so the world over, where people come to believe in the gospel and go down into the waters of baptism, they grow to love one another, and that, my brethren, is the great principle of divine love and religion. ... We are soon to have missionaries in Japan, and the day will soon come when we shall reach out to China and Russia and Portugal, and all the corners of the earth ... That is our work—to establish good things upon the earth, to spread the message of the gospel of the Lord, ... Let us be ready. Let us labor. Let us struggle hard to make the people of the earth as one great family in Zion.[22]

He completed his address by calling "for a blessing upon the people of Hawaii. ... I have not felt so keenly the fervent love and

19. "Music, Feast."
20. GQCJ, Dec. 12, 1900.
21. "The End of the Mormon Joyful Jubilee," *Pacific Commercial Advertiser*, Dec. 14, 1900, 1.
22. "End of the Mormon Joyful Jubilee."

Christian fellowship I feel for you all today."[23] Cannon had spoken mostly in English in his first speech, but now he spoke primarily in Hawaiian. He noted that he had "had great freedom in both languages. I commenced in English but the spirit rested upon me and I broke out in Hawaiian."[24]

In the afternoon, ex-Queen Liliuokalani was in attendance and sought out George Q. The two had met earlier in Salt Lake City and he had given her a priesthood blessing when she asked for it, though she was not yet a member of the LDS Church. The two now had a lengthy conversation. "In reply to my question as to her state of feeling she replied how could she feel otherwise than well after such a blessing as I had given her (referring to Salt Lake)." She asked him to visit her at her residence soon.[25]

When the afternoon celebration ended at 5:00 p.m., the "Utah Elders" and over 200 "saints of both sexes" walked up and gathered at the top of Punchbowl Hill. Cannon rode up and down the hill in a carriage and the ride afforded him "grand views of all the surrounding country and the City and Ocean. And the sun set was magnificent." One Honolulu newspaper found this gathering "the most interesting in the anniversary celebration" and the "most impressive." Cannon learned that a rumor had spread "that it was upon this hill that the first ten elders who came here had erected an altar and dedicated the islands." He instructed all that this was not correct. From where they stood on the hillside of the ancient volcanic crater, he could "see the place where the altar was erected and where we prayed and dedicated the land and our selves to his ministery [*sic*] on these islands. It is now called Pacific Heights." After more singing, he told all assembled "about the building of the altar and what we did on that occasion." After the trip up Punchbowl, the evening program consisted entirely of "stereopticon" images and musical

23. "End of the Mormon Joyful Jubilee."

24. GQCJ, Dec. 13, 1900.

25. GQCJ, Dec. 14, 1900. Liliuokalani visited Salt Lake City in September 1898 and had an extended meeting with George Q. after which she expressed amazement at how well he spoke Hawaiian. "Queen Liliuokalani a Visitor in Zion," *Salt Lake Herald*, Sep. 27, 1898, 1.

numbers. It concluded with a prayer, and Cannon once again pronounced the celebrations being "excelently [*sic*] rendered."[26]

During his mission in the early 1850s, young Elder Cannon often had trouble with government authorities, and he frequently was denied official approval for the missionaries' proselyting efforts. Now, on December 17, 1900, former Queen Liliuokalani summoned George Q. to her private residence, Washington Place, in downtown Honolulu.[27] He arrived as requested at 10:00 a.m. She told him how much good his visit to the islands "had done and would do, how the people's feelings had been aroused and their love awakened and strengthened by my visit." When George Q. arose to leave, the Queen "said she would like me to give her a blessing and led the way to another room. … I felt very free in blessing her and the spirit rested on us both."[28]

That same day he, Carlie, and the Cannon children were taken to Pacific Heights by their hostess, Minerva Fernandez. There they boarded "a new line of electric cars [that] climbs the Haights [*sic*]." Again, the view of the bay and ocean was extraordinary, and George Q. grew emotional remembering his first days in Honolulu in 1850. He knew the spot where he and his compatriots had constructed a crude altar and "had a time of rejoicing, the gift of tongues and the interpretation thereof being given to us," but he "could not locate the exact spot … as the face of the ground has been much changed by attempted improvements." Memories of this occasion clearly brought back strong feelings that he expressed to Carlie and his three young sons.[29]

American officials also welcomed President Cannon. Morris Estee, the newly appointed chief judge of the federal courts in the islands, which had just officially been made a territory of the United States, showed Cannon "great attention," often inviting him to dinner or other activities. Estee was a prominent California lawyer and national Republican leader who had advised the First Presidency on

26. GQCJ, Dec. 13, 1900; "End of the Mormon Joyful Jubilee," *Pacific Commercial Advertiser*, Dec. 14, 1900, 1; "A Fitting Close of the Mormon Jubilee," *Honolulu Republican*, Dec. 14, 1900, 1.

27. GQCJ, Dec. 17, 1900. Washington Place served as the Hawai'i territorial and state governor's mansion From 1919 to 2002.

28. GQCJ, Dec. 17, 1900.

29. GQCJ, Dec. 17, 1900.

critical political issues and played an important role in Utah becoming a state.[30] Cannon spoke with Estee several times and introduced senior local church leaders to him because George Q. believed that Estee could be "of use to them sometime."[31]

Cannon spoke often with the press during his stay. He predicted that business would flourish in the "Garden Spot of the Pacific," that facilities in Honolulu Harbor would be "enlarged to accommodate the demand" that would come with increased commerce, and that Pearl Harbor would help accommodate the growth and importance of Honolulu and Hawai'i.[32]

The following day, Samuel Wooley, the president of the LDS Hawaiian Mission and overseer of the La'ie plantation, took the Cannon party to La'ie in carriages. George was delighted by the "grand" scenery and "the tropical vegetation [that] was abundant and attractive" as they rode up Nuuanu valley. He remembered Hawaiian history when Kamehameha the First fought a battle at the "pali" (cliff) at the head of the battle. The Hawaiian leader and his warriors had driven thousands of their enemies over this precipice. He wrote that "the sight of which meets one's eye when this Pali is reached is a sudden view of the sea, the valley and the mountains on that side of the Island which is sublime beyond description. No land on earth presents a combination of which excels this in grandeur and sublimity for few lands have such a grand ocean view as this."[33] On December 19, Wooley gave him a tour of the plantation, Cannon carefully recorded the details that he found most interesting about the operation.[34] George Q. had played an integral role in the acquisition of the La'ie plantation in 1864–65.

Ever inclined to analyze and improve church administration, Cannon also reviewed the mission with Wooley. To Cannon, the mission was "clearly over stocked with sisters." Several elders showed "no promise of mastering the language," and to the church leader, it was "a waste of time for young men to spend years in this feild [*sic*]."

30. Edward Leo Lyman, *Finally Statehood! Utah's Struggles, 1849–1896* (Salt Lake City: Signature Books, 2019), 264–65.

31. GQCJ, Jan. 2, 1901.

32. "The Mormon Celebration," *Hawaiian Star*, Dec. 11, 1900, 1.

33. GQCJ, Dec. 18, 1900.

34. GQCJ, Dec. 19, 1900.

He counseled the mission president to transfer missionaries who could not "acquire the language within a reasonable period" to the California Mission. If they were "worthy" but "do not have the gift of acquiring the language," they should be able to "fill out their time" to "return home with out feeling in any way humiliated."[35]

On December 22 Cannon swam in the ocean, which he enjoyed immensely and found very agreeable. On Christmas Eve, native members of the church had a surprise luau for the Cannons to show "their good will on the eve of my departure and to show the way native feasts were conducted fifty years ago." Native speakers mentioned Cannon in the most reverential manner. He noted, "I am deeply impressed with the love and affection displayed by this people to me." On Christmas day, natives came to see George Q. again, wanting him to give them blessings. While he could not respond to all, he did bless a number with strict instructions not to tell anyone that he had done so. The party caught the train at "Ka Huku" and returned to Honolulu to catch a ship for a long-anticipated return to Maui, where George Q. had spent most of his mission.[36]

Carlie was worried about the seven-and-a-half-hour voyage to Lahaina, but Minerva Fernandez convinced her they would be fine, and "they both made up their minds to go." They arrived at the Maui port at 8:00 p.m. and were taken to a comfortable house in Lahaina. Cannon's arrival in Maui brought back many important memories—the discouraging lack of success and loneliness he initially experienced, and his vision of Jesus revealing to him that a great work would be accomplished if he and the other missionaries stayed in Hawai'i. He found the site where the most sacred experiences of his life had occurred. He then met a young man who was the grandson of Nalinanui, the woman who lent her house and garden to young Brother Cannon and his companions, James Keeler and Henry Bigler. George explained that this was where he received this extraordinary vision. As he traveled over the road in a fancy carriage, he noted that it was once a trail that he had "tramped wearily [on] foot." The next day, he met Napahaloloa, the younger brother of his "old friend Napela," whom he had baptized and who had been such

35. GQCJ, Dec. 19, 1900.
36. GQCJ, Dec. 22, 24–25, 1900.

an important part of his time in Hawai'i. They held a "meeting of the saints" and he visited the site of Joseph Napela's former house. They stopped at a small church nearby that later leaders identified as "sacred ground" to the church in the islands.[37]

It was fitting that George Q. was able to spend such an enjoyable month in Hawai'i, to see old friends and their children and grandchildren, and to see the LDS Church successfully established in the islands. He had been flattered and heartened by the accolades and love and warmth with which the Hawaiian Saints had showered him during his stay. As George Q. Cannon returned to Salt Lake City, he carried the warm sun of the islands and the love of the Saints back with him. He knew his health was failing and no doubt reflected on the extraordinary life he had lived since first arriving in the Sandwich Islands fifty years before.

37. GQCJ, Dec. 26–29, 1900.

CHAPTER ONE

A MANXMAN'S JOURNEY FROM LIVERPOOL TO ZION

"The smell of the gorse, which they sometimes burn, and the turf, … is as familiar to me as though I had only left the Island yesterday."
—George Q. Cannon, Sep. 21, 1861[1]

George Cannon (the "Q." came later) was born in the teeming port city of Liverpool on the west coast of England on January 11, 1827, six days before Arthur Wellsley, First Duke of Wellington, was made England's supreme commander of the forces. He was the oldest child of George Cannon and Ann Quayle, both natives of the Isle of Man.[2]

Many of young George Q.'s male ancestors were seafaring men. His paternal grandfather, always referred to as Captain George Cannon, was a ship owner and sea captain who prospered first as a privateer illegally transporting foreign goods into England, then as a slave trader, transporting captives from the west coast of Africa to the British West Indies. Captain Cannon was reportedly killed in a mutiny in 1811 when he was only forty-five years old. His death resulted

1. GQCJ, Sep. 21, 1861. Cannon visited the Isle of Man, where all of his ancestors had lived for hundreds of years, while he was serving as president of the LDS Church's European Mission when he made this comment in his diary. The Isle of Man lies halfway between northern England and Northern Ireland in the Irish Sea. Its residents, called "Manx," are fiercely independent. He also recalled that he had left "the Island" (Isle of Man) when he was five. His grandmother Leonora Callister Cannon lived in the Manx village of Peel until 1832, when George Q. was five and it may have been that he lived with his grandmother for a time as a small child. There is no record that he was born in the Isle of Man.

2. Family group records of George Cannon and Ann Quayle, familysearch.org (accessed Oct. 2020).

in the turn of the family's fortunes, and his children eventually dispersed to different parts of the world.[3] George Q.'s great-grandfather, Hugh Cannan (the name was spelled inconsistently), was also a ship owner who was killed by a member of his crew.[4] George Q.'s father eventually moved to Liverpool and became a skilled joiner and cabinetmaker. By most accounts, the senior George returned to Peel, Isle of Man, to woo his second cousin, Ann Quayle, in the mid-1820s, and they married in Liverpool in 1825.[5] Both George and Ann were from old Manx families on all sides, and, though their children never lived for long in the Isle of Man, their parents instilled in them all a deep love for their Manx heritage.

Young George was a precocious, lively child who learned to read early and devoured anything printed for the rest of his life. He later described himself as prone to "pranks," but attributed it to "an excess of life and spirits, a disposition to do something, if only committing pranks."[6] George's unusual energy remained with him throughout his life, enabling him to be in perpetual motion—praying, reading, writing, speaking, planning, ministering, administering, interacting, and politicking. He excelled in mathematics and, like other students, spent much of his time reading the Bible. Feeling the responsibility as the oldest child to help with family finances, George Q. left school at thirteen to work as a shipping clerk for the Liverpool and Manchester Railroad. A continuing theme in his life was his deep interest in and devotion to his family, not only with his parents, six siblings, six wives, forty children, and scores of grandchildren, but also uncles, aunts, nieces, nephews, and cousins, even distant ones.

In July 1838, LDS Church president Joseph Smith announced a revelation canonized in section 118 of the church's Doctrine and

---

3. John Q. Cannon, *George Cannon the Immigrant* (Salt Lake City: Deseret News Press, 1927), 43; *CFHT*, 13. Some question has been raised about the death of Captain George Cannon because his body was reportedly buried in the church graveyard of St. Peter's Church in Peel, Isle of Man, which would have been odd if he had been killed in a mutiny on the high seas, and because no records regarding the mutiny have been found. "Death of Captain George Cannon: By Mutiny?" *Cannundrums* (blog), cannundrum.blogspot.com (accessed Oct. 2019).

4. GQCJ, Sep. 19, 1861.

5. Family group records of George Cannon and Ann Quayle, familysearch.org (accessed Oct. 2020).

6. Bitton, *GQC*, 37n4.

Covenants that the entire Quorum of Twelve Apostles were to "depart to go over the great waters, and there promulgate my gospel, the fullness thereof, and bear record of my name" (v. 4). In the same revelation, thirty-one-year-old John Taylor was called as a member of the Quorum of the Twelve. He was sustained to this calling on October 6, 1838, and ordained an apostle on December 19, 1838 (v. 6).[7] Taylor was married to Leonora Cannon, the younger sister of George Cannon and aunt of George Q. John and Leonora had immigrated separately to Canada from England in 1832, met in a Methodist congregation in Toronto, and married in 1833. They converted to the LDS Church in 1836, having been introduced to it by Parley P. Pratt. The Taylors then joined the Latter-day Saints in Kirtland, Ohio, and subsequently moved to Missouri.[8]

The apostles were to leave for England in the spring of 1839 but were delayed by difficulties in Missouri. The first missionaries from this group, apostles John Taylor and Wilford Woodruff, landed in Liverpool on January 11, 1840. On January 13, Taylor and Woodruff visited Taylor's brother-in-law, George Cannon, and his family at No. 43 Norfolk Street in Liverpool. They carried a letter of introduction from Taylor's wife, Leonora, and were received warmly. They left the bulk of their luggage at the Cannons' home while they traveled to Preston to meet the LDS mission presidency. John Taylor was assigned to Liverpool, where he taught the gospel to the Cannon family.[9]

Ann Quayle Cannon was immediately drawn to Mormonism and sought baptism. George was more skeptical but spent much of the next month reading the Book of Mormon carefully. In the end, he was baptized with his wife in February 1840. George Q., already well-versed in the Bible, also read the Book of Mormon and remembered believing in the Mormon message from the time he first heard it. George Q.'s uncle John was impressed by the young man, and the seeds of their long, close relationship were sown. Not long after their

---

7. D. Michael Quinn, *The Mormon Hierarchy: Origins of Power* (Salt Lake City: Signature Books, 1994), 599.

8. *CFHT*, 32–33.

9. *Saints: The Story of the Church of Jesus Christ in the Latter Days, Volume 1: The Standard of Truth, 1815–1846* (Salt Lake City: Church of Jesus Christ of Latter-day Saints, 2018), 409.

parents were baptized, George Q. and his sisters Mary Alice and Ann were also baptized.[10]

The elder George Cannon was not good with money, so Ann took the lead in saving funds to gather with the other Saints to Nauvoo, Illinois. Ann not only managed the family's finances, she also found a way to set aside additional secret savings. She included her son, George Q., to whom she was particularly close, as her confidant in building their family's hidden cache of savings. By early 1842, just over two years after they joined the LDS Church, Ann had saved enough for the family of two adults and five children to book passage on a ship bound for the United States. Ann was pregnant and sick, and everyone worried about her health on the long trip to Nauvoo. She feared that traveling after the birth of the new baby would be worse than traveling while pregnant.

The entire family set sail on the *Sidney* on September 17, 1842.[11] Ann Cannon was sick for weeks as the ship plied the Atlantic Ocean, and she slipped into unconsciousness at times. Helpless to aid her, George and the children watched their beloved wife and mother slip away. On October 28, 1842, Ann died. Her still pregnant body was tied to a board, weights wrapped around her feet, and her shrouded corpse was thrown into the ocean as her husband and children watched. All of the Cannon children were traumatized by their mother's untimely death. George Q. and his siblings never forgot their mother's burial at sea and he later shared in a discourse that, at the time of his mother's death, he could contemplate death "with pleasure."[12]

The ship took another two weeks to reach New Orleans. After their eight-week ocean voyage, the Cannons boarded the steamboat *Alexander Scott* in the Crescent City and started up the Mississippi River. The boat was unable to navigate through low water in Missouri, and the Cannons and other English Saints were forced to spend most of the winter of 1842–43 in St. Louis. Finally, in the spring, a steamboat owned by the church, the *Maid of Iowa*, transported the group to Nauvoo and they arrived in April 1843. The entire trip had

10. *CFHT*, 36.
11. Cannon, *George Cannon the Immigrant*, 109.
12. Remarks by George Q. Cannon at funeral of J. S. Kimball, *JD*, 10:369, Nov. 29, 1864.

taken seven months. Upon disembarking, fifteen-year-old George Q. immediately recognized Joseph Smith as he came down to the river to meet the immigrants.[13]

In Nauvoo, George attempted to take care of his children. Fourteen-year-old Mary Alice watched her younger siblings, Angus, David, and Leonora, while George Q. and his sister, Ann, moved in with their uncle and aunt, John and Leonora Taylor. John had returned to Nauvoo from his English mission in April 1841. George worked to support his family by making cabinets and helping to build houses. Before long, George Cannon met and married Mary Edwards White, a young widow from Wales.[14]

George Q. got a job working as a printer's devil in the office of the *Times and Seasons*, the principal Mormon newspaper in Nauvoo, setting type, printing, copy editing, and distributing the newspaper, all under the tutelage of uncle John Taylor. He developed the habit of reading exchange periodicals and was eventually assigned to clip articles for republication in the *Times and Seasons*, which began a lifetime of keeping abreast of the news. He heard and read early histories of the Saints, learning the Mormon narrative of persecution. George Q. also began to learn the craft of politics as published materials supporting Joseph Smith's US presidential candidacy were produced from the office where he worked. Along with this education in political craft, young George was deeply immersed in the siege mentality of Mormonism. He began to develop skills in defending the church and its leaders as he watched his uncle and others publish articles extolling the message of the restored gospel and responding to critics.[15]

George Q. had a ring-side seat as Joseph Smith convinced the Nauvoo city council to destroy the hostile newspaper *Nauvoo Expositor*, which disclosed such secret Mormon practices as polygamy. Joseph Smith's resulting arrest, and the deaths of Joseph and Hyrum Smith at the hands of the mob, followed soon after. The events were personal to George and his siblings because their uncle was in

13. *CFHT*, 56–57; Bitton, *GQC*, 41.

14. *CFHT*, 61; James B. Allen and Malcolm R. Thorp, "The Mission of the Twelve to England, 1840–41: Mormon Apostles and the Working Classes," *BYUS* 15 (Fall 1975): 500.

15. Bitton, *GQC*, 43.

Carthage Jail at the time of the deaths of the Smith brothers. Taylor was wounded in the melee, owing his survival to Willard Richards, who carried Taylor to an inner room and threw a mattress over Taylor's body after he was wounded in the hope he would not be noticed by the mob.[16] George Q.'s father made plaster death masks of the Smiths when he built their coffins. Perhaps he told George Q. about the experience.[17]

Just months after the martyrdom of the Smith brothers, the senior George Cannon went downriver to St. Louis in search of work to support his family. After toiling in the heat on an August afternoon, he died of sunstroke, leaving behind a pregnant widow and six children. George was buried in an unmarked pauper's grave in St. Louis that has never been located. George Q. and his siblings had suffered the dual traumas of losing both of their natural parents, the murder of their prophet, and the severe wounding of their uncle. They had only known their new stepmother a little over six months. Half a year after her husband's death, Mary bore a half-sister of the Cannon children whom she named Elizabeth.[18]

In the aftermath of George Cannon's death, Mary Alice, his oldest daughter, married Charles Lambert at sixteen and essentially assumed the role of mother to her younger siblings. George Q., on the other hand, continued to work and live with his uncle. He received a special "patriarchal" blessing from John Smith in which he was told he had a gift for learning languages, and he received his sacred temple endowment in the partially completed Nauvoo Temple when he was eighteen years old. He left Nauvoo for the Rocky Mountains in early March 1846. He was scheduled to depart several weeks earlier with the Taylors, but he had fallen ill. When John Taylor returned in late February or early March, George Q. had recovered and left Nauvoo with his uncle. Within a short time, they caught up with the Taylors near Mt. Pisgah, Iowa. In July 1846, John Taylor was sent on a mission to England with Parley P. Pratt

16. Bitton, *GQC*, 44–45; Dan Vogel, ed., *History of Joseph Smith and the Church of Jesus Christ of Latter-day Saints: A Source- and Text-Critical Edition*, 8 vols. (Salt Lake City: The Smith–Pettit Foundation, 2015), 6:697; Glen M. Leonard, *Nauvoo: A Place of Peace and a People of Promise* (Salt Lake City: Deseret Book, 2002), 397.

17. *CFHT*, 62–63.

18. *CFHT*, 63–65.

and Orson Hyde to deal with some problems. Taylor asked George Q. to help care for his family. True to his word, Cannon helped the family cross to Winter Quarters where they built and lived in a log house. Food was scarce, and many suffered from hunger and starvation. Many of those living there during the winter of 1846–47 died. Ann Cannon later told how she had seen "hundreds" of graves along the hill in the area.[19]

By the following April, Brigham Young, the new leader of the bulk of Mormons, was ready to leave with the vanguard group. He postponed his departure until John Taylor arrived with scientific instruments he had been asked to bring to Winter Quarters from England. In mid-April 1847, Young left with 148 people in the advance company. John Taylor and Parley P. Pratt remained behind, preparing a very large wagon train consisting of 1,500 pioneers, 5,000 head of livestock, and 560 wagons for the trek west. The train was divided into groups of hundreds, fifties, and tens (based on the approximate number of wagons in each group). George Q., his younger sister, Ann, and the Taylor family were assigned to the fifty under the direction of Joseph Horne, which, in turn, was part of the hundred captained by Edward Hunter. Twenty-year-old George was assigned to drive a wagon. The train lost many livestock to disease and death as well as to attacks on the wagon trains by Native Americans, and the groups of fifties were soon re-consolidating. George drew the attention of Mary Jane Dilworth, a woman in the same fifty, who noticed that he "never seemed to waste his time." As soon as his oxen were unyoked and taken care of, "he could always be found sitting on the tongue of his wagon reading a book."[20]

An incident involving George's wagon brought a sharp rebuke from Charles C. Rich, an apostle who was heading another fifty. George had left his wagon and team to help other wagons through a difficult passage. George's horses started moving without him, and the "point of the hub" of his wagon "struck the rim of the wheel of one of Brother Rich's wagons and broke the axle-tree." George was running back to his team and saw what was happening but was

19. *CHC*, 3:147–51; *CFHT*, 167; Bitton, *GQC*, 51–52.

20. "Edward Hunter/Joseph Horne Company (1847)," Church History Biographical Database, history.churchofjesuschrist.org (accessed Jan. 2021); Bitton, *GQC*, 52–54.

unable to reach the moving wagon in time. The axle tree was "worth more than gold" because there was no lumber with which to fashion a new one. The young driver was profoundly sorry "and bore patiently without any attempt at justification" the tongue lashing he received. Rich later regretted his treatment of the young man and sent him an apology. Cannon was impressed by the courtesy of the church leader in making a heartfelt apology.[21]

Also traveling was a personable twelve-year-old girl named Elizabeth Hoaglund. Twenty-year-old George and the girl, the daughter of Abraham Hoagland, who had been the bishop of Winter Quarters, caught each other's eye.[22] After a long, difficult slog across the prairies, during which all of the wagon train's pioneers suffered hunger, the Horne fifty arrived in the Salt Lake Valley on September 29, 1847. There was little food for the large group for the coming winter, and housing was inadequate. Those who endured the winter of 1847–48 long remembered the difficulties they endured. The season saw insufficient snowfall to support irrigation in the spring, which made it likely there would be inadequate crops. The housing that the Taylors, with whom George and his sister Ann lived, and others built was primitive and did not keep water out when it snowed or rained. The spring of 1848 was the year of the now-famous cricket invasion and the seemingly miraculous devouring of crickets by flocks of seagulls, which George Q. Cannon watched firsthand. Drought and a poor harvest meant that there was little to eat, and 2,400 new immigrants arrived in the fall of 1848, almost doubling the local population and stretching resources even further.[23]

Unlike the mild winter of 1847–48, the winter of 1848–49 was harsh. The teeming community came close to starvation, but careful shepherding of resources avoided catastrophe. The wet winter facilitated better harvests in 1849, which provided more foodstuffs to these early pioneers.

There is little information regarding the budding friendship and romance between George and Elizabeth Hoagland from the late 1840s, but from their correspondence while he was on a mission

21. *CFHT*, 89; "Topics of the Times," *JI*, Dec. 15, 1883, 377–78.
22. Bitton, *GQC*, 54–55.
23. Bitton, *GQC*, 56–58.

in the Sandwich Islands, it appears that they had gotten to know each better and developed a mutual attraction. Elizabeth was only fourteen when George left as a missionary in October 1849. Two years later she sent him a "daguerreotype likeness" of herself. George originally referred to her as "my E—" in his journal but crossed out "my" and filled in "Elizabeth." He then noted that "E. has grown [into] a fine girl and is very pretty—it made me feel peculiar to gaze upon this likeness."[24]

There is little information about what George Q. did from October 1847 through October 1849. He worked on public projects, including roads, fences, bridges, and surveying property. He lived with the Taylors and was able to purchase a small lot and raised a crop of corn on it. He also made adobe bricks for a house he hoped to build, though the home was likely intended for his sister, Mary Alice, her husband, Charles Lambert, and their younger brothers and sisters.[25]

24. *GQCJH,* 117–18, Aug. 20, 1851.
25. Bitton, *GQC,* 61.

CHAPTER TWO

FIRST MISSIONS

1849–54

"He listened to my prayers; He revealed Himself to me as He never had done before, and told me if I would persevere, I should be the means of bringing many to the knowledge of the truth."
—George Q. Cannon, My First Mission

In January 1848, six Mormons working at Sutter's Mill in the foothills of the Sierra Nevada Mountains east of Sacramento discovered gold. John Sutter employed at least sixty church members. Word of the discovery spread quickly, and soon many Mormon Battalion members were also panning for gold in Mormon Island.[1] When some of these men brought gold dust to Great Salt Lake City, money became more "plentiful" to help pay the costs of running the community. The First Presidency urged Latter-day Saints who struck it rich in California to send donations to the church.[2] Some did; others stayed in California and ignored the directive. Recognizing that gold could help Great Salt Lake City's economy, Brigham Young sent a few individuals, including George Q. Cannon, to California in

1. Mormon Island was a productive gold field near Sutter's Mill where the Mormons discovered gold. Henry Bigler, who served missions with George Q., was there when gold was discovered and recorded the date as January 24, 1848. California's gold rush is usually dated from Bigler's journal entry. Henry W. Bigler journal, Jan. 24, 1848, copy of entry in Roberts, *CDC*, 362; Bitton, *GQC*, 60–61.

2. Eugene E. Campbell, "The Mormon Gold Mining Mission of 1849," *BYUS* 1, 2 (Autumn 1959–Winter 1960); "Second General Epistle, of the Presidency," *JH*, Oct. 12, 1849; Bitton, *GQC*, 60–61. What is today known as Salt Lake City was called Great Salt Lake City until the late 1850s.

October 1849 as "gold missionaries."[3] Little did George know, it was the beginning of an absence from Utah of almost five years.

George was an unlikely gold miner. As he later wrote, "I heartily despised the work of digging gold. … There is no occupation I would not rather follow than hunting and digging for gold."[4] After George's call, Apostle John Taylor sponsored the young gold missionary, giving him two horses and a blessing that he should prosper, be an example of "sobriety" to his colleagues, be watched over by "Angels," and return safely. After a celebration, George was riding his horse home when he passed Brigham Young. He dismounted and shook the prophet's hand. Young then told the new missionary he would remember him and pray for him. He also told George to follow his leaders, Charles C. Rich and Amasa Lyman.[5]

Given the time of year, the group of missionaries decided to travel to southern California, mostly along the Spanish Trail. They would then make their way up the coast to gold country, transporting their goods and supplies on pack animals. They were eventually joined by another group of "packers," then by several wagon trains of non-Mormon "'49ers" headed for California and guided by Mormons Jefferson Hunt and Howard Egan. Apostle Rich was traveling with Hunt's train. The journey was perilous, but became worse for the missionaries when, under Rich's guidance, they chose to turn west, off the Spanish Trail, near present-day Enterprise, Utah. They followed "Walker's cut-off," supposedly a shortcut to the gold fields based on a rough map prepared by Mormon mountain man Barney Ward. The route was dangerous; water and feed were in short supply. Animals, including George's pack horse, Croppy, were lost. Rich had been warned by Jefferson Hunt not to attempt the unproven cutoff and he eventually rethought his decision and turned the missionary packers south again. Most of the teams in the train also took the cutoff but Hunt continued to lead a reduced group of seven wagons along the Spanish Trail. About three weeks after their

3. Campbell, "Mormon Gold Mining Mission," 23.

4. "Twenty Years Later: A Trip to California," *JI*, chap. 2 (Jan. 16, 1869), 13–14. Cannon published this in installments over several months.

5. M. Guy Bishop, *Henry William Bigler, Soldier, Gold Miner, Missionary, Chronicler, 1815–1900* (Logan: Utah State University Press, 1998), 67–68; Bitton, *GQC*, 61; *GQCJ Cal*, Oct. 6, 11, 1849, Sep. 24, 1850.

routes had diverged, Rich's group rejoined Hunt's wagon train on the Spanish Trail, but they had depleted provisions and experienced a good scare. Most of the wagons who had left the Spanish Trail also eventually returned, but some of the '49ers continued along the supposed shortcut. A number died in what came to be called "Death Valley," named by these very emigrants. Near the end of 1849, Cannon's group, following the Spanish Trail, arrived at Isaac Williams's ranch, near present-day Chino, California. Cannon was grateful for the experienced leadership of Rich, to whom he gave credit for the group surviving the Walker's cutoff digression. George later counseled Mormon youth in the *Juvenile Instructor* to follow the lesson he learned from this experience, when "people follow the guidance of an inspired servant of God they can rely upon the protection and deliverance of the Lord."[6]

Williams had had good experiences with veterans of the Mormon Battalion and other church members, and employed the Mormon travelers to repair his grist mill and complete other needed tasks on the ranch. George Q. became seriously ill and "narrowly escaped death. I fully believe my life was saved through the Elders laying hands upon me and administering to me." The Mormons were there for about a month. Williams sold them two ox teams, groceries, a hundred bushels of wheat, and other provisions from funds received by Hunt "for his piloting the gold diggers," making their trip north possible.[7]

George and several of his associates traveled with the ox teams. They went to the coast at Mission San Gabriel, followed the El Camino Real northward until they reached the Gilroy Ranch south of San Jose, turned east, crossed Pacheco Pass, descended into the San Joaquin Valley, and ascended the Merced River to the Mariposa gold diggings. They reached the diggings by March 1850. Some stayed for several months, but George soon proceeded farther north to the Middle Fork of the American River, where, at the Slap Jack Bar gold field, he began mining.[8]

---

6. *GQCJ Cal*, editorial note, 32–36, Oct. 12–Dec. 9, 1849; "Trip to California," *JI*, chap. 12 (June 5, 1869), 92; Bitton, *GQC*, 61–65; Campbell, "Mormon Gold-Mining Mission," 26n17.

7. Cannon, "Trip to California," *JI*, chap. 12 (June 5, 1869), 92; *GQCJ Cal*, 77; Addison Pratt, autobiography and journal, Dec. 22, 1849–Jan. 11, 1850, as quoted in *GQCJ Cal*, 77.

8. *GQCJ Cal*, 77–81; Bitton, *GQC*, 65–66. A useful map of their trip north is in

While George was panning for gold with his fellow missionaries, his workmate, Henry Gibson, recognized George's intelligence. George would sometimes read from letters he was writing to John Taylor and friends. Gibson noted "they were beautiful letters, the composition was chaste [and] eloquent, and the purity of mind and nobility of soul of George Q. Cannon shone out in every line."[9] To distinguish himself from another George Cannon who was working in the gold fields, George decided to add his mother's birth name, Quayle, as his middle name.[10] George was no doubt relieved when he was hired by Howard Egan, an LDS frontiersman, to work as a bookkeeper in Egan's supply store, the Salt Lake Trading Company, on the Merced River. Apparently, both Egan and Cannon recognized that George Q.'s talents lay more in business than in panning. George paid someone else from his wages to take his place as a gold digger.[11]

On September 24, 1850, Rich called nine of the gold mining missionaries to the Sandwich Islands to do missionary work, at least for the winter. Gold mining was difficult and not very profitable in the winter, and it was thought that it would be less expensive for the missionaries to spend the winter in the islands. Rich had already "hinted" to George Q. the likely call to Hawai'i and asked him what he thought. George Q. responded that he had been promised by Brigham Young that he would be rewarded if he did whatever Brothers Rich and Lyman told him to do.[12] Rich then blessed each of the missionaries called to open the Sandwich Islands to "act as the spirit dictated when we got there."[13] Rich told at least some of the missionaries that he was also calling Hiram Clark, a fifty-five-year-old church member who had been assisting Rich and Lyman in California, to preside over the mission and that he would also call

---

William G. Hartley, *Faithful and Fearless: Major Howard Egan, Early Mormonism and Pioneering of the American West* (Holladay, UT: Howard Egan Biography LLC, 2017), 230.

9. Henry Gibson, from *Tullidge's Histories*, as quoted in Bitton, *GQC*, 66.

10. Bitton, *GQC*, 477–78n3.

11. Bitton, *GQC*, 66; *GQCJH*, 1n3; Hartley, *Major Howard Egan*, 241–42.

12. *GQCJH*, Sep. 24, 1850; Campbell, "Mormon Gold Mining Mission," 30; Bitton, *GQC*, 66.

13. William H. Bigler, journal, Book B, Oct. 6–16, 1850, cited and quoted in Campbell, "Mormon Gold Mining Mission," 29–30.

Hiram Blackwell, another missionary who had earlier labored with them on the Middle Fork, to serve in the islands as well.[14]

The new missionaries were not quite ready to leave the gold fields, however. They needed funds to travel to Hawai'i. The patronage at the trading store was falling off, so George began working the claim with his associates. They rebuilt their "wing dam" to divert water from the river "by means of a side ditch to expose the river bed" and thereby facilitate panning for gold on their claim.[15] By the end of the day, "they struck it pretty rich." Over the next week, the group was far more successful than they had been all season finding gold, and within a few days they made enough to pay anticipated fares to Hawai'i, retain some funds for future expenses, and even send some money home.[16]

They now "left the River" and set out on their journey, paying fares to have their possessions shipped in wagons for miles, often walking themselves. They traveled to Asahel Lathrop's Mormon Tavern on the Cosumnes River, where Egan, who was sick, was staying. They met him there, and George Q. gave him $100 to have someone returning to Utah take home to his family. Other missionaries also left money to be taken to Great Salt Lake City.[17]

Eventually the entire group made it to San Francisco. Hiram Clark arrived almost three weeks after the rest because he had been seriously ill. In the meantime, the missionaries had been fitted for new clothes that would be more appropriate for the Sandwich Islands. Once he arrived, Clark, the new mission president, worked to find acceptable passage for the group of ten missionaries. The group consisted of the eight called by Rich (one, John Berry, decided to return to Utah), Hiram Clark, and Hiram Blackwell. Clark soon booked passage on the *Imaum of Muscat* whose captain was James Riches. All the missionaries would travel "between decks" passage so they could all be together, because there were not enough berths

14. *GQCJH*, Sep. 25, 1850; Henry Bigler autobiography, "Book A," Sep. 25, 1850 (hereafter Bigler autobiography), William Farrer diary, Sep. 25, 1850, both as cited in *GQCJH*, 3n6. The missionaries told Rich that they did not know where Clark was.

15. *GQCJH*, Sept. 25, 1850, 3n7.

16. *GQCJH*, Oct. 2–16, 1850.

17. *GQCJH*, Oct. 2–20, 1850.

in cabins. They now had to wait while Riches took a week to decide that conditions were suitable to sail from San Francisco Bay.[18]

Finally, on November 22, 1850, the ship and its passengers sailed through the Golden Gate. In the prior week, the missionaries had spent much of their time on board as the anchors were raised and lowered, and as breakers struck the sides of the ship.[19] Throughout his adult life, whenever George Q. traveled across the sea, he almost always developed terrible seasickness.

Halfway through the week, George dreamed that he was on a vessel and that he and his mission compatriots were "heaving with the windlass at an anchor that was fast in the mud." Joseph Smith suddenly appeared "and went forward on to the forecastle close by the bowsprit." Cannon followed Smith and saw him kneel and pray for a few minutes aloud that the anchor might be loosened. After he did so, "one or two of the brethren took hold of the rope and pulled [the anchor] up with the greatest ease." George then spoke with Joseph and told him he wished he had "such Faith," to which the prophet replied "that it was my privilege and that I ought to have it" because George would need it to be preserved from pestilence. George awoke convinced that faith and prayer would have more effect than the windlass.[20] George never forgot this dream and its lesson "that great is the power of prayer when properly offered to the Lord."[21]

The departure from San Francisco was not without incident. A storm was approaching and the harbor pilot who had been onboard navigating the treacherous waters of San Francisco Bay left when a pilot boat came by. Darkness descended, and the crew on deck began "making a great noise" with the captain and mate shouting orders. The ship had to tack "backward and forward" frequently, and the vessel "was in a very critical situation." Breakers "were rolling very high" when all on board felt the ship "strike something pretty solid which made her tremble from stem to stern then directly a grating at the stern." George thought they had hit a reef. Instead, "a very heavy breaker" had struck the ship. The "wheel ropes" had broken "and let

18. *GQCJH*, Nov. 6–16, 1850; Bigler autobiography, Oct. 21, 1850.
19. *GQCJH*, Nov. 16–22, 1850.
20. *GQCJH*, Nov. 22, 1850
21. GQC, discourse given June 27, 1881, *JD*, 22:289–90.

the helm knock that made the grating noise we heard." George was told if the "Wheel Ropes had broke [*sic*] almost anywhere but where we were [in passing through the Golden Gate]," the vessel would have been lost.[22]

The voyage over the next twenty days was mostly uneventful, except that George and the other missionaries spent much of their time being seasick and vomiting into a common bucket. On December 11, someone sighted land, and someone else who had made the trip before announced that it was the 10,000 foot peak on Maui, Haleakala. The next morning, Oʻahu was within sight, and the passengers saw natives in outrigger canoes near the ship out fishing. A "short Heavy built man about as broad as long" came on board the schooner to steer it into the harbor. Once anchored, the ship was immediately "crowded with natives some trying to sell fruit others anxious to take us ashore. Bananas, Oranges, Cocoa Nuts, melons, &c &c were here in profusion." The water in the harbor "was beautifully clear and calm enabling us to see the bottom distinctly."[23]

The ten missionaries received their "permits" and Hiram Clark rented a house for $10 per month, where the group stayed. The next morning, the missionaries "put on our best" and made their way up towards the Nuʻuanu Valley to offer thanksgiving for their arrival. Along the way, they stopped at the Kapena Falls, and all bathed in the pool below the falls. George found it to be a "fine place to swim in and very deep." He was delighted to see "several Native boys from 10 to 15" amuse themselves by jumping from the sides of the falls thirty or forty feet up into the pool—"they were the most expert swimmers I ever saw."[24]

The missionaries crossed the stream above the falls and ascended the mountain until they found a "knob that rose precipitously on all sides and formed a table of about thirty or thirty-five feet wide." Having each picked up a stone along the way for the purpose, they made an altar of their stones and shared "what our desires are." George felt the spirit "very sensibly" and reported that all of the group hoped

22. *GQCJH*, Nov. 22, 1850. George had his memorable dream the night before the frightening passage out of the bay.

23. *GQCJH*, Nov. 22–Dec. 12, 1850.

24. *GQCJH*, Dec. 12–13, 1850.

doors would be opened for preaching the gospel, that all "opposers might be confounded," and that the lives of the missionaries might be spared.[25] This altar became legendary to Hawaiian Saints as they remembered the beginnings of missionary work in the islands.

The following day, Hiram Clark and the missionaries discussed whether they should all stay on O'ahu or be assigned to the various islands. They decided they should pair up and spread out among the more populated islands. President Clark would stay on O'ahu, and he chose Thomas Whittle to remain with him. He then chose four to be leaders of conferences (congregations) on the other islands where missionaries would be sent: George Q., the youngest, was surprised to be picked as one of the leaders. The "spirit dictated to me very plainly to choose Bro. Keeler" as his companion on the island of Maui, which George drew. Keeler later told George that he had prayed to be picked by him. Henry Bigler chose Thomas Morris and they drew Moloka'i; James Hawkins chose Hiram Blackwell and they drew the big island of Hawai'i; and John Dixon chose William Farrer and drew Kaua'i.[26]

Oddly, before anyone left Honolulu, Hiram Clark "counselled Brother Morris to go to work." Presumably, Clark believed it would be advantageous to have Morris get a job and contribute to the finances of the mission. Henry Bigler did not like the idea of going to Moloka'i alone so decided to go to Maui with Cannon and Keeler. Within several days, everyone had left for their assignments.[27]

Cannon, Keeler, and Bigler reached Lahaina after a two-day voyage, with George being seasick the entire way. When they landed in Maui, the three initially had trouble finding quarters, prompting George to experience "more feelings of despondency than I had done since I left home." There were far fewer white people—the Europeans and Americans living in the Sandwich Islands—than they had been led to expect. They found a house to rent for $4 per week—expensive but workable.[28]

25. *GQCJH*, Dec. 13, 1850.

26. *GQCJH*, Dec. 14, 1850; George Q. Cannon, *My First Mission* (Salt Lake City: Juvenile Instructor Office, 1879), 10–11. *My First Mission* is closely based on GQC's journal, but sometimes provides additional details.

27. *GQCJH*, Dec. 16, 1850; *My First Mission*, 11

28. *GQCJH*, Dec. 19, 1850; *My First Mission*, 12–13.

Once settled, the elders wanted to "have the sanction of the authorities for what they were doing and so wanted an introduction to the governor" of Maui. They sought out the American consul and later that day obtained a meeting with Governor James Young Kanehoa. He gave them his sanction "to preach as much as we wanted." The governor was unsure if he would let them use a public building for meetings. That night, several natives visited the missionaries, sang for them, and told them the Hawaiian names for many things. George afterward recorded that they were "in considerable better spirits about learning it [the language]" after visiting with these Hawaiians.[29]

The missionaries originally understood they would be seeking out "white" people. It became immediately clear to the three missionaries that "if we confined our labors to the whites, our mission to those islands would be a short one [because] the white people were not numerous at Lahaina. … Preaching to them with the hope of convincing them of the truth seemed a hopeless labor." The elders concluded that they had not been forbidden to teach the native Hawaiians and would do so. Teaching meant learning the local language, and George "made up my mind to acquire the language, preach the gospel to the natives and to the whites whenever I could obtain an opportunity, and thus fill my mission." Even if he had to do it alone, George would do so.[30]

On Sunday, December 22, the elders visited Rev. Townsend E. Taylor, chaplain for Bethel Chapel, a church in Lahaina, and asked if they could use the building for a worship service in the afternoon. Taylor reluctantly agreed, though he made clear it would not be a permanent arrangement. All three of the Mormon missionaries spoke (in English) that afternoon. One man attending the meeting asked "what additional light" the elders had compared to other churches. The missionaries used this as a helpful segue to a discussion of LDS priesthood authority.[31]

Most days thereafter, George Q. and his companions spent much of their time "studying the language." Occasionally, this would be punctuated by visits from other missionaries or locals. On December

29. *GQCJH*, Dec. 20, 1850, 35n19; *My First Mission*, 13–14.
30. *My First Mission*, 14.
31. *GQCJH*, Dec. 22, 1850.

23, Hawkins and Blackwell, on their way to the big island of Hawai'i, stopped over in Maui and visited Cannon, Keeler, and Bigler. The five shared a pleasant afternoon.[32] Later, a young couple who lived nearby, Keala and Pau, began helping the missionaries with the language. With their aid, on December 30, George Q. ordered "two vocabularys of the Native" to help their language studies. They then met Pau's mother, Nalimanui, and sister, Hoohuli. These women not only helped the missionaries learn the native language, but also washed their clothes.[33]

On Sunday, January 12, the missionaries attended a "Native meeting" in which the speaker "gesticulated" wildly. For the first time, George Q. began "to understand some little of what is said." The next day, the elders, realizing that they were almost out of money, decided to split up and seek lodging in different parts of the island because it would be easier to find a place for one person rather than three. Bigler drew the south of Maui; Keeler the east; and Cannon the north. Bigler left, then Cannon and Keeler visited Nalimanui, who had been told they were looking for a place to stay. She told the missionaries she did not know where they could find lodging, but that they were all free to live in her house. They responded that they were happy just to have a place to lie down at night, but Nalimanui insisted that she would move out of her house and live with her daughter to let the three missionaries, whom she did not know, stay. Cannon and Keeler found Bigler, and they were all delighted to remain together.[34] George Q. was overwhelmed: "The kindness of the old lady touched me, and I could not refrain from weeping. Never before in my life did I feel so thankful as I did for the shelter she offered." Not only did Nalimanui provide shelter, she and her daughter cleaned it and "fixed up the room as well as they could." George "had never been so happy in my life as I was then."[35]

What George Q. viewed as perhaps the most important experience of his life occurred in a garden near Nalimanui's house. He "sought the Lord in secret prayer" in the garden. There were so many

32. *GQCJH*, Dec. 23, 1850.
33. *GQCJH*, Dec. 24, 30, 1850, Jan. 1, 1851; *My First Mission*, 16.
34. *GQCJH*, Jan. 13, 1851; *My First Mission*, 16–18.
35. *My First Mission*, 17–18.

questions: were the missionaries supposed to teach only the white residents or the natives as well? Could they learn the difficult language? Would they have access to a meeting house? Given all the questions and challenges George faced, should he even remain in the islands? George recorded in his journal in 1900: "[the Lord] condescended to commune with me for I heard his voice more than once as one man speaks to another encouraging me and showing me the work which should be done among this people if I should follow the dictates of his spirit. … [T]he Lord revealed to me the good that should be accomplished if I should stay and work with this people. … My feelings are indescribable when I see how fully the Lord has fulfilled his words to me concerning that which should be accomplished."[36]

Soon, George Q. learned from Hiram Clark that his companion, Thomas Whittle, was going home on February 1. George found this news disheartening because "we had hoped Bro. W. would have stayed longer." George was also disappointed because president Clark reassigned George to work with him in Honolulu. Already Maui had come to feel like home, Keeler and Bigler felt like family, and Maui felt like the place where he and his associates would be most successful.[37]

Not only was Whittle preparing to leave, but John Dixon and William Farrer were also going home because they had had no success during their first few weeks. George had already developed the directness with which he often spoke and expressed his feeling to the departing missionaries that, if he were to go home "under existing circumstances the Lord in my opinion would hold me accountable for not doing my duty to this people and the people would be apt to rise up in judgment against me for not giving them the privilege of hearing the truth." Whittle and Dixon were not moved by Cannon's speech, but Farrer decided to stay and master the language.[38]

Soon, it became apparent that the reason Clark had asked George

---

36. GQCJ, Dec. 27, 1900, punctuation and spelling slightly corrected. George did not describe this singular experience in his contemporaneous journal but did on rare occasions refer to it later. See GQC, discourse given Oct. 6, 1896 reported in *DW*, Oct. 31, 1896, 610; Daniel C. Peterson, "George Q. Cannon," patheos.com (accessed Aug. 2019).

37. *My First Mission*, 18–20; *GQCJH*, Jan. 25, 1851.

38. *GQCJH*, Jan. 25, 1851; *My First Mission*, 19–20.

to join him in Honolulu was to ghost write a letter to Brigham Young regarding mission activities. George Q.'s letter to Young over Clark's signature is well-written but does note, as Clark maintained, that he would prefer to work in emigration or church finances rather than as a missionary. The letter also informs Young that at least four of the missionaries were headed home. After Clark overheard Cannon's statements to the departing missionaries, he decided that Cannon should go back to Maui to learn Hawaiian and teach the gospel. Clark also sent Farrer with Cannon "to be a partner to Brother Bigler."[39]

A few days after Cannon and Farrer arrived in Lahaina, Hiram Blackwell stopped in Maui on his way from the big island to O'ahu. He was discouraged and feared it could take a full year to learn the language well enough to preach the gospel. He had, therefore, decided to go home. His partner, James Hawkins, remained in Hawai'i.[40] On February 11, the four missionaries in Maui rose early and hiked up "the Mountain," which "was very difficult ascending and very high." Finding a quiet spot, they stopped and "spent the day in singing and prayer."[41]

Several weeks later, Hiram Clark visited the four missionaries in Maui to tell them he was going to go to the Marquesas Islands and asked them to go with him. Clark "had a testimony from the Lord that there was nothing to be done [in the Sandwich Islands]."[42] Cannon's reaction was that he and the missionaries with him "had no such testimony as Bro. Clark [in being impressed to leave]. ... I had felt my bosom warm and felt the spirit continually whispering to me if I should persevere I should be blest."[43] George Q. did not appear to have much misgiving about disagreeing with his mission president.

---

39. *GQCJH,* Jan. 27–29, 1851; Clark (written by GQC) to Young, Jan. 27, 1851, copy included in *GQCJH,* 554–56; *My First Mission* 20–21.

40. *GQCJH,* Feb. 2, 1851; *My First Mission,* 21–22.

41. *GQCJH,* Feb. 10, 1851. This was probably Paupau, a steep 3,000-foot mountain within a few miles of Lahaina.

42. *GQCJH,* Feb. 20, 1851.

43. *GQCJH,* Feb. 20, 1850. Hiram Clark's departure from the Sandwich Islands has sometimes been criticized, including by George Q. Cannon and Andrew Jenson in his "Manuscript History of the Hawaiian Mission," March 1852, CHL. Cannon is more critical of Clark in his personal journal account than in *My First Mission.* Compare *My First Mission,* 22–24, with GQCJ, Feb. 20, 1850. Historian R. Lanier Britsch is quite harsh in his assessment of Hiram Clark's brief tenure as leader of the Hawaiian Mission. Britsch, *Moramona: The Mormons in Hawai'i,* 2nd ed. (N.p.: Jonathan Napela Center

At this point, George felt prompted to "strike out to-morrow on a tramp around the Island [–] my desire to learn the language is the principal reason. I want also to see the situation of things at different parts of the Island; the brethren will remain together studying."[44] He noted he had made substantial progress in the language and felt confident he could "explain in part the first principles of the gospel." He also believed he had been inspired that he would find people prepared to receive his message and felt he was going to "meet friends" who would respond to him.[45]

At one of the first houses where he stopped and was invited in, he was offered "some Kalo and boiled Goat's flesh to eat."[46] Kalo is a plant grown throughout Polynesia. Its roots are used to make poi, a staple of the Hawaiian diet. George had previously "tasted a teaspoonful of 'poi,' but the smell of it and the calabash in which it is contained was so much like that of a book-binder's old, sour paste-pot that when I put it to my mouth I gagged at it, and would have vomited had I swallowed it." He realized, however, that if he did not eat poi, he would put the natives "to great inconvenience; for they would have to cook separate food for me every meal." This would be burdensome to those he was most interested in helping. Determined to learn to like poi, George prayed "the Lord to make it sweet to me." His prayer was answered and "the next time I tasted it, I ate a bowlful, and I positively liked it.[47] George Q. was determined to be successful among the native Hawaiians and would take, with the help of the Lord, whatever steps were required.

George was treated kindly wherever he went. As a *haole*, which he interpreted to mean "white" or "foreigner," he was something of a curiosity. Several nights he asked to stay overnight at a house and was permitted to do so, often being persuaded to sleep in a bed rather than on a mat. Yet George Q. did not feel that he had met the

---

for Hawaiian and Pacific Islands Studies, 2018), 29–32. A less critical view, which finds Cannon's *My First Mission* sometimes "self-justifying," is Donald R. Shaffer, "Hiram Clark and the First LDS Hawaiian Mission: A Reappraisal," *JMH*, 17 (1991): 94–109, which asserts that critics have been too quick to judge a man who faced a "difficult assignment in difficult times. Ibid. at 109.

44. *GQCJH*, Mar. 2, 4, 1851.
45. *My First Mission*, 23–24.
46. *GQCJH*, Mar. 4, 1851.
47. *My First Mission*, 24–26.

"friends" whom he had been inspired to believe would receive his testimony. Finally, he reached the town of Wailuku on the north side of the isthmus of Maui. It was raining, and as he crossed the swollen stream, George slipped and fell, totally drenching himself.[48]

Worried about how he looked, George found a quiet spot and changed his shirt and shaved. Feeling impressed to return, he met two women who emerged from a house as he walked by. When they saw George Q., "they called to some men who were in the house, 'E ka haole,' meaning 'oh, the white man.'" Three men came out of the house and George Q. greeted them. One asked where he was going. George told them he was returning to Lahaina, where he lived, on account of the weather. The man said "that as this was Saturday, I had better stop until Monday with him. He inquired of me who and what I was, and upon my informing him, his desire to have me stay increased." They went into his house, where the man fed George and had "some little conversation" regarding George's religious beliefs."[49]

Jonathan (Ionatana) Napela, the man who had invited George in, proposed that he take George Q. to meet "the missionary," Rev. Daniel T. Conde, affiliated with the Boston-based American Board of Commissioners for Foreign Missions, which had a number of missionaries through the Sandwich Islands. The Congregationalist missionaries sponsored by this group were generally critical of the Mormon missionaries and worked hard to undermine their efforts.[50] But for now George had a "very pleasant conversation" with Conde in which he "made many inquiries respecting Utah, my object in coming to the islands, and our belief." Conde said he could not believe in modern revelation but wished to read some LDS works. George lent him a copy of *A Voice of Warning*, a widely circulated Mormon work written by Apostle Parley P. Pratt. George had "little hope of the book having any effect on him, as he had condemned the doctrines before he had heard or read them."[51]

---

48. *GQCJH*, Mar. 8, 20, 1851.

49. *GQCJH*, Mar. 8, 1851.

50. M. Guy Bishop, "Waging Holy War: Mormon-Congregationalist Conflict in Mid-Nineteenth-Century Hawaii," *JMH*, 17 (1991): 110–19, discusses the interactions between the Mormons and the Congregationalists in Hawai'i and the critical reports made by the American Board missionaries about the Mormons.

51. *My First Mission*, 26–27.

Napela told George after the visit with Conde that if "their principles were wrong and ours were right," he would embrace the LDS principles. George learned through the weekend that his host was an "influential man, [a] judge of this side of the Island," and that he and the two men with him, H. K. Kaleohano and William Uaua, had been educated at the Lahainaluna High School for four years.[52] George later remembered that "the moment I entered into this house of this native and saw him and two friends, I felt convinced that I had met the men for whom I had been looking."[53]

On his way out of town, George stopped by to say goodbye to Conde and his wife. They invited him to eat, and they spoke for several hours, neither convincing the other of the rightness of his church's position. The twenty-five-mile walk back to Lahaina was long, and by the time George finished, his feet were covered with blisters.[54]

George Q. returned to Wailuku several times over the next few weeks, usually staying with Jonathan and his wife, Kitty Richardson Napela. They became increasingly "glad to see" him.[55] In the following days, George taught Jonathan about Joseph Smith and the Book of Mormon, leading to Jonathan's desire to read the book, although his English was not very good. Cannon and Napela agreed to help each other learn the other's language.[56] Soon after, George Q. met John Richardson, Kitty's brother, who was a circuit judge in Maui and spoke English well. Jonathan proposed that George tell John more about the teachings and history of Mormonism so that John could translate the message for him.[57]

The next Sunday, George was back in Wailuku. No doubt worried about the effect George was having on some of his congregants, Rev. Conde's sermon to his large congregation warned of the Mormon missionaries and spoke harshly about "Joe Smith" and an angel who allegedly gave Smith plates from which he supposedly translated a

52. *GQCJH*, Mar. 8, 1851.

53. *My First Mission*, 27. The three were all baptized and became the nucleus of the LDS Church in Maui. Scott G. Kenney, "Mormons and the Smallpox Epidemic of 1853," *The Hawaiian Journal of History*, 31 (1997): 1–2.

54. *GQCJH*, Mar. 10, 1851.

55. *GQCJH*, Mar. 11, 1851.

56. *GQCJH*, Mar. 20, 1851.

57. *GQCJH*, Mar. 24, 1851.

book about the Indians but which the angel later took back. Conde thought this "was an evidence of the untruth of his story." He explained that Smith was such a "notoriously bad character" and "stole so much and broke the laws to such an extent" that Smith and the "citizens" ended up fighting each other and Smith was "killed fighting, the Lord having punished him for his sins." Conde also criticized Napela for befriending George.[58]

George, who was becoming more fluent in Hawaiian every day, was outraged and asked to respond. Conde "had no idea that I could understand what he had said." Conde "assented" and George Q. told him in English that he needed to "disabuse the minds of the people of the lies he had told them." Conde refused, saying they were not lies. George Q. asserted that he had come to tell the truth: that the things which Conde "had told this people were base lies and I was a living witness that they were and that Mormonism was true; and as true as the Lord lived I would stand as a Witness against him at the Judgment seat of God for having told this people lies." The discussion lasted half an hour, and "many in the congregation, some of whom knew English, crowded around."[59]

John Richardson, Kitty Napela's brother, understood the conversation and gave a report of it "which was very favorable to [George], and altogether I think the missionary sermon did good." To George Q., "another reason of the sermon not having so good an effect was the preacher's allusions to Napela. He had called him by name, as the man at whose house I stopped, and denounced him." A few days later, Conde's congregation "had a trial upon Napela." One of the charges was that he had entertained a Mormon missionary. A family member warned Napela he might lose his judgeship if he were expelled from the Protestant church. Napela was well respected and was not frightened by the threats. George offered to leave, but Jonathan "manifested no disposition to have me leave his house." Because pressure from Conde continued, however, George Q. decided it would be wise to depart Wailuku for a time.[60]

Henry Bigler and William Farrer decided they should relocate to

58. *GQCJH*, Mar. 30, 1851.
59. *GQCJH*, Mar. 30, 1851; *My First Mission*, 29–30.
60. *My First Mission*, 31; *GQCJH*, Apr. 4, 1851.

the populous O'ahu because, with the departures of Hiram Clark and others, there were no missionaries there.[61] By fall, Farrer wrote that, despite substantial opposition, he had baptized forty new converts in O'ahu. One convert was J.W.H. Kauwahi, another graduate of Lahainaluna, a lawyer, overseer, and member of the legislature who, for a time, became one of the most effective native LDS missionaries in the Islands. George Q. would occasionally receive letters from James Hawkins, who was left by himself on the Big Island when Hiram Blackwell went home. Hawkins baptized a number on Hawai'i but felt quite "clumsy" with the language.[62]

George decided to continue his trek of Maui. He headed toward what he always referred to as Kula, which was in the upcountry on the western side of Haleakala, the 10,000 foot dormant volcano on the lower part of Maui, toward the town of Waiakoa. He learned that the Protestant missionary overseeing this part of the island, Jonathan S. Green, would be making his quarterly visit to the congregation in Waiakoa on the next Sunday, April 6. Green gave a sermon and then met Cannon, and the two had a contentious exchange.

Green began hitting George with questions: how long did the Mormon missionaries intend to stay in the islands? Didn't they believe that the gospel of Jesus Christ was already being taught there? Why had they bothered to come? George responded that he did not think the gospel was being taught and they were there to remedy that. Green countered that Joe Smith was an impostor and he would not believe Smith's words. George asked Green if he had read about the LDS Church. Green said that he had, though he admitted it had all been written by non-Mormons. George asked if he had read any materials by Mormons, and Green responded, "I would not read anything that Joe. Smith or any of his followers would write." George told him he was "incompetent to judge whether we were right or wrong" because he would not study the Mormon side of the question. He then peppered Green with questions of his own: did Green's church have offices like apostles and prophets? Did they have gifts of the spirit as well as other teachings of the original

61. *GQCJH*, Mar. 28, Apr. 17, 1851.

62. *GQCJH*, Apr. 24, Jul. 21, 1851; Kenney, "Mormons and the Smallpox Epidemic," 2–3.

church? Green became agitated and, as he left, reportedly said, "God curse you," to which George Q. replied, "Mr. Green, you have not the authority to curse me."[63]

Waiakoa congregation members heard the discussion between the Protestant missionary and the Mormon missionary. After the meeting, George went to a house nearby where Green was supposed to have stopped (but did not in his hasty departure). The "master of the house" told George Q. that Green "had told him not to entertain me." When George offered to leave, everyone told him "they would not listen to it and said I must stay until morning." George described the entire conversation with Green, and most in the house believed that "Mr. Green had done wrong."[64]

The Protestant missionaries likely viewed the Mormons as a threat. They viewed the native Hawaiians as "superstitious" and had worked hard to bring Christianity to the native Islanders over the past several decades. The Protestants had not been friendly to earlier Catholic missionaries and were successful in convincing the Hawaiian government to ban Catholic teachers.[65]

Soon after his encounter with Green, George returned to Wailuku and learned that Napela had lost his position as a judge and been cut off from his church by Rev. Conde. George also learned that Napela was having a new house built that the Mormon missionaries could use for preaching. George Q. expressed concern about giving a sermon in a church—he had only spoken "before an assembly" a few times in English; the thought of doing it in a foreign tongue made him nervous. He "almost felt to shrink from it," but did not. On Sunday, June 15, he spoke on the principles of the gospel and their restoration. "My testimony and words were favorably received by the people and they were desirous that I should continue to hold meetings." The next week, James Keeler joined him briefly in Wailuku. Soon, they were baptizing and confirming new members there. Because George would be traveling more and not returning to Lahaina, a new convert offered to collect George's things from Nalimanui's

63. *GQCJH*, Apr. 6, 1851. George noted in his journal that the LDS Church was twenty-one years old that day.

64. *GQCJH*, Apr. 6, 1851.

65. *GQCJH*, 39–40n33.

house, including letters. George Q. looked forward to reading the correspondence he received with great anticipation.[66] Always a great letter writer, he noted that he had sent notes to uncles and aunts, his quorum of Seventy in Salt Lake City, Howard Egan (still in California), Brigham Young, friends in Utah, and John Dixon and Thomas Whittle (two of the missionaries who had left the islands and who were back in the gold fields). He also recorded, for the second time on his mission, that he had written a letter to Elizabeth Hoagland.[67]

On July 13, George Q. received word that Keeler was in Keʻanae, some miles southeast of Wailuku along the coast.[68] The message Cannon preached was attractive to many Islanders. He taught that Hawaiians were descended from ancient Israelites who came to the new world under the direction of God. As Cannon told them, some of these Israelites' descendants sailed west and were the progenitors of the Polynesians, making Hawaiians special children of God. The Book of Mormon was a record of their ancestors. George Q. and other LDS missionaries also taught the prophecy in Daniel 2 regarding a stone "not cut by human hands" that destroyed earthly kingdoms and established the kingdom of God. The small stone was the LDS Church. Native Hawaiians responded to these stories and, unlike what they were taught by Catholic and Protestant missionaries, LDS beliefs made them feel included in God's plan.[69]

A week later, Keeler rode into Wailuku accompanied by Namakaiona, a man at whose home Keeler was staying, both on horses. Keeler had read scriptures to interested people in Keʻanae, and they wanted to hear more. He believed that many wanted to be baptized, and when he told them that another missionary could speak the language better than he, they pleaded to bring him as quickly as possible. George Q. had just baptized his host in Wailuku, H. K. Kaleohano, Jonathan Napela's friend, and Kaleohano and several others went to Keʻanae with Cannon and Keeler to see how

66. *GQCJH*, July 2, 1851.

67. *GQCJH*, July 2, 11, 1851.

68. *GQCJH*, July 13, 1851. The Keʻanae peninsula is today about halfway to Hana on the Hana highway.

69. Kenney, "Mormons and the Smallpox Epidemic," 2. R. Lanier Britsch attributes the view that Polynesians are descendants of Book of Mormon Israelites to George Q. Cannon. Britsch, *Moramona: The Mormons in Hawaii*, 28–29.

the church was growing. Kaleohano gave George a horse to ride. George Q. described how beautiful the scenery was as they passed through a "most romantic country." The path became rocky, hilly, and much more challenging as they turned toward the coast. When they arrived in Keʻanae, people came from all around to meet and listen to the Mormon missionaries. They met in a Calvinist meeting house where a large crowd was assembled. Kaleohano helped the missionaries by explaining gospel concepts to the Hawaiians. George Q. recorded in his journal how freely he spoke Hawaiian and how he could see the spirit in the people's faces. More Hawaiians arrived over the next few days, and Cannon and Keeler began baptizing those who requested it. "Speaking with power," Cannon and Kaleohano taught those who had not yet heard the "first principles." Over a period of five days, the missionaries baptized exactly 100 people.[70]

When one of the "lunas" ("top" in Hawaiian) of the Calvinist church asked the Mormon elders why they were teaching and baptizing people who were already baptized, George responded strongly—the baptisms they received previously were not completed with the proper authority and hence were not valid.[71]

George Q. experienced a breakthrough on Sunday, July 27. The local lunas once again let the Mormons use their meeting house. George Q. related, "I never preached with such power as I did this morning—the language came with ease and fluency and I was filled with the spirit with words and ideas. I never seen a more attentive congregation all wide awake with countenances and eyes beaming with pleasure and paying the best possible attention. … I was filled with joy. I felt like shouting Glory, Glory, Glory to the Lord God of Israel for his goodness." During the time between meetings, Cannon and Keeler baptized another thirty-one people. James Keeler recorded in his diary that "Bro. C. is able to speak the language fluently."[72] "The best of feelings seemed to exist" with the congregation's lunas. Soon they learned from one of the lunas, however, that the head missionary located in Hana, Rev. Eliphalet W. Whittlesey,

70. *GQCJH*, July 21–27, 1851.

71. *GQCJH*, July 28, 1851.

72. *GQCJH*, July 27, 1851; William Farrer diary, Aug. 20, 1851, cited and quoted in *GQCJH*, 121n49.

was furious and had forbidden the Mormons from "using the house and had condemned him [the luna] for letting us have it before."[73]

George Q. plunged ahead. In August 1851, he organized four branches in the area in and around Ke'anae, where all the baptisms had taken place: Ke'anae, Wailua, Waianu, and Honomanu. The missionaries also ordained thirteen men to the Aaronic priesthood—three teachers and ten deacons—to provide local leadership in the branches. The same day, Cannon learned that new missionaries had arrived in the islands, several with their wives. Philip B. Lewis, the new mission president, along with Francis A. Hammond and John S. Woodbury had all arrived in Honolulu. The new missionaries wanted to meet in Lahaina soon. George recorded, "It was with feelings of delight that cannot easily be described that we received the news."[74]

Soon Cannon and Keeler left Wailuku for Lahaina by horse, which made the trip easier. All the new missionaries met together, along with Brothers Bigler and Farrer who arrived in Lahaina the same day. Many letters and newspapers also awaited George Q. in Lahaina, and he was delighted not only to receive a letter from Elizabeth Hoagland but also "a daguerreotype likeness" of her. George learned that Hiram Clark and Hiram Blackwell had been "crying down" the islands and Blackwell "said we would have to leave." He also received a great deal of information about his family and matters generally in Utah.[75]

George Q. reported to President Lewis that church membership totaled 214 on Maui, with five branches (the four near Ke'anae and Waiakoa, which is what was usually referred to as Kula), and that a number of new converts had been ordained to the priesthood.[76] The new missionaries found the report "astonishing" because they had thought that no one would yet have a rudimentary command of even conversational Hawaiian "and had no idea that preaching had commenced."[77] Pratt had instructed Lewis that all of the mis-

73. *GQCJH*, Aug. 11, 1851.

74. GQCJH, Aug. 20, 1851; *My First Mission*, 38.

75. *GQCJH*, Aug. 20, 1850. Tellingly, George first wrote, "a daguerreotype likeness of my E----" but later changed it to "of Elizabeth."

76. Philip B. Lewis to Parley P. Pratt, Sep. 1, 1851, cited in *GQCJH*, 121n49.

77. Henry Bigler diary, Aug. 17, 1851, cited and quoted in *GQCJH*, 121n49.

sionaries should stay together until they "got a knowledge of the language," but finding that everyone had already "scattered out before we got here, and that they had all made a good proficiency in the language particularly Bro Cannon," they should keep things as they were.[78] Woodbury was assigned to go to the Big Island with James Hawkins, Francis Hammond set up a cobbler's shop in Lahaina to provide financial support for missionary work, and Philip Lewis would also stay in Lahaina, both with their families.[79]

George Q. had become so proficient in Hawaiian that "it was hard for me to speak in my mother tongue." It was difficult for him to pray in English "in the family circle," and he would only read books in Hawaiian other than the Book of Mormon and Doctrine and Covenants. He "had even trained myself to think in that language."[80] He had also become accustomed to being among the Hawaiians. Socializing with the old and new missionaries with whom he shared religious, national, and cultural backgrounds "made it somewhat of a trial for me to return and mix with the Natives and conform to their manner of living again — but I am laboring for a liberal master who knows that my motives are pure."[81]

While Cannon and Keeler were away, their unusual success in Ke'anae had created a sectarian war. Rev. Whittlesey, the head Calvinist minister in the area, two French Catholic priests, and Rev. Green, the Presbyterian minister with whom George Q. had had issues in Kula, were all in Ke'anae trying to make it impossible for the pair to preach and to persuade the natives who had been baptized that they needed to shun the Mormons. "[The new converts] had been assailed by enemies from every side, and those who were weak in the faith were in perplexity." To Cannon, by this sectarian strife, the "Devil had set all his instruments to work to stop the progress of the work here and turn the saints from the truth."[82]

The sectarian attacks on the Mormons grew more serious when the Protestant ministers convinced the "konohikis," the overseers of sections of land running from the uplands to the ocean, to restrict

78. Philip B. Lewis diary, Aug. 1851, cited and quoted in *GQCJH*, 121n49.
79. *GQCJH*, Aug. 21, 1851.
80. *My First Mission*, 38.
81. *GQCJH*, Aug. 26, 1851.
82. *GQCJH*, Sep. 3, 1851; *My First Mission*, 39.

Hawaiians from interacting with the Mormons. Konohikis were appointed by local chiefs and were powerful, regulating such matters as fishing rights and uses of the land.[83] The local konohiki was convinced to gather new church members together and call them out individually to tell them that they could not convene LDS Church meetings under threat of prosecution.[84]

The troubles that started in Ke'anae would not go away easily. George Q. went to Lahaina, then to Honolulu, looking for responsible government officials to complain to. The Lewises had relocated to O'ahu, and, together with President Lewis, George Q. met with numerous officials, including John Young, minister of the interior, whose permission they had asked to use the Royal Palace in Lahaina as a meeting place and who had not yet responded to their request. Young asked to have the request in writing and promised to have it considered by the Privy Council. The general reaction was that "the laws were sufficiently ample to protect us without anything further." The American consul also wrote a supportive letter. Finally, the minister of foreign affairs provided a letter condemning the actions of the sectarian ministers in Ke'anae, but he believed that the best way for the Mormons to address the problem was to apply to the courts in Maui. After describing the ten-day bureaucratic nightmare, George Q. noted simply in his journal, "Baptized 2 natives this evening."[85]

Ever resourceful, he decided to request approval for the Mormons to build a meeting house in Ke'anae, using another approach to obtain government approval. George and Lewis sought out the agent of the king's lands to make this request. They learned that the king's agent had gone to Lahaina. Cannon and Lewis followed and met with Alexander Liholiho, essentially the crown prince. He told George Q. that "we should be protected by the laws, [the sectarians] had no right to interfere with us." As for the request to build a meeting house in Ke'anae, Liholiho would learn more and then inform the konohiki what the Mormon congregations could do. George later related that "the visit, altogether, was satisfactory and resulted in good."[86]

83. *GQCJH*, 104n6.
84. *GQCJH*, Sep. 25, 1851; *My First Mission*, 41.
85. *GCQJH*, Oct. 1–11, 1851.
86. *GQCJH*, Oct. 13–20, 1851; *My First Vision*, 41.

Following Cannon's work to clarify that the Mormons could continue to engage in missionary work and protect those who joined the church, he headed to Ke'anae to calm matters. On November 11, George stopped at Makawao, near Waiakoa, in the uplands. There, he met John Winchester, an old friend of Francis Hammond, and Albion Burnham, Winchester's brother-in-law. It was rainy, and George Q. was constrained to stay in Makawao a few days. He had meaningful discussions with both men, staying up almost all night. When the weather cleared, George traveled to Ke'anae. Two days later, Winchester and Burnham, arrived from Makawao, seeking baptism. Hammond was coincidentally nearby and was delighted to baptize the pair.[87]

Others had been baptized. In addition to Winchester and Albion, there was James Kipp, who was also baptized by Hammond; a Mr. Birch, a neighbor of Jonathan Napela in Wailuku who was baptized by George Q.; and Birch's son-in-law David Rice, who was baptized shortly after. All were prosperous *haole* residents of Maui, and strengthened the church on the island. They had native and white missionaries and church members stay with them, often held conferences in their homes, and were generous to all the Saints.[88]

In spite of the sectarian strife and government issues, Cannon continued to convert new church members wherever he went, baptizing twenty-six in Lahaina during December 16–18. He created branches of the church when there were enough members. When he formed branches, he always ordained some teachers and deacons to lead.[89] George knew that branches needed leadership and he looked for strong men and women to take those roles.

The new year prompted George Q. to consider whether the "experiment … in regard to preaching the gospel among this people" had worked. "We had every reason to believe we would be sustained in attempting. The result has answered my expectations."[90] The year 1852 also brought a long-hoped-for baptism. Jonathan Napela, who contributed so much to the beginnings of the work in Maui and

87. *GQCJH*, Nov. 10–12, 21, 1851.
88. *GQCJH*, Nov. 11–13, 21, 1851; 643, 646, 692–93, 708.
89. *GQCJH*, Dec. 7, 16–18, 1851.
90. *GQCJH*, Jan. 1, 1852.

who continued to make important contributions, "came over to be baptised this morning." Five days later, Cannon and Napela accompanied William Uaua to a quiet spot and baptized him there. Now, all three of the men whom Cannon first met in Wailuku when he felt prompted to return to town in March 1851, Jonathan Napela, H. K. Kaleohone, and William Uaua, had been baptized and ordained to the Aaronic priesthood. The occasion called for a letter to Bigler and Farrer, who were living with Cannon when he initially met the three. "I told you that there were three of them together as I passed Mr. Napela's, him, Uaua, the lawyer who used to visit us at Lahaina, … and Kaleohano."[91] All three went on to serve as missionaries and play an important role in the growth and strength of the church in the islands, though Jonathan Napela occasionally went on drinking binges and sometimes "fell into transgression" (generally sexual transgression) while he was drinking. Francis Hammond and Joseph F. Smith, who served as a missionary in the islands shortly after George Q. Cannon left, were frustrated by Napela's actions. Napela was always extremely embarrassed and repentant after these episodes and he was always forgiven.[92]

In the last days of January 1852, George Q. decided to take up the task he had long contemplated: translating the Book of Mormon into Hawaiian. He was living with Jonathan and Kitty Napela and he realized that Jonathan could be very helpful. George described the situation:

> [Napela] was an educated, intelligent Hawaiian, who thoroughly understood his own language, and could give me the exact meaning of words. The meaning attached to many words depended upon the context. … [Napela] was a descendant of the old chiefs of the Island of Maui, in whose families the language was preserved and spoken in the greatest purity, and he had advantages which no other equally well educated man, at that time, possessed. He had studied the principles of the gospel very thoroughly, he had a comprehensive mind to grasp the truth, and he had been greatly favored by the spirit.[93]

91. *GQCJH,* Jan. 5, 10, 1852; George Q. Cannon to Henry Bigler and William Farrer, Jan. 12, 1852, copy in *GQCJH,* 574–76.

92. John J. Hammond, *Island Adventures: The Hawaiian Mission of Francis A. Hammond, 1851–1865* (Salt Lake City: Signature Books, 2016), 221, 238, 306, 349–50.

93. *My First Mission,* 59.

George's first journal entry on the subject, recorded January 27, 1852, read simply, "Translating Book of Mormon." Many similar entries followed over the next two years, and the mission president and fellow missionaries encouraged him. Initially, he translated only when he was not fulfilling other responsibilities. As he worked to do all of this, he noted that "the Lord seemed very near to us upon those islands in those days."[94]

George Q. described how he and Jonathan worked on the translation: George would translate a few pages and then, "when opportunity offered, explain to Brother Napela the ideas, whether historical or doctrinal, in great detail. By this means, he would get a pretty thorough comprehension of the part I was translating. I would then read the translation to him, going carefully over every word and sentence, and learning from him the impression the language used conveyed to his mind."[95]

A "general conference" for the islands was held on April 1 and 2 in Makawao and on April 6 in a beautiful canyon not far from Wailuku. The conference was to be held outdoors, but on the first day, clouds threatened rain. The Saints prayed for a "fine day," but Cannon and others planned to move the meeting into a shop in the village to avoid getting wet. Napela scolded them—"it did not manifest faith" to go indoors when they had asked for good weather. Rebuked, the missionaries "started for a grove a short distance away." The day was fine. Things were going so well in the Sandwich Islands mission that President Lewis proposed that he request nine more missionaries. All voted in favor of the proposal.[96] On April 6 the conference continued in the beautiful ʻIao Valley west of Wailuku under a large kukui tree. Over 500 natives from Maui branches were in attendance. George Q. and fellow leaders and missionaries had been nervous about broaching the subject of tithing to the members, but they did, and in response, church members unanimously approved a resolution to follow the law of tithing."[97]

In August, Napela gave George Q. a letter he had felt inspired

94. *GQCJH*, Jan. 27, 1852; *My First Mission*, 60.
95. *My First Mission*, 60.
96. *GQCJH*, Apr. 1, 1852.
97. *GQCJH*, Apr. 6, 1852; Hammond, *Island Adventures*, 91.

to write to Brigham Young to be translated. George felt "somewhat delicate" about translating the letter because Napela had used George's name liberally and George feared "lest a wrong impression might go out, as though I was blowing my own horn & anxious to have it known what I had done." George was so concerned that he prepared a few explanatory lines for the prophet.[98]

Napela's letter details the background of Napela meeting Cannon, the efforts of George Q. to establish the church in Maui and the islands, and the growth of the church. Napela iterated that "it is very plain to us that this is the church of God, … and there are many upon these islands who have obtained strong faith by the grace of God."[99] Cannon's "explanatory note" is longer than Napela's heartfelt letter and, in fact, "blows Cannon's horn" more than Napela's. Cannon explains that Napela is the "most influential man that has yet joined the church; … and embraced the work in face of all the opposition of the majority of his friends and relatives." Cannon then provides information about the mission, reporting 560 members in Maui and about 700 for all the islands, and noting that the missionaries are "striving" to "acquire" the language, "with tolerable success." He concludes that with "what leisure time I have I devote to the translation of the Book of Mormon," which "would be of incalculable benefit to the people."[100]

For the next six months, the narrative of George Q.'s mission remained largely the same. Though he generally stayed with Napela in Wailuku or Kula to be able to translate, he also continued other activities and baptized new converts. He organized branches, oversaw and facilitated the construction of meetinghouses, preached to both believers and doubters, and helped develop leaders and missionaries from among the natives. In August 1852, the Saints constructed a one-room meeting house in what Cannon described as "Kula" but sometimes as "Waiakoa." This was the first LDS chapel created in the islands. There remains today a church that is referred to as the oldest LDS building on Maui and is called the "Pulehu" meeting

98. *GQCJH*, Apr. 9, 1852.

99. Jonathan Napela to Brigham Young (translated by GQC), Apr. 8, 1852, reproduced in *GQCJH*, 581.

100. GQC to Brigham Young, Apr. 8, 1852, reproduced in *GQCJH*, 581–82.

house, which is reputed to have been built in 1852. The original part of this building is likely the Kula meeting house.[101]

About this time, it was clear to many, including his fellow missionaries, that George's project to translate the Book of Mormon was important enough that it should be his principal assignment. The other Maui missionaries blessed George that he might have the spirit both to maintain his level of righteousness and to be inspired in his translation. In October, Philip Lewis made it official, calling and setting George Q. apart to a special assignment to translate, though he also continued to travel, speak at meetings, and baptize.[102]

In November 1852, George received word from a cousin, Joseph Taylor, that members of the First Presidency sent "words of cheer, approving of what I was doing, and counseling me to persevere" "and for me not to cease until it was completed." Willard Richards, a counselor in the First Presidency, chimed in that "if I went on with it [the translation of the Book of Mormon] my name should be had in everlasting remembrance among the saints.[103]

Important matters sometimes took away from George's translation efforts. Like other LDS missionaries in Hawai'i at the time, on occasion during his mission, George was called upon to administer to those suffering from health problems. On December 15, 1852, he was with his friend, William Uaua, in Lahaina, working on the translation. Uaua woke both George and Francis Hammond, who were staying with him, saying that his wife was in the midst of childbirth, that a male midwife recognized that the baby was dead, and that the mother would soon be dead as well unless she delivered the lifeless baby. Cannon and Hammond prayed fervently with Uaua, then George went out by himself "and pled with the Lord to save both the mother and the child." As George and Francis were going outside for some fresh air, they heard a healthy cry from the newborn baby girl. The men "felt to praise the Lord for his manifold mercies."[104]

George also needed periodic distraction from the challenging work

101. *GQCJH*, Aug. 10, 1852; for photos, see Maui 24/7, "Pulehu LDS Chapel," Facebook, facebook.com/maui247/posts/pulehu-lds-chapel-the-church-of-jesus-christ-of-latter-day-saints-has-been-in-ha/913646282048713/ (accessed Oct. 2021).

102. *GQCJH*, Aug. 13, Oct. 5, 9, 1852.

103. *GQCJH*, Nov. 11, 1852.

104. *GQCJH*, Dec. 15, 1852.

of translation. He loved receiving news in the form of letters from family, friends, fellow missionaries, and church leaders, and was an excellent correspondent. George's friend, Joseph Cain, sent him months' worth of the weekly *Deseret News* at a time and he would devour each four-page issue for news.[105] Over his time in the islands, his feelings for Elizabeth Hoagland deepened. He sent her a daguerreotype of himself. Relatives and friends told him what a pretty young woman Elizabeth was becoming. George Q. noted in his journal in August 1853 that he received his first letter from her in "about two years." Her letter "breathed strong assurances of love and affection" and "conveyed peculiar feelings of pleasure to me." Her excuse for not writing more was that "she had received none from me since she last wrote." Thereafter, George and Elizabeth maintained a relatively active correspondence. In one letter she wrote that if he was not coming home soon, she would "feel like shouldering her pack and come to meet me. Bless her, O Lord for her constancy and may she be strengthened continually and kept to the end."[106]

In November 1852, George Q. received news from Joseph Cain that Orson Pratt had announced the principle of plural marriage to the world on August 31, and "the revelation together with his sermon was to be published." George commented that "this is what I have been expecting and looking for some time."[107] As close as he was to his uncle, John Taylor, who had been a polygamist in Nauvoo, Illinois, George seems to have known about the church's teaching of plural marriage for some time.

In March 1853, the nine new missionaries requested by President Philip Lewis arrived in Honolulu. Now, there were twenty-two missionaries, including Jane Lewis, Mary Jane Hammond, Elvira Woodbury (sister of Jane Lewis), and Patty Perkins, all of whom were married to four of the male missionaries who were already there. George Q. recorded that the new missionaries should be "located among the different branches and live with natives, so that

105. *GQCJH*, Nov. 11, 1852, Mar. 7–8, 26, July 21, 1853.

106. *GQCJH*, Aug. 20, 1851, July 21, Nov. 11, 1852, Aug. 18, Oct. 31, Nov. 5, 1853, Apr. 20, 1854.

107. *GQCJH*, Nov. 13, 1852.

they might learn the language and prepare themselves to fill the places of those Elders who would soon return to the Valley."[108]

About the beginning of June 1853, a smallpox epidemic broke out. Missionaries did what they could to alleviate the suffering caused by it. Parts of O'ahu were hit particularly hard and Lewis noted that "such scenes of wretchedness and misery my eyes never held before." The mission president added that many had been blessed through priesthood administration.[109] Maui was not hit as hard as some of the islands and the work of George Q. and his colleagues continued with little interruption. Nevertheless, many Saints died of this dreadful disease.[110]

George Q., despite many interruptions, always returned to translating the Book of Mormon into Hawaiian, a grueling undertaking. It forced him to understand the book in English better than he ever had. "I never could enter into the feelings experienced by those holy men who wrote the Book of Mormon as I can at present."[111] The project was monumental, the process painstaking. He and Napela would discuss each word, parsing it for understanding and connotation. According to George's later recollection, as the project progressed, it "became a very easy labor for me. I obtained great facility of expression in the language, and before I got through with the book I had a range of words at my command, superior to the great bulk of the people." Napela stayed close, however, and reviewed each sentence. Toward the end of the assignment, other men with deep understanding of the language helped George and Jonathan with their revisions. On July 22, 1853, about two and a half years after he started, George had a complete manuscript of the translation. Not satisfied, he continued to revise. Several months later, on September 27, 1853, the first round of revisions was completed, for which Cannon and Napela "felt to rejoice and thank the Lord for his goodness."[112]

The missionaries held a conference in September 1853. President Lewis blessed George Q. that he would "acquire many different

108. *GQCJH*, Mar. 7–8, 1853; Hawaiian Mission History, Mar. 9–11, as cited and quoted in Bitton, *GQC*, 26.

109. Philip B. Lewis, letter, June 30, 1853, as reproduced in part in Bitton, *GQC*, 27; Kenney, "Mormons and the Smallpox Epidemic," 3.

110. Kenney, "Mormons and the Smallpox Epidemic," 8–14; Bitton, *GQC*, 27.

111. *GQCJH*, Dec. 8, 1852.

112. *My First Mission*, 60–61.

languages and preach in power in them and also translate the Book of Mormon in many languages." At the conference, the missionaries decided to hike to the summit of Haleakala. George Q. was awed at the top of the "extinct volcano" when he and his companions "found ourselves standing on the brink of an almost perpendicular precipice which formed the sides of a vast cauldron."[113]

Three months later, in December, George Q. visited Kaua'i to further revise the translation of the Book of Mormon. William Farrer, who had come to the Sandwich Islands with George, was then serving on that island with J. W. H. Kauwahi, "a man of acute intellect and talent and good education, and who was called the most eloquent and best reasoner in the Hawaiian nation. Cannon and Kauwahi and Farrer went through the manuscript together for just over a month.[114] At the end, George was finally satisfied.

It was good to have the translation done, but the work would have little or no effect unless it was published. The question was whether to have it printed by an outside press or "to purchase a press and printing materials for the mission, with which to print that and other works necessary for the instruction of the Saints." They opted to buy a press, and fundraising followed. Edmund Dennis, a white man who had been converted in Honolulu, loaned $1,000, and Haalelea, a Hawaiian chief who had agreed to permit the Saints to use land he owned on Lana'i as a gathering place, loaned the committee $500, for a total of at least $1,500, to purchase a press, type, paper, and other necessary materials. The funds were sent to John M. Horner, a prosperous church member in San Francisco who procured the press and materials from New York City, perhaps adding some of his own funds for the purpose.[115] The press and materials were first shipped to Honolulu, but, at the direction of Parley

113. *GQCJH*, Oct. 10, 12–15, 1853. Most volcanologists believe that Haleakala is dormant, not extinct.

114. *GQCJH*, Dec. 15, 1853-Jan. 31, 1854. Kauwahi later had legal trouble. *GQCJH*, 671–72. Not long after the smallpox epidemic, he left the faith and published a letter vilifying the church, which was published in a book by John Hyde Jr. Kenney, "Mormons and the Smallpox Epidemic," 15.

115. *My First Mission*, 62, 64; *GQJH*, Nov. 9, 17, 1853. Cannon and others also raised smaller amounts from individuals.

P. Pratt, they were subsequently sent to San Francisco to print the Hawaiian Book of Mormon and a newspaper.[116]

The time drew near for the five original remaining missionaries to the Sandwich Islands to return home. Through their efforts and with help from new missionaries who joined them and members who converted to the church and shared its message, the LDS Church in the Sandwich Islands had grown from a handful of whites to over 4,000 members. One last task stood before them: finding the means to travel home. The missionaries were unwilling to ask church headquarters to pay the expenses, so they sought donations, large and small, from the Saints. Some church members donated animals, which were sold. A farewell celebration raised $15. Jonathan Napela donated $27 and a trunk to George Q.[117]

George bid long farewells to his friends in Maui, then traveled to Honolulu, where a letter was waiting for him from Elizabeth, "the best, I think, without any exception," that she had ever written.[118] The missionaries scheduled passage on the steamer *Polynesian,* even though they had not yet raised sufficient funds to pay for the voyage, which was $50 per person for second-class travel.[119] The day of their departure, George and all of his colleagues went up the Nuʻuanu Valley early "to take a bath," no doubt under the Kapena Falls, just as they had their first day in Honolulu three-and-a-half years before. As the missionaries were about to leave, the "saints got up" a final feast. Church members donated an additional $66 and a colt, which was then sold for $20. The missionaries now had enough for ship passage and a little bit more. Francis Hammond slipped George a $10 piece, which he later found in his vest pocket.[120]

George Q. was disappointed that James Keeler, George's first missionary companion, did not make it to Honolulu to steam home with his friends. By the time Keeler was ready to leave for the conference in Honolulu, he was unable to find passage from the Big Island, where he was serving. Keeler finally made it to Honolulu on August 2.[121] The

116. *My First Mission*, 62.
117. *GQCJH*, Apr. 18, May 17, 25, June 18, 24, 29–30, July 2, 5, 1854.
118. *GQCJH*, July 6, 9–10, 12–13, 16, 19–21, 24–25, 27, 1854.
119. *GQCJH*, July 26, 28, 1854.
120. *GQCJH*, July 29, 1854.
121. *GQCJH*, July 29, 1854, 521n62.

other four—Cannon, Bigler, Hammond, and Farrer—had boarded the *Polynesian* at 2:00 p.m. on July 29. The *Polynesian* attracted attention because it may have been the first steamship to visit the Sandwich Islands.[122] Scores of church members and remaining missionaries packed the wharf. Soon, the steamer left and sailed out of the harbor. By nightfall, all of the returning elders were seasick.

George Q. Cannon had served an extraordinary mission in the Sandwich Islands for forty-three months. His efforts had brought him to the attention of senior church leaders in Salt Lake City, most importantly, Brigham Young, and it would not be long before he received his next church assignment.

---

122. Passenger List of the Steamer *Polynesian*, Ancestry, Hawaii, U.S. Arriving and Departing Passenger Lists, 1843–1989, ancestry.com; Ralph S. Kuykendall, *The Hawaiian Kingdom—Twenty Critical Years, 1854–1874* (Honolulu: University of Hawaii Press, 1953), 18–19.

CHAPTER THREE

EDITOR, HUSBAND, FATHER, MISSION PRESIDENT, APOSTLE, LOBBYIST, "SENATOR"

1854-64

"To Correct Mis-Representation, We Adopt Self-Representation"
—*Motto of the* Western Standard, *1854–57*

George Q. Cannon and his fellow missionaries' trip from Honolulu to San Francisco on the steamer *Polynesian* was not without excitement. It ran out of coal before reaching San Francisco and had to "sail under canvas for thirty hours in the latter part of the passage."[1] The *Polynesian* encountered fog as it approached the Golden Gate and anchored near a small island until the fog lifted. The ship passed into San Francisco Bay and docked at the wharf about noon on August 12, 1854.[2] After an arduous two-week voyage, the missionaries had arrived; George Q. was back in the United States.

The missionaries were excited to press on to Great Salt Lake City but lacked funds and needed to find work to earn enough to make the trip. George was employed by Parley P. Pratt, president of the LDS Church's Pacific Mission, to edit and prepare Pratt's autobiography. He and the forty-seven-year-old apostle became close friends over the next few months as Cannon worked through 400 pages of the manuscript. Pratt was impressed with the talents and hard work of his young charge. With the $50 he earned for his work, George

1. "Arrival of the Polynesian," *San Francisco Daily Herald*, Aug. 13, 1854, as quoted and cited in *GQCJH*, 523n1; *GQCJH*, Aug. 8–11, 1854.

2. *GQCJH*, Aug. 12, 1854.

set out for Utah in late September, first by ship down the coast to San Pedro, then home. He arrived in Great Salt Lake City on November 28, 1854, four months after leaving Honolulu.[3]

One of the first people George Q. sought out was Elizabeth Hoagland, who had been fourteen years old when he left for the California gold fields. The two had corresponded for several years while he was in Hawai'i and were essentially betrothed. Less than two weeks after George's arrival home, the couple was married by Elizabeth's father in the family home. George wore a borrowed suit that did not fit him well. The day after the wedding, he got a job as a messenger for the legislative assembly of Utah Territory and subsequently found work as a typesetter for the *Deseret News*.[4] Just before his wedding, George Q. obtained US citizenship papers from a "judge."[5] These naturalization papers were to become controversial in future years.

George expected to return to Hawai'i, now with Elizabeth, where the printing press and related equipment purchased with loans and donations from Hawaiians were to be delivered and which he could use to print his translation of the Book of Mormon.[6] Pratt, however, had the press delivered to San Francisco and asked that George Q. be sent there to ready the Hawaiian Book of Mormon manuscript, and to typeset and print it. Pratt also anticipated that Cannon would help him publish a newspaper, using the same press.[7] From his wages as a typesetter, George Q. and Elizabeth saved enough money to pay for their journey. In May 1855, they received blessings from Brigham Young and joined a group led by Apostle Charles C. Rich bound for San Bernardino, arriving there in mid-June after a perilous journey. The couple and the two men called to assist George Q., Joseph Bull and Matthew F. Wilkie, then took a steamer up the coast to San Francisco. George did not suffer from seasickness as

3. *GQCJH*, Aug. 14–Sep. 20, 1854, 530–31; Parley P. Pratt to BY, Sep. 21, 1854, cited in Bitton, *GQC*, 69–70, 483n1.

4. *GQCJH*, 530–31; Bitton, *GQC*, 69–70.

5. Bitton, *GQC*, 72.

6. George Q. Cannon, *Writings from the Western Standard* (Liverpool, Eng.: George Q. Cannon, 1864), vi (hereafter *Writings*); *GQCJH*, 532–33; Bitton, *GQC*, 70.

7. Parley P. Pratt to BY, Feb. 1855, BY to GQC, May 7, 1855, both as cited in Bitton, *GQC*, 70, 483nn6 and 7.

much as he usually did, but Elizabeth, two months pregnant, was sick for the entire voyage.[8]

When the young couple arrived in San Francisco, Pratt had left for Great Salt Lake City, having given up the idea of publishing a newspaper and not knowing that his request for George Q. to join him had been granted.[9] George Q. learned of this from the Mowrys, church members he had met the year before and who took in an increasingly sick Elizabeth. George immediately set out to pursue Pratt and caught him at "brother Naile's," near San Jose, where the Mowrys told him Pratt might be waiting for others to join him to travel to Utah.[10] Pratt was not inclined to return to San Francisco and instead set Cannon apart as his replacement as president of the Pacific Mission (covering northern California, Oregon and Washington territories, and the British and Russian possessions in the north), subject to ratification by other members of the Quorum of the Twelve. George commented that Pratt "gave me a very good blessing indeed."[11] Apostle Orson Hyde visited San Francisco and gave George a letter written by Pratt and him (the two had met as Pratt was returning to Salt Lake and Hyde was coming to California). The letter instructed George to find a suitable building and proceed with publication of the Hawaiian Book of Mormon, but to wait for further instruction from Brigham Young before commencing publication of a newspaper. They found two rooms in a "fire proof brick building at 118½ Montgomery St., belonging to S. Brannan."[12] Samuel Brannan had led a group of Mormons to San Francisco by ship in 1846 and had stayed there and made a fortune in the gold rush, but had left the church.

Pratt's calling of George Q. to lead the mission as well as to publish the Book of Mormon and a newspaper were soon ratified, not only by Hyde in early July when he visited, but also by Charles

8. GQCJ, May 11–June 13, 1855; Bitton, *GQC*, 72. George and Elizabeth's first child, George Q. Cannon Jr. was born on January 29, 1856.

9. *GQCJH*, 534–35.

10. GQCJ, June 24–25, 1855; *Autobiography of Parley Parker Pratt*, 3rd ed. (Salt Lake City: Deseret Book Co., 1938), 426.

11. GQCJ, June 24, 1855.

12. As described in GQC to BY, July 27, 1855, printed in full in Roger Robin Ekins, ed., *Defending Zion: George Q. Cannon and the California Mormon Newspaper Wars of 1856–57* (Spokane, WA: Arthur H. Clark Co., 2002), 43–45.

Rich and Amasa M. Lyman. Lyman visited in late September and early October and presented George's name to the congregation for approval as the new mission president.[13] Not realizing that Pratt was on his way back to Utah, Brigham Young sent George Q. two letters, one in August telling him that, if Pratt left, he should take over all publishing and printing responsibilities, and a second one in September advising him to take over all financial and executive management of the printing business in San Francisco.[14]

San Francisco's "streets were filled with people." In the five years since George had first passed through on his way to the Sandwich Islands, the city had grown from about 20,000 to 50,000. Few of the local residents were members of the LDS Church and few had positive views of the Saints. George found "prospects in San Francisco for the establishment of a printing-office and newspaper … to be of the most discouraging character." Progress was soon made, however, and by July 27, 1855, George wrote to Young that the load he had felt on his shoulders lifted "when I took hold with the determination that by the help of the Lord to effect something, gleam after gleam of sunshine shone in my path dispersing the gloom."[15]

The printing press was in storage in San Francisco after its longer journey from the eastern United States to Hawai'i, then back to the mainland. Several of the press's ribs had been damaged in the voyage around the Cape of Good Horn and had to be recast, but it was otherwise "in (tolerably) good order." After the press was moved to the rooms on Montgomery Street, George Q. had repairs done and worked hard to make the press operational. Once it was working, George and Elizabeth worked together to set type for the Hawaiian Book of Mormon. Elizabeth would read passages in English while George Q. set the type in Hawaiian. The journalist missionaries—George, Elizabeth, Joseph Bull, and Matthew Wilkie—found they had too few k's, the most common letter in Hawaiian, to be able to set many pages. Cannon located a "matrix" of k's, sufficient to do

13. GQCJ, Sep. 30–Oct. 4, 1855.

14. GQC, *Writings*, vii; BY to GQC, Aug. 20, 1855, BY to GQC, Sep. 29, 1855, both quoted and cited in Bitton, *GQC*, 73.

15. Hubert H. Bancroft, *The Works of Hubert Howe Bancroft, History of California*, 39 vols. (San Francisco: Bancroft, 1888), 6:755–87; GQC, *Writings*, vii; GQC to BY, July 27, 1855.

sixteen pages, which improved operations.[16] Bull and Wilkie labored with the Cannons to prepare the typeset to publish the *Buke a Moramona*. The book was completed in January 1856. The small Brevier type needed for the title page had been ordered from New York months before but had not yet arrived. George Q. used the time to write and print an eight-page introduction in Hawaiian to the *Buke a Moramona*, 1,500 copies of which he promptly sent to the islands for use by missionaries.[17] When the book was completed, 2,000 copies were printed and sent to the islands. Hundreds of copies reportedly went unpurchased or distributed because Islander Saints believed they were to have received the book for free, although these reports suggested that only a few hundred were sent there, which is a small fraction of the number Cannon reported were printed and sent.[18] Cannon's service was extraordinary in all phases of the finished project—translating the book with the help of Joseph Napela and others (most of which occurred while Cannon was in the Islands), raising the funds from Hawaiians to purchase and transport the press, helping to typeset, and proofreading the final product. In the San Francisco printing office, only George Q. read Hawaiian, so he had to do the final edits, proofread each line, participate in typesetting, and draft a prospectus.[19] His efforts only served to further impress all of the senior church leaders, particularly Brigham Young. Cannon also specially bound a copy of the *Buke a Moramona* for Young and sent it to the prophet.[20]

As noted, Elizabeth had been ill on the trip to San Francisco. On January 29, 1856, she delivered a boy, whom the couple named George Q. Jr. George Q. Sr. copied the blessing he gave his son on February 5, 1856 into his journal. Sadly, George Q. Jr. was sickly and died ten months later.

In spite of living hand to mouth, George Q. and his colleagues did not take outside employment but proceeded to new printing and

16. Bitton, *GQC*, 73; GQCJ, July 1, 4–8, 1855; GQC to BY, July 27, 1855; *My First Mission*, 63.

17. GQC to BY, Jan. 30, 1856, quoted and cited in Bitton, *GQC*, 74; GQCJ, Jan. 28–31, 1856.

18. Scott G. Kenney, "Mormons and the Smallpox Epidemic of 1853," *The Hawaiian Journal of History*, 31 (1997): 14–15.

19. GQC to BY, Jan. 26, 1856, cited in Bitton, *GQC*, 74.

20. "Book of Mormon in the Hawaiian Language," *DN*, Apr. 16, 1856, 8.

publishing tasks. On January 4, 1855, just as the *Buke a Moramona* was being completed, George Q. issued a prospectus for a newspaper, which he called the *Western Standard.*[21] He wrote that the paper would provide correct information about the LDS Church and its members but would also print current domestic and international news. He actively sought donations. One senior church leader told George Q. that he might be able to successfully "accomplish the labors assigned" to him if he had $1,000. Finding even $5.00 was a challenge, but George persisted. One donation came from Sam Brannan, who gave George a $50 gold piece when George did not have sufficient funds to pay rent.[22]

As editor and publisher of the *Western Standard*, Cannon defended the Mormon Church, Brigham Young, and plural marriage. The *Standard's* masthead announced, "To Correct Mis-Representation We Adopt Self-Representation."[23] According to one scholar, Cannon "was a strong-willed, sometimes acerbic, even occasionally petulant man who showed no mercy to his many journalistic opponents." San Francisco was a war zone of competing newspapers in the mid-1850s, although one point most agreed on was the alleged horrors and sins of the LDS Church. Though he was combative, even pugnacious, Cannon managed to retain his "marvelous, ironic, sometimes sarcastic sense of humor through it all."[24]

From its first issue on February 23, 1856, to its last, on November 6, 1857, the periodical did, as advertised, carry news reports, humor, and culture, all reflecting its editor's interests, but its primary purpose was to defend Mormonism—its theology, practices, and leaders. The *Western Standard* did not shy away from challenging subjects, such as polygamy, the gruesome "assassination" of Cannon's friend Parley Pratt in 1857, or even the Mountain Meadows Massacre.[25] Many

21. Ekins, *Defending Zion*, 37, includes the full prospectus, which was published in various Mormon periodicals.

22. Bitton, *GQC*, 75–76.

23. A copy of the masthead is in Ekins, *Defending Zion*, 42–43.

24. Ekins, *Defending Zion*, 404–05.

25. Citations in this footnote are to Cannon's collected columns from the *WS*. All of the reprinted editorials included in *Writings* appear to have been written by Cannon. "Mormonism and Its Professors," *Writings*, Apr. 5, 1856, 59–64; "'Mormonism and Its Professors' Again," *Writings*, Apr. 19, 1856, 72–73; "'Mormons' and 'Mormonism,' and Their Opponents," *Writings*, May 3, 1856, 94–96; "Our Neighbor, The 'Golden Era,'"

of these columns were in response to articles in other newspapers. George Q. also attacked John Hyde Jr., who was called by Brigham Young on a mission to Hawai'i to help him renew his faith. Instead, Hyde realized as he sailed for Honolulu that he needed to renounce and lecture against Mormonism.[26] George Q. had a longtime distaste for individuals and groups he considered "apostate," and rarely showed them much sympathy.[27]

On April 27, 1857, Elizabeth Cannon bore a second son. Unlike his older brother, John Q. survived to adulthood and was throughout his life an unusually vigorous man who loved farming and outdoor activity and who commanded "Torrey's Rough Riders," the Second US Volunteer Cavalry, during the Spanish American War.[28]

In the fall of 1857, as reports of US Army troops marching to Utah reached San Francisco, Brigham Young wrote to Cannon, instructing him to wrap matters up in San Francisco and to be ready to leave at a moment's notice. Young suggested that George Q. might be sent to Hawai'i to oversee the binding and distribution of the new translation of the Book of Mormon and perhaps the publication of a newspaper in the Islands. Things progressed far enough by November 1857 that George Q. sent his brother, David, who had been working with him on the *Western Standard*, to accompany Elizabeth and six-month-old John back to Utah. Apostles Orson Pratt and

Writings, Nov. 29, 1856, 264–65; "The 'Alta California' on 'Mormonism,'" *Writings*, Jan. 17, 1857, 313–16; "Massacre of Emigrants—Reckless and Malignant Slanders," *Writings*, Oct. 23, 1857; "False Reports about the Mormons," *Writings*, Apr. 17, 1857, 387–88; "The Knotty Question of Utah," *Writings*, May 1, 1857, 400–402; "The 'Mormon Problem' and the 'Bulletin,' *Writings*, June 26, 1857, 454–59; "Assassination of President Parley P. Pratt," *Writings*, July 17, 1857, 465–69; "Freedom or Slavery—Which is Preferable?" *Writings*, Sep. 18, 1857, 506–12. George Q. did not include his column on the 1857 Mountain Meadows massacre in his 1864 collection of writings from the *Western Standard* likely because the tragic event had grown increasingly controversial.

26. "An Apostate and His Endorsers," *Writings*, Nov. 29, 1856, 255–59; "Society in Utah—Misrepresentations," *Writings*, Apr. 3, 1857, 382–85; KLC, "'A Strange Encounter': The English Courts and Mormon Polygamy," *BYUS* 22 (Winter 1982):73–83.

27. For example, Cannon excoriated John Hyde for leading people astray: "Previous to John Hyde's trip through the mining region, oppos<ing> the work, the people in this place were favorably inclined; but he came, and told his abominable and damnable falsehoods, and the people were turned from the truth and filled with prejudice." GQCJ, Aug. 5, 1857.

28. KLC, "Wives and Other Women: Love, Sex, and Marriage in the Lives of John Q. Cannon, Frank J. Cannon, and Abraham H. Cannon," *Dialogue* 43 (Winter 2010): 82.

Ezra T. Benson passed through San Francisco in early December and instructed George Q. that it was time for him to return to Zion.[29] George's service in San Francisco of publishing the Hawaiian Book of Mormon and editing the *Western Standard* further improved his reputation with Young and other high-ranking church leaders.

Following a difficult winter return to Utah, the group arrived in Great Salt Lake Valley on January 19, 1858. George reunited with Elizabeth and little John, who had also made the arduous journey and had arrived in the valley a few weeks earlier. Shortly afterward, George Q. gave an address in the old Tabernacle. After he and his brother, David, worked for a few weeks bringing wood into the Valley from Mill Creek Canyon, George was made adjutant general of the Nauvoo Legion (territorial militia) to be ready for the entrance of Johnston's army, sent to Utah to quell any rebellion. Realizing the serious difficulty the Saints were in, non-Mormon Thomas L. Kane obtained credentials from US President James Buchanan, traveled incognito to Utah by ocean and the isthmus of Panama. Once there, Kane met with Mormon leaders, then with new Governor Alfred Cumming and Colonel Albert Sidney Johnston. Kane was largely responsible for negotiating a peaceful resolution of tensions between the federal government and the Mormons.[30] George Q., who was soon to become a close friend and protégé of Colonel Kane, learned that the skills he had shown editing and publishing the *Western Standard* had earned him a new responsibility: leading the defense of Mormonism by editing the *Deseret News*, the central organ of the LDS Church. The press and materials for the *News* were shipped to Fillmore, 150 miles south of Salt Lake City, to which church leaders had retreated.[31]

Before he left for the "move south," George Q. met an eighteen-year-old woman named Sarah Jane Jenne. Both had the same impression that they should be married. A week later, on April 11, 1858, Brigham Young performed their wedding in Salt Lake City.[32] Elizabeth was unhappy, probably even heartbroken, about the match

29. Bitton, *GQC*, 88–89.

30. Matthew J. Grow, *"Liberty to the Downtrodden": Thomas L. Kane, Romantic Reformer* (New Haven, CT: Yale University Press, 2009), 161–90.

31. Bitton, *GQC*, 90. Actually, George was not the official editor yet, though he served in that function.

32. Joseph J. Cannon, "George Q. Cannon," *Instructor*, Dec. 1944, 576; Bitton, *GQC*, 90.

but dutifully consented to the wedding. George Q. and his two wives and son then made the trek to Fillmore, where he edited and published the weekly *Deseret News* from April to September. With the armistice negotiated by Thomas L. Kane, the federal troops marched through Salt Lake City in June on their way to quarters on the northwest end of Utah Lake.[33]

In early September 1858, George was headed back to Salt Lake City with his two wives (who were both pregnant), and his brother, David, who had helped with the *Deseret News*. Their wagons were loaded with the newspaper's presses and other materials as well as their scant material goods. George was looking forward to settling into Salt Lake City and having his life slow down. The group had stopped in Payson to rest when a carriage pulled into the home where the Cannons were staying. The driver, John Bollwinkle, gave George Q. a note. It was from Brigham Young and informed him that he had been called on a special mission to the Eastern United States and needed to leave immediately. The carriage could not carry the entire group, so George, Elizabeth, and little John Q. returned with Bollwinkle to Salt Lake City. George again placed part of his family under the care of David while he was hurriedly shuttled north. George was directed to go east to improve public and press perceptions of the Saints.[34]

The new assignment reflected the trust the president of the church had developed in young Cannon. When Brigham saw George Q., he simply asked, "Are you ready?" George responded that he was, and Brigham turned to the others assembled, "I told you it would be so."[35] Cannon was to use his "known character of sagacity, wisdom, ability, and, above all, humility and integrity" to improve public perceptions of the Mormons and their church, with the help of Thomas Kane.[36] Young, Heber C. Kimball, Daniel H. Wells, Charles C. Rich, and Erastus Snow, representing the entire First Presidency and two additional apostles, laid their hands on George's head, and Young gave him a special blessing setting him apart to this crucial calling.[37]

33. Bitton, *GQC*, 90.
34. GQCJ, Sep. 13, 14, 1858; Bitton, *GQC*, 93–94.
35. GQCJ, Sep. 13, 14, 1858; Bitton, *GQC*, 93–94.
36. *JH*, Aug. 28, 1858; BY to GQC, Sept. 15, 1858, quoted and cited in Bitton, *GQC*, 94
37. GQCJ, Sep. 14, 1858

George paid a quick visit to Elizabeth and young John, prayed with them, and gave Elizabeth a blessing for them and Sarah Jane "committing them … and all I have into the hands of the Lord."[38] He later recalled that, several months before receiving this mission call, he had dreamed that he would receive it. The dream included the words that Young would speak to him when George arrived at Young's office, and the details of what he was to do. He had told Elizabeth about the dream, and "she was so impressed with [it] that she could not shake it off. I found her crying many times alone, believing that I would have to go on this mission." Now, the dream was coming true, and he understood why she had been crying—she realized what was ahead for them all: no home, no husband, a toddler, a teenage sister wife, and needing to rely on the charity of relatives and friends who had their own challenges.[39]

Young arranged with Thomas Kane to have George Q. meet him at his home in Philadelphia and sent a letter with George introducing him to Kane. This was the beginning of what Cannon later remembered as a time when he spent about two years, partly under the charge of "Col. Thos. L. Kane," with "my duties being to allay the excitement existing in the east concerning us, and to disabuse the public mind of the falsehoods which had been circulated, and which had prompted the Administration, with President Buchanan at its head, to send an army to Utah."[40] Kane instructed Cannon how to approach specific editors: he would tell them that he was a "man of business, a 'Mormon' of course, with some means at [his] command, desirous of influencing public opinion and relieving myself and co-religionists from the weight of odium that had been so unjustly and cruelly heaped upon us" and that he "had a little means to devote to accomplish this." He would ask for their "advice on the subject": Would they publish well-written articles and letters from people in Utah to help remedy this unjust situation? Kane would then follow up with the same editors and reinforce what George had told them.[41]

38. GQCJ, Sep. 14, 1858.
39. GQCJ, May, 1, 1881.
40. GQCJ, May 1, 1881.
41. GQC to BY, Apr. 14, 1859, quoted and cited in Bitton, *GQC*, 95.

The challenges were significant: church leaders wanted the people of Utah to elect the local officials who would govern them, to convince federal officials that there was no need for the US Army to watch over the Mormons, to prevent the reduction in size of Utah Territory, to make sure that federal laws were not enacted prohibiting polygamy, and to achieve that which would facilitate all of these: statehood.[42] In an environment in which the new Republican Party had proclaimed that polygamy was, with slavery, one of the two "relics of barbarism," and in which anti-Mormon sentiment was on the rise in an increasingly tense pre-Civil War environment, Cannon was unsuccessful on each issue. Both the North and the South were against the Saints. Many Northerners were contemptuous of the strange marriage practice of the Mormons, while Southerners, who were more inclined to let local practices be regulated locally, did not want to be associated with an unpopular religion. George was disappointed that some editors and reporters would say favorable things privately about LDS practices and members but would not publish articles praising the Mormons.[43]

Cannon did get a number of articles and letters favorable to Mormon Utah published by influential newspapers and likely prevented the publication of many antagonistic reports, sometimes bribing editors for popular press coverage. Kane praised the Mormons and Utah territorial governor Alfred Cumming in a presentation to the Historical Society of New York entitled "The Executive of Utah," at which many reporters were present. George Q. attended the meeting to mingle and to distribute early press copies of the speech, but this was not the norm for his public relations efforts.[44] Ultimately, he had too few resources and too little time to curb the growing animosity.

Young continued to view the work George was performing favorably and to encourage his efforts. The church president wrote numerous letters to George in which he referred to him as "Br. George"

42. Lawrence R. Flake, "George Q. Cannon, His Missionary Years," DRE diss., Brigham Young University, 1970, 157, cited in Bitton, *GQC*, 94–95.

43. Bitton, *GQC*, 95–97.

44. GQCJ, Mar. 20–21, 1859; Grow, *Thomas L. Kane*, 198–200; "The Executive of Utah, Lecture by Col. Thomas J. [*sic*] Kane, *NYT*, Mar. 23, 1859; William P. MacKinnon, "Saving the Governor's Bacon, Thomas L. Kane's Political Defense of Alfred Cumming, 1859," *UHQ*, 89 (Fall 2021): 323–45.

and told him not to become discouraged.[45] As he learned of Cannon's efforts and continued to appreciate his abilities, the Mormon prophet encouraged his charge's efforts and reminded George that his responsibilities had been expanded to include emigration, a role that George's uncle, John Taylor, had been playing. Utilizing his organizational and administrative abilities, George Q. soon developed a system of having everything ready for church immigrants, from landing in New York or Boston or Philadelphia, to arrival at the western terminus of the railroad, which at the time was Iowa City. Immigrants were met by Mormon agents who provided resources and directed them from ship to train. On arriving in Iowa City, immigrants received supplies brought by wagon train from Utah. It was all based on a strategy developed by George and approved by Young to make the arduous trip across the country as quickly, cheaply, and efficiently as possible. Young's appreciation of George Q. continued to grow as Young came to understand that the younger man was "diligent, intelligent, articulate, and unquestionably loyal."[46]

The First Presidency and Quorum of the Twelve met in October 1859 to discuss who should fill the place in the apostolate that had been left vacant for more than two and a half years by the murder of Parley P. Pratt. Though he welcomed suggestions from all those assembled, Young stated that he wanted a man of "good natural judgment, possessing no higher qualifications than faithfulness and humility enough to seek the Lord for all his knowledge and who would trust in him for his strength." He then nominated thirty-two-year-old George Q. Cannon to the Quorum of the Twelve Apostles; the choice was unanimously sustained. Because Cannon remained in the public eye in the East, as a "man of business," the decision was kept secret for six months. Young announced the calling in the April 1860 general conference, noting George Q.'s experiences as a missionary in the Sandwich Islands, his work on the *Western Standard*, and his current assignment "assisting in the transaction of business and taking charge of this year's emigration."[47]

45. For example, BY to GQC, Sep. 17, 1859, quoted and cited in Bitton, *GQC*, 99.
46. Bitton, *GQC*,100–01; BY to GQC, Sep. 15, 1858, as cited in Bitton, *GQC*, 94.
47. Bitton, *GQC*, 101; *JH*, Oct. 23, 1859, BY to GQC, Nov. 3, 1859, as discussed in Everett L. Cooley, "A Brigham Young Letter to George Q. Cannon, 1859," *BYUS* 25 (Autumn

Cannon remained in the East for several more months, working closely with Kane, preparing for more lobbying, and working to create hope that federal troops would be withdrawn from Utah. Finally, in June 1860, he started west. He met Charles C. Rich and Amasa Lyman in Florence, Nebraska. Little did he know that he would soon be working closely with these two church leaders in a new international assignment. He then continued west in a fast carriage and caught up with Mormon businessman Horace Eldredge and territorial delegate William Hooper. The trio arrived in Salt Lake City three weeks later, on August 13.[48] He had been away from hearth and home for almost two years, and his reunion with Elizabeth, John, and Sarah Jane and his first introduction to new sons Franklin and Abraham, who had been born within six weeks of each other in early 1859, must have been especially sweet.[49] On August 26, 1860, ten months after the decision to appoint George as an apostle, he was ordained.[50] Somewhat surprisingly, the new apostle did not record the experience or his feelings in his usually comprehensive journal.

George Q. immediately reported all he had learned from his labors to Young and, a week later, spoke to the Saints in the Bowery about his activities. Young then spoke, addressed the crowd, noting that George had "accomplished all he possibly could." Speaking again three weeks later, Cannon reported that the United States was experiencing a "spirit of hatred, malice, and everything that is in opposition to the Spirit of God," likely perceiving that the country was hurtling toward civil war. He understood first hand that perceptions of Mormons based on polygamy and alleged authoritarianism were extremely negative. Cannon's faith was undeterred even as he worried

1985): 106–09. In this time before telegraph and transcontinental railroad or even the Pony Express, Cannon likely received word of his calling sometime in December 1859.

48. GQCJ, July 18–Aug. 10, 1860; *JH*, Aug. 13, 1860. Cannon crossed the country at about the same time that Sir Richard Burton was traveling by stagecoach to the "city of the saints." M. Guy Bishop, "The Saints and the Captain: The Mormons Meet Richard F. Burton," *Journal of the West* (1994):28–35. It is likely that Cannon met the famous Welsh adventurer as they were both in Salt Lake City during August and September 1860.

49. Frank was born to Sarah Jane on January 25, 1859; Abram to Elizabeth on March 12, 1859.

50. D. Michael Quinn, *The Mormon Hierarchy, Extensions of Power* (Salt Lake City: Signature Books, 1997), 647.

that the United States wanted to crush Mormonism. He regretted that Kane and he had not been able to accomplish more, although Kane reported that he had met with US President James Buchanan who hoped Congress would not enact an anti-polygamy law.[51]

On the same day he was ordained an apostle, less than two weeks after arriving back in Salt Lake City, George was called to go to Great Britain to take charge of church business, printing, and emigration in Europe. He was essentially called to serve as a co-mission president with fellow apostles Amasa Lyman and Charles C. Rich, who had been called a few months earlier and were already on their way to England.[52] Mormon leaders were careful not to take more than one of their wives with them on assignments outside Utah, and Elizabeth, who had a difficult time sharing her husband with other women, was no doubt excited about moving to England for a time and having George to herself. The couple made the wrenching decision to leave their two sons with Sarah Jane and her son, based on "counsel" they received. Perhaps this was made easier by Young's promise to Elizabeth that her sons would be well when she returned and would one day be honored men of the church.[53]

George Q. and Elizabeth left for England in late September 1860 in the company of Orson Pratt, Erastus Snow, and William H. Hooper, Utah's territorial delegate to Congress. When they stopped in Omaha, Cannon read aloud to those assembled what he referred to as Joseph Smith's prophecy about a coming war between the states.[54] The Civil War's official beginning was April 12, 1861, when Confederate soldiers fired on Fort Sumter in Charleston Harbor, South Carolina.

On their way to England, the Cannons stopped in Philadelphia to visit Kane, then headed for New York City, where they embarked

---

51. GQC to BY, Mar. 26, 1860, as cited in Bitton, *GQC*, 98.

52. Edward Leo Lyman, *Amasa Lyman, Mormon Apostle and Apostate* (Salt Lake City: University of Utah Press, 2009), 302; Bitton, *GQC*, 107.

53. Joseph J. Cannon, Notes, as referred to in Bitton, *GQC*, at 488n4; GQCJ, May 13, 1862. It may well have been Brigham Young, whose counsel George Q. was most likely to heed.

54. GQC, Discourse, Apr. 21, 1867, *JD*, 12:41. In this 1867 discourse, George Q. talked about reading Joseph Smith's December 25, 1832 "revelation … respecting the secession of the Southern States" in Omaha as he and Elizabeth traveled toward Europe in the fall of 1860.

on December 8, 1860, for Southampton on the wooden-hulled side-wheel steamship *Arago*.[55] Elizabeth must have had a difficult passage, missing her two sons and being four months pregnant. George almost certainly was anxious remembering his mother's difficulties on the Cannon family's voyage to America in 1842 and her burial at sea after she died. Once they arrived in England, they set up residence on the second floor of the famous "old" 42 Islington Road building in Liverpool, where the Mormon Church's European mission was headquartered for almost fifty years.[56]

Europe was the center of Mormon missionary efforts in the early 1860s even though the announcement of plural marriage in 1852 required significant explanation and caused disruption. The European Mission at this time was unique because Apostles Amasa Lyman, Charles C. Rich, and George Q. Cannon served as co-presidents.[57] The men worked together well, and Cannon later attributed their success to the care of his co-leaders.[58] Not surprisingly, Cannon was assigned to oversee publication and emigration. Liverpool was the center of Mormon publishing, and Cannon jumped in, providing contract printing services, purchasing a steam-powered press, and taking charge of the publication of the *Millennial Star*, the *Journal of Discourses*, and other publications. George also realized that thousands of volumes of earlier-published Mormon works were not selling. On the instruction of Brigham Young, Cannon remaindered many copies of seldom-sold books, disposed of unbound volumes, and sent the bound books to Utah.[59] Not many months after the Cannons arrived in England, Elizabeth bore the couple's first daughter, Georgiana.[60]

As editor of the *Millennial Star*, George Q. not only wrote editorials defending the church but also received letters from missionaries and church members, becoming the center of communication among

55. GQCJ, Dec. 2–6, 1860.

56. Ronald G. Watt and Kenneth W. Godfrey, "'Old 42': The British and European Mission Headquarters in Liverpool, England, 1855–1904," *Mormon Historical Studies* 10 (Spring 2009): 87–99.

57. Lyman, *Amasa Lyman*, 303.

58. [GQC], "Topics of the Times," *JI*, Dec. 15, 1883, 378.

59. Peter Crawley, *A Descriptive Bibliography of the Mormon Church*, 3 vols. (Provo, UT: Religious Studies Center, Brigham Young University, 2012), 3:23.

60. Bitton, *GQC*, 463.

European Saints. He learned much from this correspondence and set about addressing missionary discipline, which he found to be lax, by establishing rules and procedures without being unduly harsh. He applied principles and systems he had developed as he led emigration efforts in America to make the long trip to Utah easier for the thousands who wished to gather to Zion while helping members understand the costs of emigration. George's journal is replete with references to negotiations for places on ships, inspecting ships that Mormon emigrants would take passage on, and the numbers of emigrants leaving from all over Europe. Cannon also took control of church finances and sought to avoid disparities in the way contributions were dealt with by local authorities by centralizing the collections of tithes and offerings to the mission office in Liverpool. He also created transparency by giving access to the records of the church's operations to local leaders. He set up a fund to help all missionaries in the area.[61]

In September 1861, George Q. demonstrated his love of the Isle of Man when he visited there. He felt a revival of *amor patriae* and exhibited considerable familiarity with and affection for extended family members whom he met or saw again, and recalled the sights, sounds, and smells of the island. He visited the historical Cannon family farm and heard stories about family members. From a cousin of his father, he learned that George Sr. had had a drinking problem and liked convivial company. He was told that, not only had his slave-trading paternal grandfather been killed in a mutiny on the Atlantic, but his grandfather's ship-owning father had also been killed by one of his crew.[62]

As the Cannons settled into Liverpool, seven Southern states seceded from the Union, and the Civil War broke out. Some of the men who had referred to the Mormons as treasonous during the Utah War, such as General Albert Sidney Johnston and Secretary of War John B. Floyd, were part of the Confederacy's open rebellion against the US government. Some in Utah saw the Civil War as an opening to seek statehood. With support from a few federal officials in Utah,

61. Bitton, *GQC*, 110–14; on arranging ships to carry emigrants, see, *e.g.*, GQCJ, Mar. 7, 18–21, 24, 27, Apr. 8, 17–19, 21–24, 30, May 3, 6–8, 13, 1862.

62. GQCJ, Sep. 18–30, 1861.

such as acting Governor Frank Fuller, church leaders prepared for a statehood initiative in 1862. A proposed state constitution was drafted and adopted at a constitutional convention. Brigham Young was elected as proposed initial governor, while George Q. Cannon and William H. Hooper were elected as the initial US Senators. Cannon's service in Europe was interrupted when he was directed to return to the United States to lobby for statehood. He was not informed of his proposed position in the would-be state, though he was told that the two tentatively elected senators would deliver the statehood memorial and constitution.[63]

George's breath was "literally" taken away at the instruction he received from Young in a telegram received on May 5, 1862. The prophet instructed him to be in Washington, DC, on May 25 to pursue statehood. He was still not informed that he had been elected as a "senator" by the recent constitutional convention. He did not know what he would be asked to do in Washington, but knew it "would require faith and perseverance and the blessing of the Lord." All of this was complicated because Charles Rich and Amasa Lyman were being released and were leaving England at the same time as George. He hurriedly called Jacob G. Bigler as acting president of the European mission until he returned. On May 14, 1862, George Q. left Elizabeth, because her health was not good, almost one-year-old Georgiana, and a ten-year-old girl, Rose Matthews, whom the Cannons had recently taken in, in Liverpool and traveled to New York City, where he arrived on May 29. His voyage on the *Kangaroo* had been eventful, with numerous icebergs (which George found to be "beautiful") and fog. George suffered from seasickness for much of the trip. It was not until May 31 that Cannon and William Hooper, whom George knew had been designated as a senator, met. Hooper told George that he, too, had been elected as a senator and gave him a letter from Brigham informing him of this. Together, the two "senators-elect" met with editors of the *New York Times*, *Herald*, and *Tribune*, trying to convince them that Deseret should be made a state. Horace Greeley, editor of the *New York Tribune*, was noncommittal but assured Cannon he would not oppose it.[64]

63. GQCJ, Mar. 6, 1862; Bitton, *GQC*, 116–25.
64. GQCJ, Apr. 8, 21, May 5, 9, 15, 29, 31, June 4, 1862; Bitton, *GQC*, 119–20.

The principal lobbyists for Utah statehood were the elegant and polished John M. Bernhisel, Utah's territorial delegate (who had served 1851–59 and was serving another term, 1861–63), who presented the proposed state constitution; William H. Hooper, who had been Utah's territorial delegate from 1859–61; and George Q. Cannon. Cannon and Hooper were permitted to circulate on the floor of the House of Representatives in Congress and even spent an afternoon with Abraham Lincoln.[65] George described Lincoln's face as "plain, but shrewd and rather pleasant." He was "very tall" and "awkwardly built, heightened by his want of flesh." To Cannon, the president looked better than expected given the "cares and labors of his position, and is quite humorous," always "uttering some joke." Lincoln knew something of Utah, asked smart questions, but was non-committal about supporting statehood for Deseret.[66] They also met many senators and representatives who supported statehood, and even enjoyed strawberries and ice cream with some of the officeholders. Cannon argued at some length with Massachusetts Senator Charles Sumner, who opposed Utah statehood because of polygamy and what he considered to be the inordinate priestly power of the Mormon leaders. Cannon also met with firebrand Thaddeus Stevens, who did all the talking as he criticized Lincoln and William Seward, and did not mention possible Utah statehood. In all, Cannon and Hooper were courteously treated by all but Kentucky Senator Garrett Davis.[67]

Not only did Congress not seriously entertain possible statehood for Utah, members of Congress worried about Mormon loyalty, equated slavery with polygamy, the "other" relic of barbarism, and enacted the Morrill Anti-Bigamy Act of 1862, the first federal legislation intended to eradicate polygamy in the territories. It was signed by President Lincoln on July 8, 1862, just days after the Mormon emissaries finished their Congressional rounds. A few months later, on January 1, 1863, Lincoln issued the Emancipation Proclamation, which was part of a series of abolitionist victories.[68] Shortly after the enactment of the Morrill Act, George Q. was told by Benjamin

65. GQCJ, June 9, 13, 1862; Bitton, *GQC*, 119–20.
66. GQCJ, June 13, 1862; Bitton, *GQC*, 120.
67. GQCJ, June 18–21, 23–28, 30, July 1, 1862; Bitton, *GQC*, 120–22.
68. Bitton, *GQC*, 123–24.

F. Wade, chair of the Senate Committee on Territories, that Deseret statehood had no chance.[69]

George traveled to see his friend and mentor, Thomas Kane, who was recovering from wounds suffered in a battle at Harrisonburg, Virginia, and had a no-holds-barred conversation with this gentile friend of the Saints. Kane was delighted to see and converse with Cannon. Among other subjects, Kane described how horrified he was by the Civil War—how he found "that butchering men was debasing." George had a hard time leaving this conversation and almost missed his train.[70]

All in all, Cannon's mission to Washington had some positive effects, just as his last assignment had. He built on his experience from 1859–60. Having spent an intense ten weeks in the United States, Cannon boarded the "splendid steamer" *Scotia* on July 16 and returned to Liverpool. He was seasick some days, "but not as bad as usual." He and Brigham Young Jr., who travelled with him, were treated as celebrities, the New York papers having reported on their visit to Washington. When they arrived in Liverpool on July 26, George Q. assumed his new role as the sole president of the European Mission.[71] He spent the next two years exhorting in publications and in speeches, editing the *Millennial Star*, assigning and reassigning missionaries and local leaders, interacting with the Saints, and planning and carrying out emigration.

George Q. directed emigration efforts as part of his responsibilities. He chartered ships, organized emigrants into companies, and received reports. He made George Reynolds, future general authority and famous defendant in *U.S. v. Reynolds*, the Supreme Court's landmark 1879 decision on free exercise of religion, his personal secretary, emigration clerk, and protégé. Cannon often personally supervised and organized final boarding of ships.

In early June 1863, George Q. was in London organizing emigrants who would travel on the *Amazon*, which he had engaged to

69. GQCJ, July 10, 1862; Bitton, *GQC*, 124.

70. GQCJ, July 14, 1862; Bitton, *GQC*, 125. "Gentile" is a term sometimes used by Mormons and people who live in close proximity to Mormon communities to refer to someone who is not a member of the LDS Church. Mormons perceive themselves as part of the House of Israel and adopt the term for outsiders. It is a synonym of "non-Mormon."

71. GQCJ, July 16, 26, 1862.

transport approximately 900 Mormons to Zion, the largest group to that date. Most LDS groups left from Liverpool, but no suitable ships were leaving from there at the time so he engaged the London-based *Amazon*.[72] As George Q. was overseeing final preparations and boarding of the ship, Charles Dickens came to the docks to witness the departure of a Mormon emigrant ship. Dickens went on board the ship to talk to the captain and some of the passengers. Unlike other emigrants he had observed as their departure drew near, "nobody is in an ill-temper, nobody is the worse for drink, nobody swears an oath or uses a coarse word, nobody appears depressed, nobody is weeping. Many of the passengers were writing—letters, diaries, notes." Dickens and the captain agreed that, far from deserving censure, the largely working-class LDS emigrants and their "Mormon Agent" (Cannon) had experienced "some remarkable influence [that] had produced a remarkable result." Dickens described the emigrants as, "in their degree, the pick and flower of England." Ultimately, he approached the "Mormon Agent, who had been active in getting them together, and in making the contract with my friends the owners of the ship to take them as far as New York on their way to the Great Salt Lake."

Dickens described George as a "compactly handsome man in black, rather short, with rich-brown hair and beard, and clear bright eyes. ... Probably, a man who had 'knocked about the world' pretty much. A man with a frank open manner, and unshrinking look, withal a man of great quickness." Dickens was certain that Cannon did not recognize him and was "wholly ignorant of my immense Uncommercial importance."[73] In fact, Cannon had recognized Dickens and reported to Young that the famous novelist had spent several hours watching the Mormon emigrants' preparation on the *Amazon* and had "a great many questions for me, appearing to be much interested in us and free from prejudice."[74]

---

72. Richard L. Jensen and Gordon Irving, "The Voyage of the Amazon: A Close View of One Immigrant Company," *Ensign*, Mar. 1980, 16–19, says there were 891 LDS emigrants on board the Amazon, GQCJ, June 4, 1863, estimates there were 896 LDS emigrants.

73. Charles Dickens, "Bound for the Great Salt Lake," in *The Uncommercial Traveller* (New York: Charles Scribner's Sons, 1905), 260–65.

74. GQC to BY, June 24, 1863, CHL. Cannon did not mention Dickens in his journal. It was no surprise that Cannon recognized Dickens. Cannon was familiar with

Dickens took a fair amount of creative license in his description of the discussion with Cannon and made the Mormon agent out as a "rough American" in his speech. By contrast, the first professional American diplomat, Benjamin Moran, who worked in the US Embassy in London, met with Cannon about the same time and described him as "a very clever Englishman by the name of Geo. Q. Cannon, ... who has ... great intellectual force."[75]

Unsurprisingly, George had gone to hear Dickens read from his works in London. Throughout the remainder of his life, he attended plays, concerts, scientific lectures, horse races, the circus, and visited historical sites. While in England, he even showed himself to be a bit of a "royals watcher" when he hurried to Windsor Castle with "Bro. M.B. Shipp" to review the rooms where Prince Edward and Princess Alexandra had been wed in the royal wedding of the era a day or two before.[76] He visited a Turkish bath to try to resolve acute pains in his knees that he feared "must be rheumatic." He visited Lorenzo Niles Fowler and had his phrenological chart done by the famous American. Fowler may have recognized Cannon.[77] George Q. also stayed abreast of travel accounts chronicling visits to Utah, including ones by Sir Richard Burton, Jules Remy, and Horace Greeley. Burton visited Cannon in Liverpool seeking photographs of Utah that he could use to illustrate his *City of the Saints* and George Q. obtained for him "portraits" of Brigham Young and the twelve apostles.[78]

On May 19, 1863, Elizabeth bore a son, whom the couple named George Hoagland.[79] A month later, George Q. sent Elizabeth, Rosina (Rose) Mathews, an eleven-year-old orphan whom George and

---

the author's writings, and several months before meeting him on the *Amazon*, Cannon attended a reading by Dickens from *Nicholas Nickleby* and *The Pickwick Papers* in London. Cannon was delighted with Dickens's use of "eight or nine different voices in the first and five or six in the second readings pieces." GQCJ, Mar. 11, 1863, June 4, 1863.

75. Dickens, "Bound for the Great Salt Lake," 260–65; Sarah Agnes Wallace and Frances Elma Gillespie, eds., *The Journals of Benjamin Moran, 1857–1865*, 2 vols. (Chicago: University of Chicago Press, 1949), 2:1059 (Aug. 27, 1862).

76. GQCJ, Mar. 13, 1863. This was on the same trip to London during which Cannon heard Dickens read from his works.

77. GQCJ, Sep. 28, 1863

78. GQCJ, Aug. 24, 27, 30, 1861. After first being visited by Richard Burton, who was on his way to "Fernando Po" where he has been appointed consul, George met with Burton's wife, Isabel.

79. GQCJ, May 19, 1863.

Elizabeth later adopted, and his two small children, Georgianna and George Hoagland, home to America. As he watched Elizabeth and Rose holding his small children on the deck of the *City of Washington*, he felt very blessed. He had decided to send his family home out of concern that possible difficulties between the U.S. and England during the ongoing Civil War could disrupt travel between the two countries. He also worried about leaving her in England alone again if he should have to return to the United States quickly. It was also reassuring that Joseph F. Smith and other friends were on the same ship and would travel to Utah with them.[80]

During his last days in England, Cannon faced widespread agitation against the LDS church by apostates, schismatics, and others. George Q. combatted these disrupters. He labored hard to convince British Mormons to ignore those criticizing the church. He gave stirring talks and wrote biting editorials seeking to inspire British Saints to greater faith, service, and commitment. He alternated between characterizing his charges as "nobility" and telling them they had far to go before they were truly the people of God.

In September 1863, George received a letter dated August 5 from Elizabeth in Wood River, Nebraska. She assured him that the children were well and that George was getting so big that it made his mother's arms ache to hold him. Elizabeth, on the other hand, was "getting very thin, the heat & the care and fatigue" wearing upon her. He was "completely stunned and overwhelmed" a month later, when he received a letter from George Peacock, in the same pioneer company, reporting that the small children had come down with whooping cough and Georgianna had passed away on September 2. George could not contain his grief and distress and worried that Elizabeth's health would worsen "that she might not be able to live." He "fancied [she] was in the room with him and when I lit my candle … by the bedside I looked around the room almost expecting to find her there." George received a soothing blessing from "the brethren" and acknowledged a tinge of guilt when he noted that his motives were pure and he had felt prompted by the spirit to send his family home.[81] When he

80. GQCJ, June 24, 1863.

81. GQCJ, Sep. 7, Oct. 8–9, 1863; George Peacock to GQC, Sep. 4, 1863, pasted into GQCJ, Oct. 9, 1863.

received word in February 1864 that little George H. had succumbed in December to whooping cough and measles, he lamented the loss of three children that he and Elizabeth had suffered. Nevertheless, he felt blessed to have three healthy children.[82]

George Q.'s service in Europe and Washington, DC, demonstrated his single-minded focus and deep reserves of energy in spite of heartache and worry. He was a brilliant organizer and administrator who was also a veritable whirlwind of activity. He had no fear of frankly and openly dealing with anyone and everyone, from the most powerful people in the world to the most impoverished emigrants. He wrote and spoke harshly (and eloquently) from the pulpit and from the *Millennial Star* against enemies of the church, particularly those whom he viewed as apostates. And yet, he also had a deep faith and carefully searched for faith in others as he wrote and spoke from the *Star* and the pulpit to uplift and inspire the Saints.

82. GQCJ, Feb. 9, 1864.

CHAPTER 4

BRIGHAM'S PROTÉGÉ AND MORE

1864-70

"President Young's admiration for Cannon had grown with each experience, and now Brigham wanted his brilliant younger associate by his side."
—Davis Bitton

In May 1864, George Q. Cannon received a letter from Brigham Young's chief clerk and private secretary, David O. Calder, confidentially informing him that Daniel H. Wells would arrive in July to replace him as president of the European Mission and that George Q. would leave in mid-August. He also noted that Wells would be accompanied by Brigham Young Jr. George Q. was surprised that a member of the First Presidency (Wells was second counselor) would be assigned to a foreign mission and, yet, also thought it appropriate for one of the presidency to oversee church and mission operations in a foreign land.[1] Characteristically, upon Wells's arrival, Cannon spent several weeks with him introducing the older man to church leaders and others in Great Britain, explaining the financial records that Cannon had organized, and discussing the operations and importance of the *Millennial Star*. George then left Liverpool with another son of Brigham Young, John W. Young, on August 27, 1864, bound for the states on the *Scotia*, the same ship he had taken when he returned to Liverpool from Washington, DC, two years earlier. Anticipating Cannon's departure, George Reynolds noted in the British Mission history how much he admired the former leader,

1. GQCJ, May 1, 1864. Cannon received a letter confirming the information from Brigham Young on May 7, 1864.

adding: "I do not think it too much to say he was universally beloved. His kind, tender, unassuming disposition, ... rendered him an object of affection. Wherever he went or whatever circumstances he was placed in, he gained friends."[2]

After landing in Jersey City on September 6, 1864, Cannon and Young stayed at the Metropolitan Hotel in Manhattan.[3] The country was very much at war—Atlanta had recently fallen to the troops of General William Tecumseh Sherman and was burning, and General Philip Sheridan was marching up the Shenandoah Valley in a series of bloody battles. The war created travel concerns that were exacerbated by reports of "Sioux, Cheyennes and Arapahoes ... [attacking] settlements, [wagon] trains, etc., killing hundreds of people and carrying off and destroying immense quantities of goods and other property on the prairies." George Q. worried that both the Civil War and disputes with Native Americans might disrupt Mormon trains, but was reassured when he learned that the last train of the season had 500 well-armed men and was expected to reach Salt Lake City by October 1.[4]

Cannon and Young stayed in the East for ten days and visited various people, including now-General Thomas L. Kane, still suffering from his leg wound but full of inside political information that George Q. might find useful. Kane offered to help the Saints however he could. While in the Philadelphia area, Cannon, Young, and several others attended the play *Richelieu* starring Edwin Booth at the venerable Walnut St. Theatre. George admired Booth's acting style.[5]

On September 16, Cannon and Young obtained railroad passes for free travel as far as the train went and passes on the stage "by an Order on President Young," and set off for the West. The two passed without serious concerns until they reached the Mississippi and Missouri Rivers, both of which had had a number of bridges destroyed. Ferries across the rivers encountered trouble because the water was low. On one leg, the train was so crowded that the two

2. George Reynolds, in British Mission History, Aug. 27, 1864, as quoted in Bitton, *GQC*, 139.

3. GQCJ, Sep. 6, 1864.

4. GQCJ, Sep. 6, 15, 1864.

5. GQCJ, Sep. 7–15, 1864. Some of the Eastern press began to call George the "Mormon Richelieu" in the 1890s.

Mormon leaders had to stand "nearly the whole way," and George was appalled at the "dreadfully" profane and blasphemous expressions they heard from the "very rough crowd" of "Western people." To him, it seemed ungrateful for people who were the beneficiaries of a "lovely land," "unequalled advantages of government and for every thing necessary for comfort" to act this way. The "change produced by the war" was very apparent to George.[6]

After reaching the end of the rail line in Atchison, Kansas, Cannon and Young encountered more delays, with stagecoach travel periodically interrupted by reports of shootings, burning buildings, and stagecoach drivers refusing to travel through troubled areas. This led George to record in his journal that if the trip was to be made successfully, it "must be made by faith and through the protecting care of our Heavenly Father."[7] What should have been a two-week trip extended to a month. Cannon and Young finally arrived in Salt Lake on October 10. He and Young were excited to reach the valley and first stopped by Brigham Young's office. Learning that the president was at a party for members of Zions Camp in the Social Hall, the two immediately went there. Everyone was delighted to see George. Brigham embraced him, then sent his son and George home to "clean ourselves," but also invited them to come back to the party and "bring our wives with us." George Q. was taken home in a carriage, where he received a "fond welcome from my wife Elizabeth and my children, John Q. and Abraham H and our adopted daughter, Rosey … my wife Sarah Jane, and my son Franklin J. and my brother Angus." Even though there was a happy reunion once he made it home, his wives may have been perturbed or hurt George did not visit them immediately upon arriving in the valley and that he wanted to return to the party to be with Brigham Young. The best indication of this is that neither of them returned with him to the celebration. George Q. may have let his physical and social energy and finely tuned political instincts cloud his better judgment by returning to the party alone and staying until 2:00 a.m.[8]

Although he had missed October's general conference, Cannon

6. GQCJ, Sep. 16–23, 1864.
7. GQCJ, Sep. 24–Oct. 9, 1864.
8. GQCJ, Oct. 10, 1864; Bitton, *GQC*, 140.

gave a long talk in the "Old Tabernacle" on October 23, telling the Saints how good it was to be back in their midst and how reassuring it was to see them growing spiritually. He counseled them not to dwell on the past, but on present prophets, who would continue to lead the church by a continuing "stream of revelation."[9] Young's admiration for George Q. had grown as he followed his activities in Europe and lobbied for statehood in Washington. The church president now decided to keep his talented associate nearby. Young made George his personal secretary and also gave him special assignments. Cannon soon became the spokesman for the president and traveled everywhere with him, sometimes writing speeches and serving as the prophet's confidante. George also worked as editor of the *Deseret News*, became the leader of the church's Sunday school youth program, started and managed the *Juvenile Instructor*, and pursued entrepreneurial enterprises.[10]

In spite of his failure to visit them first upon his return to Utah, George Q. was delighted to be home with his immediate and extended families. His financial situation improved, making it easier to provide for his growing families. He spent parts of most days with Brigham Young, and was an integral part of the central administration of the church.

Heber C. Kimball, who had been Brigham's closest advisor for many years, felt threatened by and perhaps jealous of some younger leaders, particularly Cannon.[11] Kimball once predicted that George Q. "would go up like a rocket and come down like a stick."[12] When Kimball died in 1868, George Q. was one of the speakers at his funeral and lionized the long-term First Presidency member as a wonderful man who always gave good counsel, as a leader and as a father.[13]

George Q. did not forget his beloved Sandwich Islands. In November 1864, he sent Francis A. Hammond and George Nebeker, who had earlier served in the islands as missionaries, to O'ahu to negotiate the purchase of the Dougherty plantation in Lai'e on the northeast

9. GQC, Discourse, *JD*, Oct. 23, 1864, 6:340–48. The new (and current) Tabernacle was begun the same year and completed in 1867.

10. Bitton, *GQC*, 140–41.

11. Stanley B. Kimball, "Brigham and Heber," *BYUS* 18 (Spring 1978): 407.

12. As quoted in Bitton, *GQC*, 142.

13. GQC, funeral sermon, *JD*, June 24, 1868, 12:183–85.

shore. The two negotiated the purchase of the 6,000-acre plantation ranch with a large number of livestock, farm equipment, a large frame house, and other homes, barns, and outbuildings. The purchase closed on January 26, 1865, for $14,000. Since its acquisition, the plantation has been the focal point of LDS Church culture and operations in the islands and used as the site of agricultural operations, the mission home of the Hawai'i mission, the Hawai'i Temple, the church college of Hawai'i (now BYU–Hawai'i), and the Polynesian Cultural Center. This purchase was initiated by George Q., and was important enough that Young and Kimball (the two members of the First Presidency in the country at the time), Wilford Woodruff, and George all participated in setting apart Hammond and Nebeker.[14]

Cannon's life was filled with many leadership and regular church meetings, during which he gave hundreds of sermons. In spite of having a busy life in Utah, staying close to home for much of the last half of 1860s permitted George Q. some stability with his wives and sons and with two new wives. Difficulties continued, as two of the three children Elizabeth bore in the 1860s died within two years of their births. Sarah Jane had a son in 1867.[15] In mid-summer 1865, during a trip with Young to the southern colonies in Utah, twenty-year-old Eliza Tenney of Payson caught George's eye. In August, Young married the pair, and the next day they honeymooned on a trip with Young through northern Utah. When Eliza later met Sarah Jane in Salt Lake City, Sarah reportedly asked her if she knew who she was. Indicative of the sometimes challenging living conditions in polygamy, Eliza responded, "Yes, I suppose you are one of the Mrs. Cannons."[16]

In February 1868, George Q. met a twenty-one-year-old schoolteacher named Martha Telle. He sent her an invitation to a play at the Salt Lake Theatre. He suggested that because her "duties are confining and in some respects probably harassing, under such circumstances amusement and relaxation are necessary to health." He ended with the hope that his "mode of evincing my thoughts may not be distasteful to you." Martha's response showed even more

14. GQCJ, Nov. 9, 10, 1864; Francis M. Hammond to Daniel H. Wells, May 7, 1865, in *MS* 27 (Aug. 19, 1865), 527; R. Lanier Britsch, "The Church in Hawaii," in Daniel H. Ludlow, ed., *Encyclopedia of Mormonism* 4 vols. (New York: Macmillan, 1992), 2:578–79.

15. Bitton, *GQC*, 463.

16. As quoted and cited in Bitton, *GQC*, 143.

tartness than Eliza's reply to Sarah Jane. She wondered how it would be if she could "avail myself of the advantage which Leap Year grants to ladies? Were such my privilege, or did it belong to my sphere (women's sphere) to do so, I would invite the sender of the tickets to accompany me." She slightly tempered the tartness with her next statement, no doubt realizing she was writing to a forty-one-year-old apostle and editor: "now please do not think me audacious or fill your editorial columns with criticisms on the improprieties of young women nowadays." The two married shortly after, on March 16, 1868, in the Endowment House.[17]

As the decade wore on, George Q. assumed responsibility over many aspects of religious education and academic education among Latter-day Saints. Having watched younger people in Britain lose interest in their church and believing much of that was caused by Protestant ministers and teachers, he encouraged Mormon families not to send their children to Protestant schools. At the same time, he took measures to improve both religious and academic education by publishing the *Juvenile Instructor* and other publications, sponsoring the establishment of the Deseret Sunday School Union, and training teachers. After he had learned the ins and outs of printing and publishing in Nauvoo, San Francisco, Liverpool, and Fillmore, he started the *Juvenile Instructor* and soon began his own publishing company under the imprint of the Juvenile Instructor Office. George Q.'s nephew, George Cannon Lambert, apprenticed at the Juvenile Instructor Office beginning in 1867 and took over operations when his uncle was elected as Utah's territorial delegate to Congress in 1872. Lambert continued to operate the office until 1882, when he was called as a missionary and George Q.'s son Abram took over most of the publishing duties. The Juvenile Instructor Office printed books, periodicals, reports for unrelated entities such as the territorial legislature and other organizations, and the *Deseret News*.[18]

During this time period, George entered other business ventures. In the late 1860s, he became treasurer of Deseret Telegraph, a director of Utah Produce, and a director of the Zion's Commercial Mercantile

17. GQC to "Miss Telley," Feb. 25, 1868, CHL; Martha Telle to GQC, Feb. 25, 1868, as quoted and cited in Bitton, *GQC*, 153; Bitton, *GQC*, 463n67.

18. Craig S. Smith, "Utah Book Publishing in the 1880s: The Juvenile Instructor Office and the Cannons," unpublished paper in my possession.

Institution. In 1867, George also resumed his position as editor of the *Deseret News* and continued to influence public opinion and interests. One of his first acts as editor was to begin publishing a daily paper while keeping the venerable weekly version of the *Deseret News*, whose name was eventually changed in 1888 to the *Deseret Weekly*.[19]

Even though Abraham Lincoln had signed the Morrill Anti-Bigamy Act in 1862, Latter-day Saints were shocked when they learned by the new telegraph that the US president had been assassinated. Mormons mourned the murder of the man who had worked hard to end the Civil War. George Q. Cannon gave one of the addresses at a meeting held in the Old Tabernacle on Temple Square. In his speech, he compared the assassination of Lincoln to the murder of Joseph Smith in Carthage, Illinois, in 1844.[20]

LDS leaders continued to elect a shadow "state of Deseret" government each year. While federally appointed officials governed in Utah Territory, secret conventions of Mormons elected full slates of proposed would-be governmental leaders. The local officers were generally the same as those elected to the territorial legislature, but the territory-wide officers of Deseret were different from those appointed by the federal government. In 1865, George Q. was made the "secretary of state" of Deseret and Young delivered the "Governor's Message," even though he had not been the official territorial governor of Utah since 1858.[21]

Cannon's desire to defend the church through its publications took an uneasy turn as the two ends of the anticipated transcontinental railroad continued to bear inexorably toward each other. In most ways, the church and George Q. fully supported completion of the railroad for many reasons. The railroad would facilitate immigration of Latter-day Saints to Utah by making travel quicker, cheaper, and safer for all. Many church members were employed in surveying and building the railroad as it approached Utah. On the other hand, the railroad would bring outsiders and disrupt the local economy by impairing home industry, reducing agriculture, and

19. *DN*, Nov. 21, 1867. The daily edition was called the *Deseret Evening* News to distinguish it from the semi-weekly and weekly editions. *Deseret Weekly*, Dec. 29, 1888, 1.

20. "Our Nation Mourning," *DW*, Apr. 19, 1865, 228.

21. "Home Items," *News Supplement*, Jan. 25, 1865, 132; "State of Deseret, Governor's Message," *News Supplement*, Jan. 25, 1865, 133.

expanding mining.[22] Young was worried about what worldly effects improved transportation and an increasingly diverse local population could have on the Saints. Young contemplated retrenchment, which eventually became the cooperative movement in Utah. Mormon businesses and businessmen and women were encouraged to be self-sufficient and not to trade with gentiles (as non-Mormons have often been called in Utah) to avoid being corrupted by outside society. This caused friction with non-Mormon merchants of Utah.[23] Cooperatives sponsored by the church mined for coal and iron, grew sheep for wool, raised cotton, and farmed. Stores offered everything from groceries to clothes to furniture to construction materials. ZCMI became the central cooperative store. George Q. was a leading voice in the cooperative movement, providing enthusiastic support and urging the same from his fellow church members.[24]

The cooperative movement and its removal of the church and its members from commercial interaction with non-LDS merchants also resulted in one of the most important dissident movements in nineteenth-century Mormonism. The dissident group, the New Movement or Godbeites (named for William Godbe, a leader in the movement), consisted of Mormon merchants and intellectuals who opposed Brigham Young's economic separation from the world. Members of the movement founded the *Mormon Tribune*, which evolved into the *Salt Lake Tribune*. In October 1869, a unique church court was convened publicly in City Hall against Godbe and E.L.T. Harrison, the intellectual leader of the Godbeites. George Q. Cannon, who always felt disdain for dissenters in the church, was assigned the role of "prosecuting" the charges against Godbe and Harrison. He charged the two men, whom he knew well, with "harboring a spirit of apostasy" and accused the brilliant Harrison of "sophistical speech." Cannon also defended Brigham Young and

22. Leonard J. Arrington, *Great Basin Kingdom: An Economic History of the Latter-day Saints, 1830–1900* (Cambridge, MA: Harvard University Press, 1958), 236–40; idem., "The Transcontinental Railroad and Mormon Economic Policy," *Pacific Historical Review* 20 (May 1951): 145–46.

23. Leonard J. Arrington, Feramorz Fox, and Dean May, *Building the City of God: Community and Cooperation among the Mormons* (Salt Lake City: Deseret Book Co., 1976), 79–110.

24. Bitton, *GQC*, 162.

the church. Ultimately, Godbe and Harrison were cut off from the church, but the whole disciplinary action left many Saints uncomfortable. Apostle Amasa Lyman drifted out of the LDS Church and into the "New Movement" (the Godbeites) and was more quietly excommunicated on May 12, 1870. [25]

Cannon also served as one of the leading public defenders of the Mormons. On July 4, 1870, he gave a grand Independence Day oration in the Salt Lake Tabernacle before 10,000 listeners. In this and other speeches Cannon invoked the American concept of liberty and referred repeatedly to the US Constitution and the Declaration of Independence.[26]

A curious editorial written by Cannon in the *Deseret News* in 1868 can only be explained in the context of concerns about the worldly influences that Young and the Saints worried about. A murder case that had become famous in Utah involved an 1856 homicide committed by Howard Egan, George Q.'s associate and friend from the California gold fields, who was both a devout Mormon and rough frontiersman. In September 1856, Egan killed his friend James Madison Monroe, who had had an affair with Egan's first wife. Egan had found out about the liaison and a child born as a result when he returned to Utah after guiding a wagon train to California. Egan's defense was that he was justified in killing his wife's seducer. Egan was represented at his trial by First Presidency member George A. Smith, who argued that the "mountain common law" demanded that a man kill the seducer of his wife or daughter. The jury found Egan not guilty. A number of defendants in similar homicide cases invoked "mountain common law" over the years after 1856 and were also found not guilty.[27]

Now, writing in the columns of the *Deseret News*, Cannon warned

---

25. Ronald W Walker, *Wayward Saints: The Godbeites and Brigham Young* (Urbana: University of Illinois Press, 1998), 92–108, 152–69; 207; Edward Leo Lyman, *Amasa Mason Lyman: Mormon Apostle and Apostate, A Study in Dedication* (Salt Lake City: University of Utah Press, 2009), 421–32.

26. "The Celebration, Oration," *DN*, July 5, 1870, 2. The *Salt Lake Herald* noted the loud applause by the huge audience after the oration. "Celebration of the Fourth," *SLH*, July 6, 1870, 2.

27. KLC, "Mountain Common Law, Redux: The Extralegal Punishment of Seducers in Early Utah," *UHQ* 89 (Spring 2021): 38–55; Argument of George A. Smith, *JD*, October Term 1851, 1:95–100.

outsiders that, while Mormons might practice plural marriage, they held the sacred vows of marriage to be of supreme importance, and, if a man were to "seduce" a Mormon woman (which in practice often involved mutual consent rather than coercion), her husband or father should seek out the seducer and kill him, just as a shepherd would hunt and kill a coyote or wolf that had harmed one of his sheep.[28] It is likely that most Americans, appalled as they were by plural marriage, thought that a Mormon man's murder of his polygamous wife's seducer was more serious than the seducer's adultery with the polygamist's wife.

The 1860s was an era of technological innovation and development. The most obvious was the transcontinental railroad, which revolutionized cross-country travel in the United States after 1869. Not long after the transcontinental railroad was completed, the Utah Central completed a spur from Ogden to Salt Lake City. Young had a cold (though he was at the dedication of the railroad), so George Q. read the church president's speech (though Cannon likely wrote it anyway). Cannon noted that the Mormons had just completed the line without "the Territory, or any county or city in it having incurred debt." They could do this because the Union Pacific had paid for work done on that road by the Mormons by supplying "iron and rolling stock" to the Utah Central line. He said they "were now asking the parent Government for a State Government and thought the work they had just completed without subsidy or aid was evidence they could care for themselves."[29] Other developments were also important. In 1862, the telegraph was completed across the United States. By 1867, local telegraph lines stretched between more populous cities of Utah.[30] By 1866, a permanent oceanic telegraph line was successfully installed, reducing the time for international communications.

Cannon's families grew slowly during the 1860s: Elizabeth lost four of the seven children she bore between 1856 and 1867, while Sarah Jane bore two children (though both lived into old age). Neither Eliza nor Martha had a child before the 1870s. By contrast, eighteen children were born into the Cannon household in the 1870s, all but

28. [GQC], "Inviolability of Virtue," *DN*, Feb. 26, 1868, 2.
29. "Salt Lake," *NYT*, Jan. 19, 1870, 2.
30. GQC, "Editorial Thoughts," *JI* 2 (Feb. 1, 1867), 20; Bitton, *GQC*, 157.

one of whom lived into adulthood. Martha Telle eventually bore nine children, five in the 1870s, all of whom reached adulthood.[31]

With Young's encouragement, and in the midst of a growing family, George Q. built a grand Second Empire mansion on the northwest corner of First West (today's 200 West) and South Temple in about 1868. Though George Q. later expressed some regret about building such an elaborate residence, the "Big House," as it came to be called, became home to him and his four wives and all his children for about a decade.[32]

The influx of "outsiders" to Salt Lake City brought new calls nationally to force Mormons to comply with the 1862 anti-bigamy law. Gentiles who saw polygamy up close were either offended by the practice or, as George Q. Cannon sometimes thought, criticized the practice in an attempt to co-opt power or gain control of the natural resources and resulting prosperity that Utah enjoyed. Some of the federal appointees to Utah were quite harsh in their attitudes towards and treatment of Mormons in an effort to wipe out this remaining "relic of barbarism," according to Republicans in 1856. Schuyler Colfax, who had visited Salt Lake City in 1865, was Ulysses S. Grant's vice-president and continued his diatribes against the Mormons. He refused to concede that polygamy could be a question of religion. John Taylor exchanged written statements with the vice-president that were later published by George Q. and the *Deseret News* in a pamphlet called *The Mormon Question*.[33]

A series of public debates held in Salt Lake City pitted Reverend John Philip Newman, chaplain of the US Senate and important Methodist minister in Washington, against LDS Apostle Orson Pratt. Newman was powerful and a close adviser to several US presidents. He hated polygamy and encouraged the appointment of federal officers in Utah who would treat polygamy harshly. Pratt argued in response that God had instituted polygamy in Old Testament times. In the final debate Newman became increasingly scornful of Pratt, to the point where Mormons began hissing during the last session. Young gave a sign for the Saints to stop.

31. See appendix.

32. Bitton, *GQC*, 155.

33. Bitton, *GQC*, 145, 158–59; *The Mormon Question* (Salt Lake City: Deseret News, 1870).

Each session of the debate began and closed with a prayer. Newman thought he had arranged it so that the opening prayers were always given by Mormons and the closing prayers by his supporters. In the last session, however, Mormons were left to close. George Q. offered a powerful benediction in which he made clear who he believed was "on the Lord's side"–"We beseech Thee, our heavenly Father, to pour out Thy Spirit upon this congregation." He then thanked the Lord for enabling part of the audience to "distinguish between truth and error, between right and wrong, … We thank Thee … that we are not left to the vague opinions, and assumptions, and assertions of uninspired men; but that Thou hast, in Thy goodness and mercy, revealed Thyself from the heavens and bestowed the knowledge of thy mind and will upon men. … We thank Thee that we are in this land of freedom; that we can welcome our friends and extend to them a liberty which has been denied to us; that they can come into our tabernacles … and plead their cause." The *New York Herald* reported that it was the Mormons who, "under the pretense of religious services, induced [Newman] to change the order of exercises, so that one of the Mormons would make the closing prayer. The Doctor's courtesy was taken advantage of to pronounce in favor of polygamy, which Apostle George Q. Cannon did by closing the proceedings with the … remarkable prayer."[34]

The Liberal Party, a "gentile" political party created in response to LDS political control of Utah, was organized in February 1870 and was made up largely of men who were antagonistic to Mormons. George R. Maxwell, Robert Baskin, and others delivered biting criticisms of the church. Chief Judge James McKean and other federal appointees aligned themselves with the Liberal Party, as did Colonel Patrick Connor, former commandant of Camp Douglas located on the east bench of Salt Lake City. Mormons cynically referred to these closely connected groups as the "Ring," and spent several decades defending themselves from the Ring. Members of the Ring, on the other hand, believed they were rooting out a barbaric practice.

34. "Mormonism," *New York Herald*, Sep. 3, 1870, 11–12; GQC, "Topics of the Times," *JI* 18 (July 15, 1883), 211–12; Bitton, *GQC*, 159–60. The *Herald* included a transcript of the entire prayer and the background. Later, George Q. disputed the *Herald's* account and discussed who he thought had acted inappropriately.

At the forefront of the Mormons' work to combat the actions of the Ring was Cannon, editor of the *Deseret News*. As a result, he was often criticized and attacked by the Ring and its principal newspaper voice, the *Salt Lake Tribune*.[35]

Col. Connor, who commanded Camp Douglas during much of the Civil War, encouraged his soldiers to hunt for precious metals. Connor also wanted gentiles to move into Utah and dilute or undermine Mormon influence. Some of Connor's troops were instrumental in discovering and mining precious metals in the mountains surrounding the Salt Lake Valley. The attraction of mining brought many gentiles; by 1873, non-Mormons made up about a quarter of Salt Lake City's population.[36] This further created conditions that Cannon fought to mitigate.

Congress enacted the Morrill Anti-Polygamy Act in 1862. After the Civil War, egged on at least in part by the Ring, Congress considered passing laws that were even more harsh. In early 1870, separate bills were introduced in the Senate and House of Representatives that would have been more punitive for Mormons who practiced or even believed in polygamy. Rep. Shelby M. Cullom of Illinois sponsored a bill drafted by non-Mormon Utah lawyer, Ring member, and firebrand Robert Baskin. The bill would have removed most local control from Utah Territory in the appointment or election of officials; excluded believers in polygamy from jury service in polygamy and cohabitation trials; prohibited polygamists from voting, holding office, or being naturalized; stripped criminal jurisdiction from local probate courts; permitted wives to testify against husbands; and authorized the president of the United States to enforce these provisions by the military.[37]

As many as 25,000 Mormon women around Utah Territory held indignation meetings denouncing the Cullom Bill and defending plural marriage. George Q. condemned the proposed law in a mass

---

35. John Gary Maxwell, *Gettysburg to Great Salt Lake, George R. Maxwell, Civil War Hero and Federal Marshal among the Mormons* (Norman: Arthur H. Clark Co., 2010), 148–51; Bitton, *GQC*, 169–75. The People's Party was organized about the same time as the semi-official political party of Mormons.

36. Jeffrey D. Nichols, "Colonel Conner Filled a Varied, Dramatic Role in Utah," History to Go, Apr. 21, 2016, historytogo.utah.gov (accessed Aug. 2021).

37. Bitton, *GQC*, 164.

meeting held in the new Tabernacle by taking issue with the underlying assumption of the bill that Mormon women were "the degraded, spiritless and ignorant creatures that their traducers have represented them." Cannon applied his motto for the *Western Standard*, "to correct mis-representation, we adopt self-representation" to argue against the Cullom Bill. He asserted that it violated many provisions of the US Constitution: the prohibition against bills of attainder, guarantee of a right to trial by jury of one's peers, and prohibition against excessive fines and prison sentences. According to Cannon, the bill would have taken property from church members that they had already paid for by reclaiming it from "barrenness." It would have also "disfranchised" and "proscribed" American citizens for no act other than *believing* in plural marriage and it would have offered "a premium for prostitution and corruption" by forcing "husbands and wives to violate the holiest vows they can make and voluntarily bastardize their own children."[38]

The Cullom Bill passed the House on March 23, 1870, but was never brought up by the Senate and so died. One proposed harsh anti-polygamy bill had failed, but the fight was not over.

George Q. supported woman suffrage. Writing in the *Deseret News* shortly before women were given the right to vote in Utah in February 1870, he stated that he believed Mormon women could be part of "the great cause of reform." He viewed Mormon women as capable of great things and argued that women should be given both opportunities and responsibilities, including the franchise, and that neither women nor men should be required to labor under the disability of not being permitted to vote.[39] After Utah women were given the franchise, Elizabeth Hoagland Cannon with other leading women submitted a letter of gratitude.[40]

---

38. "Mass Meeting, Remonstrance against the Cullom Bill," *Ogden Semi-Weekly Junction*, Apr. 2, 1870, 2.

39. "Woman and Her Mission, *DW*, May 26, 1869, 186; Thomas G. Alexander, "An Experiment in Progressive Legislation: The Granting of Woman Suffrage in 1870," *UHQ* 38 (Winter 1970): 22; Bitton, *GQC*, 164, Lola Van Wagenen, "In Their Own Behalf: The Politicization of Mormon Women and the 1870 Franchise," *Dialogue* 24 (Winter 1991): 41.

40. Orson F. Whitney, *History of Utah*, 4 vols. (Salt Lake City: George Q. Cannon & Sons, 1892–1904), 2:404; Bitton, *GQC*, 163.

CHAPTER FIVE

TERRITORIAL DELEGATE

1870-80

"No matter how thick the clouds of darkness have been, or how much Satan and his servants have raged, the Lord has been my rock of refuge."
—George Q. Cannon, June 16, 1880

Even before his visit to Utah and debates with Orson Pratt in August–September 1870, US Senate chaplain John Philip Newman convinced President Ulysses S. Grant to appoint firebrand James B. McKean as Utah's chief judge to bring the Mormons to heel. Soon after McKean arrived in Salt Lake City in August 1870, he worked to establish federal authority, first by ruling that the territorial courts were federal courts and the US Marshal was the appropriate person, not territorial officials elected by popular vote, to empanel grand juries.[1] The Mormons protested what they saw as federal encroachment on their local sovereignty. An unrelated case involving the same federal vs. territorial jurisdiction issue was on appeal to the US Supreme Court at the time in the case of *Clinton v. Englebrect* that would soon resolve the question of whether local territorial courts were subject to the control of the federal courts in Utah.

In the fall of 1871, a federal grand jury empaneled by McKean issued warrants for the arrest of Brigham Young, George Q. Cannon, and others on charges of "lewd and lascivious cohabitation" under territorial law. US Marshal M. T. Patrick arrested the defendants.

1. Thomas G. Alexander, "Federal Authority versus Polygamic Theocracy: James B. McKean and the Mormons, 1870–1875," *Dialogue* 1 (Autumn 1966): 85–100; Robert Joseph Dwyer, *The Gentile Comes to Utah, A Study in Religious and Social Conflict (1862–1890)* (Salt Lake City: Western Epics, 1971), 63, 123–27; Bitton, *GQC*, 170–71.

McKean required bonds of $5,000 for each man to go free pending trial. As Young stood before McKean at his arraignment and bail hearing, the judge announced that "while the case at bar is called, '*The People versus Brigham Young*,' its other and real title is '*Federal Authority versus Polygamic Theocracy*.'"[2] Several weeks later, the same grand jury issued arrest warrants against Young and others, implicating them in the 1857 murder of non-Mormon trader Richard Yates during the Utah War.[3]

Young sent George Q. to California to seek support for the church president, principally in connection with the murder and lewd and lascivious cohabitation charges, but also to lobby for support of possible statehood for Utah. Over several days, Cannon met with many prominent politicians and judges in Nevada and California, all Republicans, to assess their willingness to encourage withdrawal of the cohabitation and murder charges against Young and other Mormon leaders. Cannon met with US senators from Nevada and California, current and former governors of California, a US senator from Indiana who was visiting in California, trial and appeals court federal judges, and others, including Theodore H. Hittell, a prominent California historian of significant influence. All of these men were critical of the heavy-handed treatment by McKean. All promised to use their influence to stop the prosecutions of Young and other leaders.[4] It is not clear what discussions, if any, these Western politicians and jurists had in Washington about McKean. McKean was not removed from office for several years, and the lewd and lascivious cohabitation and murder charges were not dismissed at this time.

On the way home from California, some of the cars on George's train, including his sleeping car, derailed. The cars pitched down an embankment and rolled one-and-a-half times. George had "a good shaking up," but many were badly injured. George believed his life

2. "Opinion of Judge McKean," *SLH*, Oct. 13, 1871, 1; Alexander, "Federal Authority"; Bitton, *GQC*, 170–71.

3. For more on the Yates affair, see John G. Turner, *Brigham Young, Pioneer Prophet* (Cambridge, MA: Harvard University Press, 2012), 285–86, 364–68.

4. GQC to BY, Oct. 31, 1871, CHL. This letter illustrates what a political *tour de force* George Q. Cannon could be—he sought out and sat with leading politicians on the same train and talked to them for hours along the way before reaching San Francisco. On Hittell, see Robert W. Righter, "Theodore Henry Hittell: California Historian," *Southern California Quarterly* 48 (Spring 1966): 289–306.

was spared because Young had blessed him before his trip to "return in safety."[5]

Young also contacted Thomas L. Kane, who suggested the he "retain the best legal counsel in the United States without regard to expense" and go into hiding. If necessary, Young could live with Kane, who would provide personal protection.[6]

At the end of 1871, George Q. was sent once again to Washington, DC, to assess what the post-Civil War American government thought of Utah and its people. Cannon met with Attorney General George H. Williams, a prominent lawyer, judge, and politician from Oregon who had just been appointed by Grant. Williams worked to enforce Reconstruction policies in the South. He asked Cannon if the Mormons were ready to accept any legislation Congress passed regarding Utah. George Q. replied they would so long as any such law did not limit their religious freedoms. Williams also wondered if the Mormons were prepared to agree to the prohibition of future polygamous marriages in exchange for recognition of existing plural marriages and legitimization of children from those marriages as well as for Utah statehood. Cannon, ever the politician, responded that any compromise would need to be proposed by Washington.[7]

Shortly after his return to Utah, George Q. participated in another statehood initiative. A new constitution was ratified that included woman's suffrage, which garnered support from national suffrage groups. Cannon and non-Mormons Frank Fuller and Thomas Fitch[8] were assigned to present the petition for statehood. The three met with President Grant, who told them that, unless gentiles would be in control or Mormons forsook polygamy, he would veto any bill proposing Utah statehood even if Congress were to pass it.[9] Can-

---

5. GQC, "Editorial Thoughts," *JI*, Nov. 11, 1871, 180.

6. Matthew J. Grow, *"Liberty to the Downtrodden": Thomas L. Kane, Romantic Reformer* (New Haven: Yale University Press, 2009), 260–61.

7. "Washington," *New York Tribune*, Dec. 19, 1871, 1; "George Henry Williams," US Department of Justice, justice.gov (accessed Oct. 2021).

8. Fuller was a non-Mormon Utah politician friendly to the Mormons and a close friend of Mark Twain. Fitch was also a lawyer and former congressman from Nevada who was retained by the church.

9. John Gary Maxwell, *Gettysburg to Great Salt Lake: George R. Maxwell, Civil War Hero and Federal Marshal among the Mormons* (Norman, OK: Arthur H. Clark Co., 2010), 161–62.

non met with committees and congressmen to plead Utah's case, and, although he found that many members of Congress had been "softened" and many presented a "seemingly kind and fair exterior," the national legislators were not interested in approving statehood unless the Saints "relinquished" celestial marriage (another term for plural marriage), at least for future unions.[10] While in Washington, Cannon also spent some time lobbying for the replacement of Judge McKean and waited impatiently for a decision by the Supreme Court in the *Clinton v. Englebrecht* case.[11]

In April 1872, the Court opined that that the US Marshal in Utah was not vested with the right to summon federal grand juries to consider and bring charges under territorial criminal law. The *Washington Star* correctly interpreted this to mean that since a grand jury "summoned by the United States marshal was illegal, the [trial] juries summoned in the same way to try Mormons for 'lewd and lascivious cohabitation,' under the territorial statute, are also illegal, and all proceedings had against them fall to the ground."[12] Mormons were delighted at the victory. McKean, who was in the Supreme Court's courtroom when the decision was read, "sat stone-faced, 'almost in despair,' as he tried to grasp the extent of the death knell of everything he had done."[13] There were over 130 illegal indictments issued by the federal grand jury, including the lewd and lascivious cohabitation and murder charges against Young, Cannon, and others that were effectively dismissed by the high court's unanimous decision.[14]

William H. Hooper, who had served as Utah's territorial delegate since 1865, now announced his retirement. To no one's surprise, the LDS-controlled People's Party soon nominated Cannon as its candidate. His opponent was Liberal Party candidate George R. Maxwell, a federal appointee who was a critic of the Mormons. Cannon received 20,969 votes (over 90 percent), Maxwell 1,942 votes, about 8 percent. Maxwell contested the election on grounds

10. GQC to BY, Mar. 31, 1872, CHL; Bitton, *GQC*, 171–72; Edward Leo Lyman, *Finally Statehood! Utah's Struggles, 1849–1896* (Salt Lake City: Signature Books, 2019), 67–79.

11. Lyman, *Finally Statehood*, 73–75.

12. *Clinton v. Englebrecht*, 80 U.S. 434 (1872); "End of the Mormon Prosecutions," *Washington Star*, Apr. 16, 1872, 1.

13. Lyman, *Finally Statehood*, 74, Whitney, *History of Utah*, 2:685–86.

14. Alexander, "Federal Authority," 86–87.

including the following: a majority of votes for Cannon were cast by women, including unnaturalized foreign and underage women; the election was "not free and fair" because of intimidation by Brigham Young; ballots were numbered and could be identified; and because Cannon believed that the revelation on polygamy trumped human law, Cannon would believe that he was not bound by any oath of allegiance to the United States.[15] Cannon did not immediately respond, prompting the *Salt Lake Tribune* to wonder when the "apostolic, Polygamistic editor of the *News*" might favor the public with a reply. Several weeks later, Cannon denied each claim and stated that he was a proper candidate and had been duly elected.[16] Having received only 8 percent of the popular vote, Maxwell had no choice but to cast every possible aspersion on his opponent if he wanted to be declared the winner. His contest of the election and attacks on Cannon created the blueprint that was followed for the next five territorial delegate races in Utah. Because of the start and end dates of congressional sessions of the period, Hooper remained in office until March 1873. Since the new Congress did not begin until December 1873, Cannon would not be sworn until then. In the meantime, Cannon served as William Hooper's understudy to understand the ins and outs of Congress, develop relationships, and learn how to be an effective member of Congress.[17]

Thomas L. Kane, who had tutored George Q. in statecraft and politics from 1858 to 1860 while Cannon worked in the East to improve the image of the Saints, came to Utah with his family just as Cannon was preparing to leave for Washington. When the two met, Kane provided indispensable advice on how to address the seemingly insuperable challenges of furthering the interests of Mormons.[18] Soon thereafter, Hooper and Cannon boarded an eastbound train. After arriving in Washington, DC, several days later, George immersed himself in the work of a territorial member of Congress, learning all he could from Hooper.

In December 1872, Cannon returned to Utah for a winter recess.

15. "The 'General' Protests," *SLH*, Oct. 31, 1872, 2; Bitton, *GQC*, 172–73.
16. "The Delegateship," *SLH*, Nov. 26, 1872, 2.
17. Bitton, *GQC*, 175–82.
18. Bitton, *GQC*, 174.

He spent a few days with his family, then was summoned to St. George to meet with Young and Kane as quickly as possible. After a brisk four-day ride—first on the train to Lehi, then in John W. Young's buggy with changes of horse teams every ten or fifteen miles—John Young and Cannon arrived in St. George.[19]

There, Young and Kane met with George Q. For three days Kane provided "valuable help on public affairs." Among other practical advice, Kane counseled George to "keep myself neutral from all entanglements [and to] make the acquaintance of at least one man on each committee from whom I could get information as to what was going on." Young made clear that he recognized that George Q. was the best choice for the territory.[20] Cannon was able and canny, but he also believed that God was leading his church and would protect the Saints. As a result, he was fearless in defending the church, its leaders, its precepts and practices, and in using his personal abilities and charm in seeking out and meeting some of the most powerful men in America. Over the next decade, he developed relationships with congressmen, senators, and other government officials that would pay dividends over the next thirty years as Utah sought and finally attained statehood.[21] Cannon's abilities and hard work only increased the Ring's suspicions and distaste for him. As a result, the Ring consistently worked to characterize him as a dangerous person. As Cannon quoted Young: "Next to himself I [Cannon] was the most [hated] of any of the authorities."[22]

After returning home for a few more days, Cannon travelled to Washington to continue shadowing William Hooper to prepare for the day when he would take over as territorial delegate. George Q. came to believe that Hooper, although a Mormon, did "not believe in special providences" involving the LDS Church and that this hurt him in his position.[23] In contrast, Cannon consistently saw God's hand in protecting the Saints. His faith gave him confidence in his ability to work to persuade others. George's fearlessness in taking positions he viewed as correct made him impatient with congressmen

19. GQCJ, Dec. 30, 1872, Jan. 1–4, 1873.
20. GQCJ, Jan. 7, 1873.
21. Bitton, *GQC*, 175–76.
22. GQCJ, Jan. 4, 1873.
23. GQCJ, Jan. 29, Feb. 20, 1873; Bitton, *GQC*, 181.

who he believed were sympathetic to Utah but were "moral cowards" for worry of offending their constituencies.

In January 1873, Cannon saw God's hand stopping proposed new legislation through a series of unlikely events. After meeting with several men from Utah who were critical of the Mormons, President Grant made clear that he wanted legislation addressing affairs in Utah. In response, Senator Frederick Frelinghuysen of New Jersey introduced a wide-ranging bill which, among other provisions, would have reversed the *Englebrecht* decision by permitting federal courts to hear cases under territorial law and empanel grand juries, prohibiting probate courts from hearing criminal cases, and repealing all territorial election laws, including woman suffrage and numbered ballots. Cannon was told by a member of Congress that the "intention was to 'go for' me first thing under this Bill when it passed." Suffragists decried the provision ending woman suffrage in Utah. Just days after former Mormon Fanny Stenhouse gave a lecture in Washington on the evils of polygamy, the Senate passed a somewhat softened bill which, according to the *New York Times*, caused "increased anxiety in Utah."[24]

The House was expected to pass the bill as well. As it was coming to a vote, Cannon noticed that his rival George Maxwell was seated next to William Clagett, the territorial delegate from Montana, who supported Frelinghuysen's bill. Clagett and other members of Congress left the chamber for some refreshments. The punch had been spiked, and soon many of the congressmen were tipsy. They decided they could not take up the bill in their condition. The following day, many bills awaited consideration. After a long day, the Frelinghuysen bill was about to come up at about 2:00 a.m. when an impeachment case involving two federal judges pushed it aside. The next morning, when the bill would have come up, a representative from California objected to consideration of the bill on the basis that there was not a quorum present. The effect was that the session ended without passage of the Frelinghuysen bill. Maxwell and his allies were unhappy; some

24. Stephen Eliot Smith, "Barbarians within the Gates: Congressional Debates on Mormon Polygamy, 1850–1879, *Journal of Church and State* 51 (Autumn 2009): 611; GQCJ, Feb. 7–8, 12, 15, 19, 21, 26, 1873; "The Frelinghuysen Bill," *Corinne Reporter*, Feb. 18, 1873, 2; "The Frelinghuysen Bill," *DN*, Mar. 12, 1873, 8; "Anxiety in Utah as to Frelinghuysen's Bill," *NYT*, Mar. 2, 1973, 1; Maxwell, *George R. Maxwell*, 164–65.

accused the Mormons of bribing the Speaker of the House. Cannon, on the other hand, saw the hand of Providence which had by "seemingly small and insignificant means" produced "marvelous results."[25]

While George Q. was spending much of his time in Washington, fighting congressional battles, his family was growing. With four wives, the number of his children grew during the 1860s and 1870s. By mid-1872, he had thirteen living children. Ten years later, he still had four wives (Elizabeth had died, and Cannon married her sister, Eliza) and twenty-two living children.[26] Providing for this large family created challenges and worries for George.

The United Order, an LDS retrenchment program, was instituted in response to the growing non-Mormon population and the likelihood that more would enter the territory with the completion of the transcontinental railroad. The level of cooperative activity in towns and congregations varied in the early 1870s but remained in operation to some extent for the next decade or so. Institutions such as ZCMI were overseen by general church leaders. Some local wards and stakes (organized congregations of Saints divided into geographical areas) created their own United Orders. The purpose of the order, treating members equally in an attempt to minimize disparities in wealth and income, was viewed favorably by Cannon, who worried about the economic disparity between rich and poor. He believed that wealth could debase the rich and that poor people could become servile, ignorant, envious, and were thus also demeaned.[27] This seems inconsistent for a man who had built and lived with most of his four wives and many children in one of the largest personal residences in Utah.[28]

In April 1873, Young called Cannon and four others as assistant counselors in the First Presidency. With the additional workload of being Utah's territorial delegate to Congress and of serving in the First Presidency, George Q. temporarily gave up his job as editor of the *Deseret News*.[29]

25. Bitton, *GQC*, 178–80.

26. See appendix.

27. Arrington, Fox, and May, *Building the City of God*, 79–335.

28. Bitton, *GQC*, 155. The family called it the "Big House" which stood on the northwest corner of 200 West (then called "First West") and South Temple Streets.

29. Bitton, *GQC*, 182–83. Unfortunately we have no journal entries from Cannon to learn how he felt about receiving this calling.

In November 1873, Cannon and others newly elected to Congress were sworn in. When George Q.'s name was called, Clinton L. Merriam, a Republican congressman from New York, proposed a resolution excluding Cannon because he had made oaths "inconsistent with citizenship of the United States" and was guilty of violating federal law. Cannon stepped aside while others were sworn in. His calm demeanor and "pluck" impressed many of the congressmen, and when Milton Sayler, a Democratic congressman from Ohio, objected to the proposal to exclude Cannon on the basis that there was no proof, all but one of the assembled legislators voted to table Merriam's resolution.[30]

George Q. was outgoing and kept busy in Washington visiting senators, representatives, newspaper editors, and others to discuss Utah, legislation that would affect Utah, and general matters. He was soon known to many of his colleagues as engaging, well informed, and articulate. He kept abreast of current events by reading newspapers and other periodicals voraciously. In Washington, as he had in England and elsewhere, he attended plays and lectures and was conversant with popular culture. He missed his family in Utah and wrote often, mostly to Elizabeth, who he expected would share the letters with the other wives. He would also sometimes send letters to different wives and to his children. He always provided advice to his children when he wrote, encouraging them to pursue service to others.[31]

George Q. faced two daunting tasks: keeping his seat and finding a way to defeat the latest anti-polygamy bill, the Poland bill. A few months after Representative Merriam had unsuccessfully sought to exclude George from Congress, the House's Committee on Elections took up Maxwell's challenge to Cannon. Maxwell's lawyer argued that George was a polygamist and that some votes cast for him were illegal. Maxwell's attorney demonized Mormons and characterized George Q. as a founder of a "system of murder and inaugurator of bloodshed." Cannon's lawyer had to restrain Cannon from shouting at Maxwell. Having calmed down, George

30. *Congressional Record*, 43rd Congress, 1st Sess., Dec. 2, 1873, as cited in Bitton, *GQC*, 184.

31. Bitton, *GQC*, 185–86; undated letter (either Jan. or Feb. 1874), GQC to John Q. Cannon reproduced in part in Bitton, *GQC*, 185–86.

then made his argument which was "clear, forcible, and incisive." He asserted that Maxwell could not have been elected because he had received less than 10 percent of the 22,911 votes cast and that Cannon had received the remaining 90-plus percent. Cannon was lawfully elected and sitting in Congress, and no proof or admission had been introduced that he was a polygamist. If the argument was that George had committed a crime (i.e., practiced polygamy), his exclusion could only be on the basis of trial and conviction, and he had not even been charged. A new lawyer for Maxwell was smoother but even stronger in bitterly denouncing Cannon in his closing argument. George Q. wrote in his journal that "I never suspected I was the monster they wished to make me out to be."[32] He consistently recorded that he did not believe he would be expelled and often prayed that he would retain his seat.

Not long after this committee hearing concluded in late March, Ann Eliza Webb Young visited Washington, DC, to lecture on the horrors of polygamy. Webb, who had married Brigham Young in 1868 as his "wife no. 19," made national headlines when she sued for divorce in 1873. Her "next best friend" in court filings was George Maxwell. Webb's case was originally assigned to a probate judge in Salt Lake City and was pending when she lectured in Washington in April 1874.[33]

The timing of Webb's lectures in the capital city was not coincidental. Maxwell was in town lobbying for the exclusion of Cannon from Congress and for passage of the Poland bill, the same matters that were occupying most of Cannon's time. As novelist Irving Wallace fancifully narrated, Maxwell escorted Webb into the House of Representatives where Speaker James G. Blaine and most of the other Representatives gathered around to talk to her. She gave two lectures to audiences made up mostly of congressmen and other officials and their wives. She blamed Congress for "the system that makes a plurality of wives possible in the Mormon country" and complained that "George Q. Cannon, of Utah, a polygamist with four wives, sits there [in Congress]." President Grant and his wife,

---

32. GQCJ, Mar. 30–31, Apr. 2–6, 1874.

33. Ann Eliza Webb Young, *Wife No. 19, or the Story of a Life in Bondage,* (Salt Lake City: n.p., 1875); Maxwell, *George R. Maxwell,* 178; Alexander, "Federal Authority," 91.

Julia, sat in the front row of Webb's second lecture. When she had finished, Wallace wrote, Grant shook Webb's hand and said, "It will be an everlasting disgrace to the country if Cannon is allowed to take his seat in Congress."[34]

In June 1874, the Committee on Elections voted 4-3, with one abstaining, against expelling Cannon. The *Tribune* suggested that a congressman from North Carolina whose vote might have made a difference had been bribed.[35] When the issue was brought before the entire House, the vote was 109-76 that Cannon had been elected and would be seated. This good news was tempered, however, by another House vote of 131-51 to investigate the accusations of Cannon's alleged polygamy and disloyalty to the Union.[36] The *Salt Lake Herald* opined that the Ring had created the impression that Cannon was "really a dangerous man, given to vice and immorality, and unfit to sit in their immaculate midst. But of late they have learned to the contrary. They have watched our Delegate narrowly and have decided that he is a much worthier man than any of those who have defamed and vilified him. They have been compelled to admit, that for gentlemanly bearing, honorable deportment, and attention to duty, he is the peer of the best of them."[37] It was not the last time that Cannon's qualification to serve in the House was contested.

Six months earlier, in January 1874, Vermont congressman Luke Poland had proposed a bill to make it easier to prosecute and convict a man of polygamy, to authorize a federal grand jury to bring cohabitation-like charges under territorial law, and to change certain voting laws. As originally filed, it also excluded Mormons from grand and trial juries for believing in polygamy. The Morrill Anti-Bigamy Act was twelve years old, but no one had been charged with a crime under it for three reasons: it required prosecutors to

34. Irving Wallace, *The Twenty-Seventh Wife* (New York: Simon & Schuster, 1961), 327–30. Wallace gives no citations for any of his account, which is replete with factual misstatements regarding GQC's life. Maxwell's account of Webb's visit to Congress is based on Wallace's book. Maxwell, *George Maxwell*, 178–81.

35. "The Corruption Fund, a North Carolina Congressman Is Greased," *SLT*, June 16, 1874, 4. The *Tribune* routinely accused Cannon and his colleagues of bribing journalists and politicians.

36. "No Expulsion," *SLH*, June 18, 1874, 2; "More Carriage Grease," *SLT*, June 19, 1874, 2; Bitton, *GQC*, 186.

37. "No Expulsion," *SLH*, June 18, 1874, 2.

prove that a polygamous marriage had been solemnized, which was difficult; grand juries that would issue an indictment for the crime of polygamy were made up mostly of Mormons; and trial juries made up mostly of Mormons would have to convict the accused. Mormons were not inclined to indict or convict members of their church of polygamy or illegal cohabitation. McKean tried to change these dynamics by working to exclude Mormons from grand and trial juries and by directing a federal grand jury made up mostly of non-Mormons to indict alleged polygamists under a territorial law making "lewd and lascivious cohabitation" (i.e., polygamy) a crime. The US Supreme Court upended McKean's ploy by ruling in the *Englebrecht* case that a federal grand jury could not bring an indictment for crimes under territorial law and that a federal court could not hear such a charge.[38]

The Poland bill as filed was similar in many respects to the Frelinghuysen bill: probate courts lost criminal jurisdiction; federal grand juries could issue indictments for violations of territorial criminal laws; federal courts could hear cases involving territorial law; polygamists could not hold office. At least one historian sees a different focus in the Poland bill from earlier anti-polygamy legislation: it was not intended to demonize Mormons; rather, it was intended to permit the prosecution of a practice that Congress and America at large found offensive, even barbaric—polygamy and polygamous cohabitation. Many Americans had watched the Mormons help to complete the "Pacific railroad" and had seen what industrious people they were.[39] The Poland bill did not provide for the end of woman suffrage in Utah and thereby avoided a controversy with the suffrage movement.

Based on negative reactions from some House members, Representative Poland toned down his original bill. Under the revised proposal, grand juries would be appointed through a cooperative procedure between federal authorities and county officials. Judgments entered by probate courts before the Poland Act would not be disturbed. Convictions in polygamy cases could be appealed directly to the US Supreme Court.[40]

38. GQC to BY, Jan. 6, 1874, CHL.
39. Smith, "Barbarians within the Gates," 611–13.
40. Whitney, *History of Utah*, 2:738–40.

After the House passed the Poland bill, the Senate made several last-minute changes, including cutting a proposed disqualification of jurors and officeholders who believed or even practiced polygamy. The sponsors did not oppose the changes, and the bill passed into law.[41]

In the midst of Congress's consideration of the Poland bill, Thomas Kane summoned Cannon to meet him. Over several days, George Q. received both reassuring and helpful words from Kane and also learned that Elizabeth Kane had kept a journal of her visits to Mormon homes in Utah and Arizona during their 1872–73 visit. She had had pleasant experiences in Mormon households and had shared her notes with Eastern friends, who reacted favorably to her accounts. After reviewing her journal, George heartily agreed with Thomas that Elizabeth should publish her experiences. He believed that the published work "would do good and dissipate many prejudices and misconceptions." Elizabeth Kane's *Twelve Mormon Homes* was published in March 1874.[42] In June, Kane sent copies to George to distribute to politicians and journalists "in hopes of heading off the 'rascally Congress which favors the Poland Bill.'" Cannon provided copies of the book primarily to senators on the Judiciary Committee, which was considering the Poland bill. Positive press reviews "explicitly connected [*Twelve Mormon Homes*] with the congressional deliberations" and likely contributed to amendments that softened the proposed bill.[43]

Cannon viewed members of the Ring as enemies of the church who wanted to rule Utah. To him, these people wanted to displace the large majority to control the resources and development in Utah for their own economic benefit. George felt that the only reason to make allegations of blood atonement and murder was to frighten and outrage the public at large. Most Americans did not like polygamy, but charges of violence were far more serious.

The 1874 election was held in August of that year, on the heels of the enactment of the Poland Act. A new Liberal Party candidate,

41. Lyman, *Statehood Finally*, 89–92; 18 Stat. 253 (1874); Mark Wilcox Cannon, "The Mormon Issue in Congress, 1872–1882, Drawing on the Experience of Territorial Delegate George Q. Cannon," PhD diss., Harvard University, 1960, 57–60.

42. Elizabeth Wood Kane, *Twelve Mormon Homes* (Salt Lake City: Tanner Trust Fund, 1974).

43. Bitton, *GQC*, 189; Grow, *Thomas L. Kane*, 268–69.

attorney Robert N. Baskin, was chosen to run against Cannon. The result of the election was another lopsided result, with Cannon receiving 24,864 votes and Baskin 4,518. Governor George Lemuel Woods disallowed votes from Cache County, where Baskin received only three votes, because the county clerk had been appointed by the local probate judge. Even with the exclusion of these votes, the final result was 22,360-4,515. Nevertheless, Woods refused to certify the victory for Cannon.[44]

The same day that the voting results were announced, Baskin contested the election utilizing arguments against Cannon similar to those made by Maxwell in 1872. To these, Baskin added new claims, arguing that George was not a US citizen, that he had violated federal law by marrying two polygamous wives after 1862, when the Morrill Anti-Bigamy Act was enacted, and that he was ineligible to serve as a member of Congress under the Poland Act, which prohibited any bigamist or polygamist from serving.[45] The allegation with respect to Cannon's citizenship was based on the alleged issuance of an invalid naturalization certificate in 1854 shortly after Cannon's return from Hawai'i, at a time when George Q. was not yet eligible for citizenship.[46]

Just days after the election results were announced and Baskin filed his contest, Chief Judge McKean charged the sitting grand jury to remember that the practice of polygamy "goes hand in hand with the murderous doctrine of blood atonement."[47] Taking its lead from McKean, the *Tribune* noted that "the most ardent advocate of Blood Atonement who ever raised his voice in the Tabernacle, is George Q. Cannon; that he is the most vindictive, and theoretically, the most blood-thirsty of all the Mormon Priesthood."[48] Two weeks later,

44. "Complete Election Results," *SLH,* Oct. 8, 1874, 3; "Why He Did Not Give the Certificate," *DW,* Feb. 10, 1875, 8; Bitton, *GQC,* 191–92.

45. "Contested Election," *SLT,* Nov. 15, 1874, 4; "Congressional Contest," *SLH,* Nov. 17, 1874, 2. Bitton, *GQC,* 192. In his contest, Baskin relied on a version of the Poland Act that passed the House in April but not the Senate and never became law. There was no prohibition in the act of a polygamist holding office in Congress. 18 Stat. 253.

46. John Gary Maxwell, *Robert Newton Baskin and the Making of Modern Utah* (Norman, OK: Arthur H. Clark Co., 2013), 172–74.

47. "Chief Justice McKean's Charge to the Grand Jury," *SLH,* Oct. 8, 1874, 3.

48. "The Blood Atoner," *SLT,* Oct. 13, 1874, 4. The "doctrine of blood atonement," as it was understood by the Ring and the *Salt Lake Tribune,* involved the Mormon

it was announced in McKean's courtroom that the grand jury had returned a new indictment against Cannon accusing him of "lewd and lascivious cohabitation" under territorial law, just as Ring proponents had vowed to do as soon as the Poland Act passed.[49] This appears to have been an orchestrated attempt to make it impossible for George Q. to argue that he had not been charged with a crime for practicing polygamy.

When Cannon appeared at his arraignment with his lawyer, future US Senator and US Supreme Court Justice, George Sutherland, the court required bail of $5,000. The US district attorney, William C. Carey, indicated that he did not have time to prosecute this criminal matter during the current term and the jury pool was too small to proceed with trial. Sutherland argued that the case should be tried immediately, asserting Cannon's constitutional right to a speedy trial and noting that his client would be in Washington, DC, the following term, serving as the territory's delegate to Congress. At the next hearing a month later, when a trial on the lewd and lascivious cohabitation charge was to be scheduled, Cannon was served with a new indictment under the Morrill Anti-Bigamy Act for the crime of polygamy. George Q. was arraigned on this charge and McKean imposed an additional $5,000 bail.[50]

Cannon responded to Baskin's charges, which were more sophisticated than most that Maxwell had raised. George acknowledged that he was foreign born, but he identified the date that he had taken the "oath of allegiance and fidelity to the United States" and had received a certificate of full citizenship. George addressed the issue of marrying since 1862 obliquely, arguing that no one had been charged with violating the Morrill Act, an argument that was undermined by the new pending charges against him. On the lewd and lascivious cohabitation claim and, by extension, any polygamy claim that might

"church-instigated violence directed at dissenters, enemies, and strangers." The church has always denied that it participated in such activity, though church members sometimes engaged in "occasional isolated acts of violence" in nineteenth-century America. Lowell M. Snow, "Blood Atonement," in Daniel H. Ludlow, ed., *Encyclopedia of Mormonism*, 4 vols. (New York: Macmillan, 1992), 1:131.

49. "Another Lie Nailed to the Counter," *SLH*, Oct. 22, 1874, 2; Bitton, *GQC*, 192.

50. "Third District Court, Justice McKean Presiding," *SLT*, Nov. 13, 1874, 4; Bitton, *GQC*, 192.

follow, he argued both that he enjoyed a "constitutional pledge of toleration and immunity from religious test," and that he had not been convicted of any such crime. On the Poland Act, Cannon correctly asserted that the portion of the Poland bill prohibiting polygamists from serving in Congress had been deleted before it was enacted by Congress. Going on the offensive, George hinted at a statute of limitation defense by stating that "his matrimonial status has been unchanged for many years." Cannon also pointed out that Congress had engaged in a "most searching investigation" of his right to be seated and had come to the conclusion that he was not disqualified. Finally, he reminded everyone that he had received more than five times the number of votes than Baskin. It was abundantly clear that Baskin had not been elected to office and could not take office.[51]

Baskin, in spite of not carefully reading the final version of the Poland Act, was a talented lawyer. He scheduled an "inquest" for January 4, 1875, in which witnesses were sworn and deposed and documents were reviewed with the goal of showing that Cannon was not eligible to become a naturalized citizen on the date of the naturalization certificate he had received.[52] This was probably Baskin's best argument, and continued to be raised against George for years, though no court with jurisdiction ever determined that he was not a citizen.

Before Baskin's inquest could take place, Cannon caught the train for the East on November 28, 1874. The *Salt Lake Herald*, sometimes referred to by the *Tribune* as "Zion's Echo," noted his departure and assured him that his "thousands of constituents wish him a safe journey and a pleasant winter, and will joyfully welcome him on his return home next spring."[53] Even federally appointed judges did not have the courage to keep Utah's popularly elected territorial delegate from going to Washington to serve in Congress.

As had happened in the previous session of Congress, the House Committee on Elections, urged on by Baskin and others, decided to investigate Delegate Cannon. George Q. met with many congressmen. The reaction of James G. Blaine, the powerful Republican

51. "Congressional Contest," *SLH*, Nov. 17, 1874, 2; Bitton, *GQC*, 192–93.
52. Maxwell, *Baskin*, 159–60.
53. "Off for Congress," *SLH*, Nov. 28, 1874, 3.

Speaker of the House, was that the attacks on Cannon were "tremendous folly." In January 1875, the committee recommended that Cannon be expelled from Congress as "unworthy to occupy a seat."[54] In the next few months, newly appointed Samuel Axtell replaced George Woods as governor of the Territory of Utah. Axtell reversed his predecessor's refusal to certify the election. He did not feel he had any choice—the vote tally was clear.[55] The Ring accused Axtell of being friendly with the Mormons. Much to the chagrin of anti-Cannon agitators in Utah, the proposal to expel him was never voted on in the 44th Congress.[56]

February 1875 was also the month of McKean's downfall. His removal was likely imminent because of criticism leveled against him by many in Washington, but his actions that month ensured it. Under the Poland Act, Ann Eliza Webb's divorce suit against Brigham Young had been transferred from a territorial probate judge to McKean. McKean ordered Young to pay Webb alimony.[57] The ruling had serious legal inconsistencies and was ultimately reversed on appeal, but McKean incarcerated the Mormon prophet for a night for refusing to pay. Within a week McKean was removed from office by President Grant, to the fury of many members of the Ring and to the joy of Mormons and their allies.[58]

When George Q. returned home the next month, he told how he had been received cordially by most members of Congress, with only those "who sought to do us injury" being difficult. He had been invited to more dinner parties than he could attend. On a substantive level, he had worked hard on a new railroad bill that was important to Utah.[59] Soon, the *Juvenile Instructor* published an editorial written by George Q. against the deposed McKean. Cannon characterized the "late" McKean (who had lost his position but was not dead) as the most "striking" example of one who relentlessly sought to "destroy the people and overthrow the work of God." Just when McKean

54. GQCJ, Jan. 15–20, 1875; Bitton, *GQC*, 194.

55. "Mr. Cannon's Certificate," *SLH*, Feb. 6, 1875, 3; Maxwell, *Baskin*, 160

56. Maxwell, *Baskin*, 160.

57. Alexander, "Federal Authority," 91–92.

58. Dwyer, *Gentile Comes to Utah*, 83–93; Bitton, *GQC*, 195.

59. "Welcome Home," *SLH*, Mar. 14, 1875, 2; "Delegate Cannon at Home," *SLH*, Mar. 16, 1875, 2; Bitton, *GQC*, 95.

thought he was succeeding, "he was hurled from his position. If death had struck his downfall could not have been more sudden." As always, Cannon found divine intervention in this change: "The Lord has overruled the conduct of this man for the good of Zion."[60]

When the polygamy charge against Cannon was addressed in court in April, it was quietly dismissed because the prosecutor knew that Cannon had a good statute of limitation defense: the indictment against him would have had to have been brought within three years of the criminal act, in this case, the marriage.[61] George Q. had not entered into any new marriages in years. The procedural changes effected by the Poland Act did not change the Morrill Act, which only made a polygamous marriage criminal, not marital relations after the marriage.[62]

The Saints believed that their religious practices, which they averred were not damaging to others, were protected by the First Amendment. As McKean began to take serious steps to enforce the anti-polygamy laws, George Q. considered the possibility of creating a test case on the constitutionality of the laws. His old secretary from the British mission, George Reynolds, was indicted for polygamy under the Morrill Act on October 21, 1874, and an agreement was supposedly made with prosecutors to make this a test case, with a promise that Reynolds would not receive a prison sentence.[63] Cannon and Reynolds later realized that either no agreement existed or the prosecutor had decided not to honor it. Reynolds was convicted. The conviction was later overturned on procedural issues but was brought again shortly afterward.[64]

President Grant visited Utah in October 1875. He and his party, including his wife, Julia, were met by Young and Cannon in Ogden. Mrs. Grant chatted with Young while Cannon, Grant, and another

60. GQC, "Editorial Thoughts," *JI*, Mar. 6, 1875, 54.

61. The federal statute of limitations in 1871 appears to have been two years, which was increased by statute in 1876 to three years. Paul D. Swanson, "Limitless Limitations: How War Overwhelms Criminal Statutes of Limitations," *Cornell Law Review* 97 (September 2012), 1563; 19 Stat. 32, 32–33 (1876).

62. "Court Proceedings," *SLH*, Apr. 3, 1875; 3, "Judicial Persecution," *DN*, Apr. 14, 1875, 6.

63. George Reynolds Journal, Oct. 16, 1874, quoted in Bruce A. Van Orden, *Prisoner for Conscience' Sake: The Life of George Reynolds* (Salt Lake City: Deseret Book Co., 1992), 58–65.

64. "Court Proceedings," *SLH* , Apr. 3, 1875, 3; Bitton, *GQC*, 218.

new governor, George Emery, spoke together. As Grant and his entourage were transported from the train depot to Temple Square, the streets were lined with children from LDS Sunday schools, no doubt orchestrated by Cannon. Grant reportedly asked who these children were, and, when told Mormon children, he reportedly stated that he had "been deceived." William Hooper took Julia Grant to an organ recital in the Tabernacle. She was reported to have said to the ex-delegate, "Oh, I wish I could do something for these good Mormon people." Nevertheless, Grant spent most of his time with federal officials and members of the Ring and impressed on all that he wanted to see the Poland Act enforced.[65]

George started for Washington for his second-term congressional duties in November 1875. A month later, Elizabeth and their daughter, Mary Alice, left to join him. He met them in Chicago, and the three traveled to the capital city together. They rented rooms near the Capitol Building and enjoyed American centennial festivities for much of the next year in Washington, Philadelphia, and New York City. Cannon not only wanted Elizabeth and Mary Alice in Washington to enjoy themselves, he was interested in showing government leaders that Mormons were not so different from other Americans. So many horror stories of Mormon family life were circulated among Americans of the time that George wanted his colleagues to see what a real LDS family looked like. Elizabeth and Mary Alice attended receptions and parties, and Elizabeth got to know some of the important women in Washington. They were invited to centennial activities where members of Congress had the best seats and watched various activities, including the "grandest" fireworks George had ever seen. On May 17, Elizabeth received a "beautiful basket of flowers" from First Lady Julia Grant.[66]

During the congressional proceedings of 1876, Baskin testified before the Committee on Territories. George reported to Young that Baskin asserted that Cannon and the Mormons were guilty of polygamy, blood atonement, and incest; that the people were

65. Whitney, *History of Utah*, 2:777–79; Leonard J. Arrington, *Brigham Young: American Moses* (New York: Alfred A. Knopf, 1985), 374; Bitton, *GQC*, 195–96.

66. GQCJ, Nov. 25, 29, Dec. 23, 25–27, 1875, Feb. 9, 22, May 9, 15, 17, 27, June 13, 20, 24, July 4–5, 8, 15, Aug. 12–13, 1876.

ignorant and were mostly made up of foreigners; that "the women [are] driven from the harems in droves to the polls"; that theocracy reigned in "terror and blood"; and that people were in danger of assassination and were "always excommunicated if they did not vote the Church ticket." Cannon responded, stating among other things that the fact that Baskin had not been assassinated was proof positive the Mormons were not murdering their enemies.[67] Baskin had also done more due diligence on Cannon's supposed citizenship and reviewed the naturalization records, finding no indication that George Q. had been made a citizen in 1854 as he had claimed.[68] Baskin made his arguments before the Committee on Elections and impressed all by his legal skills and preparation. Cannon ably responded.[69] More bills were filed regarding Utah and the Mormons, from ones that would regulate elections to ones that would bar any believing Latter-day Saint from sitting on a jury. Some included provisions ending woman suffrage in Utah, which raised the ire of national suffragists Sara Andrews Spencer and Belva Lockwood of the National Woman Suffrage Society. George Q. was at the center of all the fights over these bills.[70] He sometimes worried that Baskin had convinced Congress to expel him. On July 31, however, members of the committee confided in him that the committee had voted unanimously that "there was no case against me." The next day, the subcommittee chair confirmed that but told George the decision would not be announced until the next session.[71]

George was reelected to Congress again in 1876, this time by a vote of 21,101 to 3,833. From August to November, he spent a good deal of time with Young, who continued to look to Cannon for advice. Elizabeth was grieved and Mary Alice "wept sorely" at not returning to Washington with him. This time, he took his eldest son, nineteen-year-old John Q., to serve as his personal secretary. John

---

67. GQC to BY, Mar. 23, 1876, as quoted and cited in Bitton, 198–99.
68. GQCJ, May 5, 1876.
69. GQCJ, May 25–26, 1876.
70. GQC to BY, Mar. 11, 1876; GQCJ, Feb. 4, 25, Mar. 9, 1876; Bitton, *GQC*, 198.
71. GQCJ, July 31, Aug. 1, 1876. No one wanted to have the decision raised against them in the fall elections.

had previously learned shorthand at the request of Brigham Young and was well prepared for his time in Washington.[72]

Just before Christmas, George Q. took John to New York City and the two saw several Broadway shows, visited the Metropolitan Museum of Art, and reviewed the ongoing construction of the Brooklyn Bridge. It was clear to many that George was grooming John to follow in his footsteps. Heber J. Grant later wrote that no "young man in the whole church … has had more opportunities and advantages extended to him educationally, spiritually, and every other way than John Q. Cannon."[73] The real reason for George's Christmas trip to New York, however, was to meet Samuel Tilden, the Democratic governor of New York. Tilden had just run for president of the United States in the most hotly contested race in the history of the presidency, and the one with perhaps the most controversial outcome. Cannon took a letter of introduction from a mutual friend to Tilden.[74]

On January 2, 1877, Cannon and Tilden had a "very free talk" about Utah Territory in Tilden's mansion in New York City. Cannon expressed the frustration that Mormons felt in being the dominant population in Utah yet subject to federal appointees whom they believed ruled in a heavy-handed manner against the interests of the majority. Cannon recorded in his journal that Tilden promised to review issues in Utah shortly after taking office, to visit the territory early in his term, and to consider making changes that would be favorable to the Mormons. As it turned out, however, Samuel Tilden never got to serve as president.

In the contentious November 1876 presidential election, Tilden, the Democratic nominee, received more popular votes and was ahead by nineteen votes in the Electoral College. A total of twenty votes in four states were disputed, however, and the Electoral College was deadlocked. A special fifteen-member electoral commission, five senators, five representatives, and five Supreme Court

72. GQCJ, Nov. 27–Dec. 4, 1876; Bitton, *GQC*, 202; KLC, "Wives and Other Women: Love, Sex, and Marriage in the Lives of John Q. Cannon, Frank J. Cannon, and Abraham H. Cannon," *Dialogue* 43 (Winter 2010): 74–75.

73. GQCJ, Dec. 23, 26–27, 29, 1876; KLC, "Wives and Other Women," 75; Bitton, *GQC*, 203.

74. GQCJ, Dec. 22, 28, 30, 1876.

justices, was appointed to decide the election. Cannon had a good seat from which to watch as commission members negotiated the Compromise of 1877, which counted all disputed electoral votes from the four states as cast for Republican Rutherford B. Hayes in exchange for the withdrawal of federal troops from the former Confederate states, effectively ending Reconstruction.[75]

No one knows how helpful Tilden might have been to Utah, but he almost certainly would have been more favorable than the president sometimes called "His Fraudulency." Hayes was a teetotaling Methodist and a devotee of the Reverend John Philip Newman, a known critic of the Mormons. Though Cannon was able sometimes to present proposals to Hayes, and while Hayes was both disciplined and astute enough to listen carefully, he showed more inclination to take notice of the Ring in Salt Lake City, who were intent on destroying Mormon polygamy, political hegemony, and cooperative economy.[76]

George Q. spent the summer of 1877 in Salt Lake City. He was ill for much of the season, but, when he heard that Brigham Young was ailing, he immediately went to his side. Young was concerned that Cannon was too ill to minister to him, but Cannon insisted. Though Cannon was sick, he returned each day to watch over the Mormon prophet who had had such a profound influence on his life. Finally, on August 29, 1877, Young passed away, likely of a ruptured appendix.[77]

Young's death created challenging issues. Because of the Morrill Act's prohibition on the church owning more than $50,000 in assets, Young had comingled church assets with his own. His estate, with assets valued at $1,626,000 but offset by many debts, had a net value of $224,242. George had helped Young prepare his will and was one of three executors of Young's estate. Many of Young's wives and children may have expected to inherit more than they did. Some of his children were estranged from the church and challenged the executors' decision to deem much of Young's estate to be property owned by the church. The Brigham Young Trust Company, created

75. Eric Foner, *Reconstruction: America's Unfinished Revolution, 1863–1877* (New York: Harper & Row, 1988), 579–601; GQCJ, Feb. 1, 17, 19, 23, 28, Mar. 1, 5, 1877; Bitton, *GQC*, 204–5.

76. Bitton, *GQC*, 216.

77. GQCJ, Aug. 23, 29, 1877; Bitton, *GQC*, 210; Lester E. Bush Jr., "Brigham Young in Life and Death: A Medical Overview," *JMH* 5 (1978): 102–3.

to administer the estate, lasted for decades as heirs and executors worked to resolve the issues.[78]

After the death of Young, the church was led for a period of three years by the Quorum of Twelve Apostles. John Taylor, the senior-most apostle, became the general leader of the church by reason of leading that quorum. George Q. was a relatively junior apostle, and his position of assistant counselor to Young ended, although his relationship with Taylor and his natural gifts meant that he continued to play a prominent role

Many, if not most, of the "Utah" bills introduced in Congress during this time proposed to end women's suffrage. An important exception, and the only bill enacted, was the Poland bill. Congressmen and the lobbyists who egged them on believed that Mormon women should not vote because Mormon men would simply instruct their many wives on how to vote. This was both a misapprehension of most LDS women and a miscalculation of national suffragists' views. They were not pleased and took the unexpected role of opposing the legislation. One of them, Isabella Beecher Hooker, sister of Harriet Beecher Stowe and Henry Ward Beecher, who had recently quoted a statement Cannon made on woman suffrage when she testified before Congress, related to George Q. that she had "told many of my friends that I would rather be your 50th wife than be the only wife of hundreds of men whom I know."[79]

Cannon's old friend George Reynolds was convicted of polygamy (again) in 1875, and this time the Utah Supreme Court affirmed the decision, in June 1876, finding no evidence of prejudice from the trial judge's negative remarks about polygamy. The court ruled that the trial court was not in error, "especially too when we remember that this crime has a blighting and blasting influence upon the consciences of all it touches."[80] That decision had been appealed to the US Supreme Court but was not heard in 1876 or 1877. Now, in early 1878, the Supreme Court decided to hear Reynolds's appeal

78. Bitton, *GQC*, 212–31.

79. GQCJ, Jan. 30, Feb. 3, 1878; Bitton, *GQC*, 217. Cannon noted that he "replied that I thanked her for the compliment and I accepted it as such more to my religion than to me personally." GQCJ, Feb. 3, 1878.

80. George Reynolds, diary, June 1876, as cited and quoted in Van Orden, *Prisoner for Conscience' Sake*, 78–79.

quickly, leaving the church little time to find competent counsel to represent Reynolds in what promised to be (and ultimately became) the first important decision on free exercise of religious freedom under the Constitution's First Amendment. Reflecting a different era, George met with Chief Justice Matthew R. Waite to seek to slow the appeal down. The Chief Justice offered little help. Ever the problem solver, Thomas Kane suggested that the church hire George W. Biddle, a prominent Philadelphia lawyer, who did not have the time to prepare for the appeal that session. The Supreme Court could deny an informal continuance request from Utah's territorial delegate but not from a distinguished eastern lawyer, and when George Biddle requested a continuance of oral argument, the justices reluctantly postponed argument in the Reynolds case to November 1878.[81]

Reynolds, through Biddle, maintained in both briefs and oral argument that the Morrill Act violated the First Amendment.[82] On January 6, 1879, the Supreme Court issued its unanimous decision. It distinguished between belief and action, holding that citizens were free to believe what they wanted so long as they did not engage in inappropriate action based on their religious beliefs. The government could not regulate belief, but it could regulate certain actions. As to what constituted sufficiently inappropriate action not to be protected by the First Amendment, the court ruled that all would agree human sacrifice would not be countenanced. According to the court, polygamy, long considered "odious" in the Western world, was close enough to human sacrifice that it was not protected by the Constitution.[83]

George Q. was profoundly disappointed. He firmly believed that God had instituted plural marriage and that he had personally been inspired by God to enter "the principle." It was deeply troubling to him that the US Supreme Court had not recognized the right of the Mormons under the Constitution to practice a form of marriage that, he believed, did not harm others. Cannon was also unhappy

---

81. GQCJ, Mar. 16, 30, Dec, 28, 1878, Jan. 11, 1879; Grow, *Thomas L. Kane* , 279–80; Bitton, *GQC*, 219.

82. Sarah Barringer Gordon, *The Mormon Question: Polygamy and Constitutional Conflict in Nineteenth-Century America* (Chapel Hill: University of North Carolina Press, 2002), 122–32; Bitton, *GQC*, 219–20.

83. *Reynolds v. U.S.*, 98 U.S. 45 (1879); GQCJ, Jan. 11, 15, 1879; Bitton, GQCJ, 220–21.

because it was he who had urged Reynolds to have his case be the test case and it was Reynolds who would be imprisoned.

Cannon approached Justice Stephen Field, who had concurred in the decision but found that certain evidence at the trial should not have been admitted, about a rehearing. The court did not rehear the case generally but did determine on a limited rehearing that Reynolds should not have been sentenced to hard labor. Cannon then requested that President Hayes pardon Reynolds. The president refused, but Hayes and his attorney general, Charles Devens, expressed a willingness to grant amnesty to Mormon polygamists who had married before the Supreme Court had upheld the constitutionality of the Anti-Bigamy Act and to legitimize children born to these polygamous couples, so long as these parents would obey the law prospectively. Cannon sent a telegram to John Taylor indicating that the Hayes administration would consider amnesty. Taylor recognized that this would mean the end of polygamy and was not prepared to agree. Not surprisingly, government leaders in Washington were not willing to push for amnesty when it was apparent the LDS Church and its members were not prepared to stop plural marriage going forward.[84]

Cannon soon prepared a commentary on the Reynolds decision, addressing only the issue of whether polygamy should be protected as part of the First Amendment's right to free exercise of religion. He spent many days in the library researching and several months writing the review. The Supreme Court issued its opinion on January 6, 1879, George Q.'s commentary on the decision was published shortly after he finished it, in mid-1879.[85]

On the home front, in 1876, George Q. and his families began constructing homes and other buildings on property he had purchased some years before from his brother Angus near where Emigration, Red Butte, and Parleys Creeks all drained into the Jordan River. George gave his wives the choice between living in one

84. GQCJ, Jan. 18, 22, 1879; Bitton, *GQC*, 223–24.

85. GQCJ, Feb. 15, 26, Mar. 8, 12, 15, May 14, June 8, 1879; GQC, *A Review of the Decision of the Supreme Court of the United States, in the Case of George Reynolds vs. the United States* (Salt Lake City: Deseret News, 1879). George Q. circulated a draft of the review to a number of legal scholars and Congressmen, many of whom commented that they thought his analysis was sound and persuasive. GQCJ, June 8, 1879.

large home together or of each having her own home. They voted for separate homes. There George Q. and his family originally planned and developed a family compound with the largest house for Elizabeth called the "Farm House," three other homes for Sarah Jane, Eliza, and Martha, and a school house. It was several years before many of the buildings were habitable, but wives and families slowly migrated from the "Big House" on South Temple to the family compound known as the "farm." All but the oldest children spent most of their years growing up at the farm, attending the family school and living with many brothers and sisters.[86] Many of the buildings from the Cannon compound remain today along the west side of 1000 West, just south of California Avenue (about 1300 South), in Salt Lake City. Two still-standing homes include the Farm House where Elizabeth Hoagland Cannon and her children lived, and a large Victorian house built by George Q. about 1890 for his last wife, Caroline Young Cannon.

86. GQC to Eliza Tenney Cannon, Apr. 18, 1878, cited and quoted in Bitton, *GQC,* 390–91; Bitton, *GQC,* 390–96.

CHAPTER SIX

HOPE AND OPTIMISM DURING TROUBLED TIMES

1880-87

"The devil has tried a good many ways to destroy us. ... But God has spoken. His word has gone forth concerning his work and it must prevail."
—George Q. Cannon, December 19, 1881

At the beginning of 1880, George Q. was in Washington, DC, attending to his duties as Utah's territorial delegate to Congress. He had brought his first wife, Elizabeth, and their two young daughters, Mary Alice and Emily, with him. On January 15, the Cannons received a letter from their oldest son, John Q., informing them that he had just become engaged to Elizabeth Ann "Annie" Wells. Annie was the accomplished daughter of Daniel H. Wells, sometime First Presidency member and Salt Lake City mayor, and Emmeline B. Wells, feminist editor of the *Woman's Exponent* and Relief Society leader. It came as a total surprise, though a pleasant one.

The congressional docket turned out to be busy as George fought against anti-polygamy legislation and the Ladies' Anti-Polygamy Society of Utah's petition for his expulsion from Congress. As a result, George, Elizabeth, and John's two sisters were unable to attend the Mormon wedding of the year—at which Daniel Wells officiated in the Endowment House—and were able only to send their "warmest congratulations to Annie and [John Q.]." While they rejoiced "exceedingly," the "drawback" was that "we are not with you."[1]

While George did not disclose it to family in Utah, their doctor

1. GQCJ, Jan. 7–8, 15, Mar. 17, 1880; "Wedded," *SLH*, Mar. 18, 1880, 3.

in DC, Mary Parsons, found a spot on Elizabeth's lung and signs of weakness in her heart. George had often worried about Elizabeth's health. Now his concern grew that she did not have much time to live.

On January 6, the Ladies' Anti-Polygamy Society of Utah submitted a memorial to the House of Representatives asking for the expulsion of George Q. from Congress. The society called George "one of the ablest and most strenuous upholders of this disgraceful institution [polygamy]." The reasons he should be excluded were familiar: he was a polygamist, he had believed that the Morrill Anti-Bigamy Act was unconstitutional (now the Supreme Court had ruled otherwise), and he had continued to "urge polygamy upon" "his followers," even recommending that "they marry wives in pairs." In addition to requesting the expulsion of Cannon, the memorial asked for an amendment to the Morrill Act to make "the continuous living together of men and women in polygamous relations" criminal.[2]

During the session, George Q. saw threats to himself and the church from the Ring and the Ladies' Anti-Polygamy Society, whose *Anti-Polygamy Standard* was established to challenge Emmeline Wells's *Woman's Exponent*, which defended plural marriage. These challenges needed to be met head on, which George felt he was doing. As he left for Utah with his family, George hoped that, with the responses he and others had made, the "dark and threatening clouds" were clearing. In a speech he gave a few weeks later, he noted how those who actually visited the city of the Saints did not afterward believe the stories of Mormons' disloyalty to the country or harsh domination by the "priesthood."[3]

US President Rutherford B. Hayes was making a coast-to-coast tour and stopped in Utah. Mormon dignitaries met the presidential party in Ogden and took them to Salt Lake City in special railroad cars reserved by the Mormon-dominated city council, but, once Hayes reached Salt Lake City, Governor Eli Murray, other federal officials, and other prominent gentiles preempted the Mormons. The best showing by the Saints was large groups of LDS Sunday school

2. Memorial, copy clipped inside GQCJ, Jan. 8, 1880; "Defiant Mormons," *New York Herald*, Jan. 5, 1880, as copied into GQCJ, Jan. 8, 1880; Barbara J. Hayward, "Utah's Anti-Polygamy Society, 1878–1884" (MA thesis, Brigham Young University), 1980.

3. GQCJ, June 11–13, 16, 19, 1880; "Tabernacle Services," *SLH*, Sep. 6, 1880, 2; Bitton, *GQC*, 237.

children holding banners and singing as they lined the streets that the president passed.[4]

In November 1880, George once again ran for reelection as territorial delegate, this time against Allen G. Campbell. Campbell, like Robert Baskin before him, asserted that Cannon was not a naturalized citizen and that he had four wives. In all the earlier contests, Cannon had argued successfully that no one had ever brought a criminal charge against him for polygamy and that no one had ever proven he was not a naturalized citizen. Campbell also revived a third argument that George Maxwell had made in 1872: that Utah women had voted in the election and their votes should not be counted. Cannon responded as he had before, and Campbell, in a strongly worded reply, got personal with George:

> you are not a man of good moral character; you are not attached to the principles of the Constitution of the United States; nor well disposed to the good order and happiness of the same and you are not a citizen of the United States; you have been many years a polygamist, living and cohabiting with four women as wives, to whom you have joined yourself by a pretended ceremony of marriage; you do not loyally yield assent and obedience to the act of Congress against polygamy; you have for many years long past publicly endeavored to incite others to violate that statute in the Territory of Utah: therefore all the votes given you at said election are void.[5]

Cannon retrieved his certificate of citizenship, but the Liberal Party candidate and his supporters were not content. Like Baskin, they argued that the certificate was not valid on its face, notwithstanding that it was issued in 1854. As always, Cannon won the popular election by a wide margin. Even though Cannon had received over 93 percent of the vote, Governor Murray issued Campbell a certificate of election on the basis of his views that Campbell was an American citizen while Cannon was not. Murray's certificate also provided the vote totals from the election, which George M. Adams, the clerk of the US House of Representatives, took to mean that the winner of the popular vote was George Q. The result was

4. "The President's Visit, Grand Reception," *DN*, Sep. 6, 1880, 2.

5. Feb. 26, 1881, *Cannon vs. Campbell Contested Election Case*, 47th Cong., 1st Sess., Rept. No. 559 (Washington, DC: Government Printing Office, 1882).

that Murray's certificate had declared both candidates the winner. Because the certificate recited that Cannon had won the popular vote, the clerk of the House of Representatives enrolled his name. This was contested by Campbell, so Cannon gave notice that he was entitled to the office.[6]

During this period, C. C. Goodwin was hired as the new editor of the *Salt Lake Tribune*. Writing in the popular periodical *North American Review*, Goodwin argued that Utah needed to be checked or it would "dictate the elections in all the region between the Rocky Mountains and the Pacific Ocean, except California and Oregon," because George Q., "the sweetest, smoothest, and most plausible sophist in all this round earth," would manipulate matters in such a way that Mormons would someday control elections in six Western states from Cannon's desk in Salt Lake City.[7]

Elizabeth's medical condition remained precarious. She did not join George in Washington in 1881, and her health continued to deteriorate while he was gone. Elizabeth would sometimes ask her sister, Emily Hoagland Little, to stay with her and help with the children. George and Elizabeth had six living children, the youngest of whom was three-year-old Sylvester, who also was quite sickly that summer. Emily was divorced from Jesse Little and had six children of her own. Emily lived downtown, but when she stayed with Elizabeth, she brought her children with her.[8]

During this time, Emily told George that she had always loved him and wished she had married him at the same time as her sister. There had been discussions between George and the Hoaglands' father, LDS ward bishop Abraham Hoagland, before George left on his mission in 1849 about marrying both sisters at the same time. George was, however, "going to preach the gospel and … was very shy and extremely destitute during this time" and was not ready to marry either sister, let alone both. Emily then married Jesse Little at the suggestion of Heber C. Kimball in 1856. George Q. noted in his journal that he had always loved Emily and he conferred with

6. Roberts, *CHC*, 6:12–14.

7. C. C. Goodwin, "The Political Attitude of the Mormons," *North American Review* (Mar. 1881): 276–86; Bitton, *GQC*, 243–44.

8. GQCJ, Apr. 9, June 10–13, 19, 1880.

John Taylor about marrying "the younger sister of my first wife" who was a divorcee. Taylor "agreed wholeheartedly without any hesitation," though he advised George to do it "quietly" so others would not know about it. George and Emily married on July 11, 1881, in his first marriage in thirteen years, with Joseph F. Smith officiating. George Q. continued to refer to Emily most of the time as "my sister-in-law" to help keep their marriage "quiet." George rarely spoke of Emily's six children, even though the four younger ones likely often stayed in the house he shared with Elizabeth. Elizabeth would sometimes stay with Emily in her downtown house.[9]

As George Q. faced the challenges of Elizabeth's ill health, he experienced for the first time serious troubles in the life of one of his children. Franklin Jenne Cannon, George's second oldest child and second wife Sarah Jane's oldest child, was a clever, brilliant young man. Sarah's aunt, Jane Snyder Richards, was married to Apostle Franklin D. Richards—in fact, Frank J. Cannon was named after Richards. The Richardses recognized Frank's talents from a young age and asked George Q. if the thirteen-year-old could live with them in Ogden and work with his cousin, Franklin S. Richards, who eventually became one of Mormondom's most prominent attorneys. George agreed, though he later regretted his decision because Frank developed drinking and carousing habits with friends in Ogden. Frank always claimed Ogden as his home town after living with the Richardses.[10]

In 1878, Frank married the talented, vivacious Martha "Mattie" Anderson Brown, daughter of prominent Ogden parents. He took a job as the editor of a newspaper in Logan, and he and Mattie moved there. In June 1880, Mattie bore a daughter, Dorothy Brown Cannon. The Cannons hired a nanny, Ellen Maud Baugh (called Maud), to help.[11]

In October 1880, William B. Preston, the LDS stake president in Logan, sent George Q. a letter, indicating that Baugh's father had met with him and informed him that his daughter was pregnant,

---

9. GQCJ, June 6, 14, July 11, 14, 21, Aug. 1, 12, 16, 17, Oct. 30, 1881. George was nervous that he had actually violated the Morrill Act and could be prosecuted. George did refer to Emily in his journal as "my new wife" on their wedding day.

10. KLC, "Wives and Other Women: Love, Sex, and Marriage in the Lives of John Q. Cannon, Frank J. Cannon, and Abraham H. Cannon," *Dialogue* 43, no. 4 (Winter 2010): 83.

11. KLC, "Wives and Other Women," 83–84.

that the father was Frank, and that the relationship may not have been entirely consensual. George T. Baugh also told Preston that Frank had told Maud that they would not be getting married because "he was not Mormon enough to marry two wives yet." Frank sent both his parents letters, asking them not to "proceed in relation to that terrible affair." George Q. angrily told the family that "he did not care if Frank never came near him again." Within a few weeks, Frank and his wife and daughter moved to San Francisco where Frank took a job as a reporter for the *San Francisco Chronicle*.[12]

Within the next few months, Maud Baugh was brought to the Cannon farm southwest of Salt Lake City, where she lived with Sarah Jane Jenne Cannon. There, on April 24, 1881, Maud gave birth to a son. Coincidentally, Sarah was pregnant at the same time and delivered her last child, Preston J., just twelve days earlier. She and George Q. took in Maud and Frank's child, named him Karl Q., and raised him as the twin of their own infant.[13]

As George was dealing with Frank's problems in Logan, Democrat James A. Garfield was elected president of the United States in a razor-thin victory over Rutherford B. Hayes. From their time in Congress together, George Q. believed that Garfield understood the "Mormon question" better than anyone else, and that he was an ally.[14] In his inaugural address, however, Garfield disappointed George when he made it clear that he opposed polygamy and believed it needed to be prohibited because it was a criminal practice "of that class which destroy the family relations and endanger social order.[15] Cannon had hoped Garfield would say nothing, and believed that Garfield had betrayed the Saints after he was elected, dealing "us a severe blow."[16]

George Q. met with Garfield the following week. The president informed him that he had said what he believed about polygamy. He did not favor retroactive measures to existing relationships and "was not in favor of harshness, but polygamy must cease." Cannon explained that his people did not expect favors but did expect fair treatment. He then told Garfield that he did not want officials

12. KLC, "Wives and Other Women," 84–85.
13. KLC, "Wives and Other Women," 85.
14. GQCJ, July 2, 1881.
15. James A. Garfield inaugural, quoted in Bitton, *GQC*, 243.
16. GQCJ, July 1, 1881.

appointed who would use the country's hostility toward polygamy as a basis for punitive treatment.[17]

On July 2, 1881, Garfield was shot. He lingered for two and a half months, but succumbed to his wounds on September 20, becoming the second president to be assassinated, after Abraham Lincoln. The Saints had not liked his views on polygamy, but he was the president of the United States, and on September 26 they held a memorial service for him in the Tabernacle. Members of the church attended the service, while gentiles generally did not. George Q. was the concluding speaker. A few days after Cannon's address at the memorial service, prominent Brooklyn clergyman DeWitt Talmage asserted that the Mormons had prayed for Garfield's death because of his views on polygamy and that the assassin Charles Guiteau must be a Mormon. In an extraordinary statement, Talmage expressed his view that Garfield's assassin must have had "the spirit of Mormon licentiousness, of Mormon cruelty, Mormon murder."[18] It was indicative of the country's view of the Saints.

Shortly after Garfield's death, George Q. returned to Washington to face the most serious contest over his congressional seat yet. He understood that LDS Church leaders and members were counting on him to continue to fight against harsh anti-Mormon legislation. He hired non-Mormon attorneys Arthur Brown, from Salt Lake, and Halbert Paine, a former prominent member of Congress from Wisconsin. Allen Campbell published a pamphlet against Cannon. With the help of Mormon journalist Charles Penrose, George responded. In the flexible legal ethics of the day, George Sutherland, who had previously represented Cannon in defending his seat, represented Campbell.[19]

The most serious claim against George was again that his naturalization certificate was not valid and that he was not a citizen.

17. GQCJ, Mar. 14, 1881.

18. GQCJ, July 2, Sep. 20, 1881; "Obsequies of President Garfield, Services in the Tabernacle, *SLH*, Sep. 25, 1881, 4; Roberts, *CHC*, 6:26–27; "General News – Talmage on Mormonism," SLT, Oct. 5, 1881, 1. DeWitt Talmage also suggested that if Guiteau "was not a Mormon, he was one of the Oneida Community, whose chief doctrine was, right to a profusion of wives." In fact, Charles Guiteau was a member of the Oneida community. Susan Wels, *An Assassin in Utopia, The True Story of a Nineteenth-Century Sex Cult and a President's Murder* (New York: Pegasus Crime, 2023).

19. GQCJ, May 10, 20, 23, 26, 28, 1881; Bitton, *GQC*, 249.

Campbell filed a suit in equity in federal court in Salt Lake City seeking a determination that the certificate was invalid and obtained by fraud and that, as a non-citizen, Cannon could not be a member of Congress. Cannon, through his lawyers, filed a procedural "demurrer" asserting that only the US Attorney General had standing to bring such a claim. Judge John A. Hunter dismissed the suit on the basis that the court did not have subject matter jurisdiction, but he also purported to dismiss the suit on the basis of Cannon's demurrer. There was no record that George Q.'s naturalization and the invalid certificate were obtained by fraud. Having found no jurisdiction, the court could not make an enforceable determination of the invalidity of the certificate or of fraud. The judge's ruling, therefore, was legally meaningless. It may have been that Cannon's naturalization certificate was not properly issued, but the question was not determined by Hunter's decision.[20]

In the midst of George's fight to retain his seat, he learned that Elizabeth's health had continued to decline. She was the love of his youth, his first and legal wife, and the hostess of dinners and celebrations at the Big House and the farm. It was Elizabeth who accompanied George to San Francisco and to England on missions and who made positive impressions on women and men at events she attended. When her health permitted, George brought her to Washington and took her to parties and galas and dinners hosted by presidents, senators, and other influential people. Cannon had enormous influence over choices for new general authorities, though he disclaimed attempts to do so. Like many of the apostles, however, Cannon had sons who were called to senior positions at young ages. Only Elizabeth's sons were made general authorities. Stranded in Washington, fighting for his position and his people, he thought often of Elizabeth and wanted to go to her, but he was 2,000 miles away. As he wrote in his diary, "Were I to yield to my feelings I would be plunged in grief, and if here on private business, I would start for

20. "Cannon–Campbell Matter, A Bad Crow by a Black Crower," *SLH*, Nov. 2, 1881, 5; "Campbell–Cannon Decision," *SLT*, Nov. 1, 1991, 2; "Cannon Busted," *SLT*, Nov. 1, 1881, 4; "The Campbell–Cannon Case," *Ogden Herald*, Nov. 2, 1881, 2; John Gary Maxwell, *Robert Newton Baskin* (Norman, OK: Arthur H. Clark Co., 2013), 169–78. Both the *SLH* and the *Ogden Herald* understood that Hunter's decision had no effect. The *Tribune* and Baskin's biographer did not.

home by the first train; but I cannot desert my post. All I can do is to cry unto the Lord." He received word from his brother Angus that Elizabeth felt the same way: "notwithstanding Elizabeth was very bad all day, indications are better now. She says, stand to your post. God can raise me up in answer to your prayers there as well as here."[21]

George's role in defending his church was more important to him even than Elizabeth. He and Elizabeth had been happy the first few years of their marriage before he married Sarah Jane, and they remained devoted to each other and their children. As George Q. acknowledged, his obedience to celestial marriage tried her faith and made her sad at times. Elizabeth remained committed to their faith against these challenges and stood by her husband. On January 25, 1882, as George Q. was losing his battle to remain in Congress, Elizabeth died.[22] He could not be with her in her last days and could not even attend her funeral. He wrote to Angus to help the children "not yield to grief." His devotion to his God and his prophet took precedence. Campbell, Campbell's lawyer, and Governor Eli Murray were working hard to lobby representatives to deny George's seating. Fourteen bills against the Mormons had been introduced in the House, and a constitutional amendment and four bills in the Senate, and Cannon needed to address each.[23]

The contest to retain George's seat continued. Chester A. Arthur, who became president when Garfield was assassinated, was critical of the Mormons. Lobbyists claimed they could get sufficient numbers of congressmen to support Cannon's retention, but they wanted thousands of dollars in fees and to make bribes to do it. George Q. was occasionally not averse to authorizing bribes to journalists at important times, but he was unwilling to seek any funds to pay these "sharks."[24]

Those opposed to Cannon in Washington, urged on by those opposed to Cannon in Utah, sought different ways to exclude him from Congress. The House suspended its rules to permit the consideration and unanimous passage of a bill introduced by Julius C. Burrows that forbade polygamists from serving as members of Congress. Cannon

21. GQCJ, Jan. 18, 24, 1882.
22. GQCJ, Jan. 18, 25, 26, 1882; Bitton, *GQC*, 251.
23. GQCJ, Jan. 17, 20, 26, 1882.
24. GQC to Eliza Tenney Cannon, Jan. 5, 1882, cited and quoted in Bitton, *GQC*, 250.

believed this was an *ex post facto* law that could not be applied to him. He mused that he should have proposed an amendment to the bill which would have excluded anyone who was guilty of adultery or fornication, which he knew would not be approved but might result in Congress's modifying the rule to apply to him.[25]

In fact, the public supported punishment of the Mormons for their marriage practice and for their cooperative economic policies and political hegemony, and that support was growing. This bipartisan support for anti-Mormon legislation was evident. Even though the president (first Garfield, then Arthur) was a Democrat, the Senate was deadlocked with equal numbers of Republicans and Democrats, and the House had a small Republican majority, there was wide support for anti-polygamy legislation introduced by Senator George F. Edmunds, a Republican from Vermont. George Q. had a "long and full discussion" with Edmunds, whom he described as "like a block of ice—polished, cold and hard." Edmunds knew of Cannon's "adroitness and ability" and was determined that George would "'get no advantage of'" him.[26]

George Q. met with numerous senators and recorded that many were friendly, but only a few Southerners were willing to stand up to the momentum carrying Edmunds. One senator asserted the bill violated equal protection, another attacked the bill as an *ex post facto* law, still another argued that the creation of a Utah Commission constituted carpetbag rule. One senator claimed that the Edmunds bill was the first bill of attainder (prohibited by the Constitution) proposed "in all history."[27]

Edmunds was canny—his bill originally proposed ending woman's suffrage in Utah, but, in a "brilliant stroke," he recognized that this could result in the loss of suffragists' support as it had with some earlier proposed legislation. Only Mormon men and women involved in polygamy would have their right to vote rescinded. National suffragists supported the bill with this change. The Edmunds

25. GQCJ, Feb. 6, 9, 10, 1882.

26. GQCJ, Feb. 11, 13, 1882; Bitton. *GQC,* 252.

27. *Congressional Record,* 47th Cong. 1st Sess., vol. 13, part 2, 1199, 1200, 1211; Bitton, *GQC,* 253.

bill passed the Senate on February 13, the House on March 14, and Arthur signed it into law on March 22, 1882.[28]

The enactment of the Edmunds Act meant the end of George Q.'s service in Congress. The House's Committee on Elections addressed three questions with respect to Cannon's reelection as Utah's Delegate: whether he had won the popular vote, whether he was a citizen of the United States, and whether he was a polygamist and, therefore, under the Edmunds Act, ineligible to serve. The committee answered all three questions in the affirmative. Only one dissenter voted against the first two questions. Putting Judge Hunter in his place, the committee report took a swipe at Campbell lawyer John McBride's "own style of special pleading ... being but a repetition of his sophisms." What Cannon could not get around was section 8 of the Edmunds Act, which prohibited a polygamist from holding office. Some congressmen suggested that, if he had been seated before the enactment of the act, they might have decided the after-the-fact removal of him would not have been condoned.[29]

George Q. was permitted to give one last speech on April 18 before the floor vote was taken on three proposed resolutions: that Campbell was not entitled to the seat, that Cannon was not entitled to the seat, and that the Utah delegate's seat was therefore vacant. Though "in some respects it was like addressing a mob, for many had all the spirit of a mobocracy," Cannon proceeded. As he described it, "The Lord took away all fear and I was calm and self-possessed." In his hour-long valedictory, he reviewed the history of the Saints and likened their treatment to the persecution of early Christians. He remembered former Utah delegate William H. Hooper, a Mormon monogamist, who was attacked for being a Mormon, not a polygamist. He attacked Governor Murray, who had certified an election for the losing candidate despite that candidate receiving less than 10 percent of the popular vote. He argued for freedom of religious conviction.[30]

---

28. Lola Van Wagenen, "Sister Wives and Suffragists: Polygamy and the Politics of Woman Suffrage, 1870–1896" (PhD diss., New York University, 1994), 345; GQCJ, Feb. 16, Mar. 14, 1882; Bitton, *GQC*, 253.

29. "The Case of the Delegate from Utah," *DN*, Mar. 17, 1882, 2; Bitton, *GQC*, 254.

30. GQCJ Apr. 19, 1882; "Speech of George Q. Cannon of Utah," *DN*, Mar. 27, 1882, 1; Bitton, *GQC*, 254

At the conclusion of the hearing, the House passed all three resolutions, that neither Campbell nor Cannon would be seated and the delegate's seat from Utah was vacant. Cannon was complimented on his speech and some congressmen admitted they had been "cowardly."[31] In his journal, he complained that "the devil is stirring up the people against us," detailing unfavorable newspaper articles, preachers' discourses, speeches attacking polygamy by the president, senators, cabinet members, congressmen, and governors, and anti-Mormon rallies in large cities. Everywhere Americans were attacking the Mormons and their marital practice. He felt alone and without anyone "with whom I can sit down and unbosom myself."[32]

How successful had George Q. been as delegate to Congress? Preeminent historian of the American West Howard R. Lamar found him to be ineffective by certain standards, though he had gotten some bills favorable to Utah passed such as a railroad bill.[33] He ultimately prevailed in most of his attempts to block anti-Mormon legislation, but he did not stop the Poland bill (though he and others succeeded in watering it down) or the Edmunds bill. He had done this by "parliamentary maneuvering" before bills made it to the floor of Congress, convincing groups of congressmen to support his position or abstain from voting, and to argue persuasively against arguments supporting the bills. He was tireless in meeting with members of Congress and presidents and cabinet members, whether friend or foe. He had not succeeded in his test case on First Amendment free exercise of religion through his friend George Reynolds.

George Q. had, however, forthrightly, unambiguously, and eloquently sought to protect his religion and its people, and it was for this that he was always returned to Congress with overwhelming majorities. Once Utah achieved statehood and was governed by local rule, Utahns would have plenty of time to obtain legislation favorable to it. Cannon had used his skills and charisma to ingratiate himself to many people, and had changed many minds about the Mormons

---

31. Roberts, *CHC*, 6:50; GQCJ, Apr. 19, 29, 1882.

32. GQCJ, Jan. 24, 26, 1882.

33. Howard R. Lamar, *The Far Southwest, 1846–1912* (Albuquerque: University of New Mexico Press, 2000), 333; John Gary Maxwell, *Gettysburg to Great Salt Lake: George Maxwell, Civil War Hero and Federal Marshal among the Mormons* (Norman, OK: Arthur H. Clark Co, 2010), 177–78.

as a people if not about their practices. He had many friends, but, as was probably inevitable, he ultimately failed in his legislative pursuits. Because he was successful for most of a decade in blunting legislation that modern civil libertarians would have found shocking, he was the principal point of attack for journalists, carpetbag federal officials in Utah, and a largely white, Protestant population in the East who were offended by the exotic practices of the Mormons. He came to be called the "Mormon Richelieu" and the "Mormon Premier" by the Eastern press. To his enemies, he was not the talented representative of a persecuted people, he was the one who controlled them for the political ends of a small Mormon elite.

Though he felt lonely and saddened by the loss of Elizabeth, by the attacks on the church and people he cherished, and by the sins of at least one of his children, George did not give up or stop trusting in God. He could pursue other approaches. Thomas Kane, always a supporter of George Q., met with and consoled him. John Taylor had him remain in Washington to continue the fight. His Utah opponents did not succeed in installing Campbell in Congress. The House of Representatives was not going to seat someone whose opponent received over 90 percent of the vote.[34] Rather, after months of jockeying, Utah elected and the House seated John T. Caine, a monogamous Mormon, to serve out George Q.'s term as delegate and to remain for the next session of Congress as well.[35]

The fight over polygamy in Congress and his central part in it made George Q. famous outside of Utah. The popular *Harper's Weekly* published two Thomas Nast cartoons of Congress dealing with him. In one, appearing on January 28, 1882, two Saints holding umbrellas stand in front of the House of Representatives manning a cannon pointed at the door the House guarded by Columbia. A sign next to the door reads "Notice. No Polygamist Shall Be Admitted to a Seat in this House. U.S." The caption reads, "Even (G. Q.) Cannon shall not open these Doors to you." Three-and-a-half months later, following the expulsion of Cannon from the House, in another cartoon Columbia still stands in the doorway and the cannon, with the name "The Mormon (G.Q.) Cannon" exploded and sent

34. Roberts, *CHC*, 6:50.
35. "The Election," *SLH*, Nov. 10, 1882, 5.

the two Mormons and their umbrellas flying in different directions. The caption reads, "Burst the Other Day at Washington, D.C."[36] As he traveled, however, George Q. was recognized and "treated ... with marked respect by everyone" he met.[37]

The Edmunds Act did much more than ensure the dismissal of Cannon from Congress. It made polygamy a felony; it criminalized "unlawful cohabitation," which became relatively easy to prove; and it created a five-member "board"—the "Utah Commission"—to oversee everything related to voting: registration, conduct of elections, allowance of votes, canvassing and returning votes, and issuing certificates of election.[38]

In the first months after the Utah Commission arrived in Salt Lake City in mid-1882, Cannon hosted a dinner at the family Farm House for three of the commissioners. All three members of the First Presidency—John Taylor (who brought a daughter), Cannon, and Joseph F. Smith (who each brought one of his wives)—as well as Brigham Young Jr. and one of his wives, former delegate William H. Hooper, and prominent Mormon businessman William Jennings attended. An array of Cannons was also there: brother Angus, son Frank and wife, son Abraham "Abram" and a wife, son John Q's wife, Annie, and her sister, the talented Louie Wells. All sat for four hours eating a multiple-course dinner prepared by new LDS convert and chef, "Bro. Ball, late of London."[39] The commission was entertained by some of the best and brightest of Utah. Church leaders' attempts to ingratiate themselves with Commission members were not particularly successful.[40]

One of the first acts that the Utah Commission took was to impose a voting test oath that required any man who desired to vote to avow that he was not a bigamist or polygamist, did not live or cohabit with more than one woman, or, if a woman, that she was not the wife of a bigamist or polygamist or entered into any relation forbidden by the polygamy laws of the United States. The commission

36. *Harper's Weekly*, Jan. 28, 1882, 61; *Harper's Weekly*, May 4, 1882, 288.

37. GQCJ, July 3, 1882.

38. 22 Stat. 30b (1882).

39. GQCJ, Sep. 19, 1882.

40. Stewart L. Grow, "A Study of the Utah Commission, 1882–1896," PhD diss., University of Utah, 1954, 254.

(and Congress) assumed that good Latter-day Saints would not take the oath, given their continuing resistance to federal legislation. No doubt many monogamist Mormons felt disinclined to take the oath. However, in an "Address" from the First Presidency in August 1882 written by George Q., and in an October 1882 general conference discourse, Cannon encouraged monogamists to take the oath and vote. The First Presidency counseled non-polygamous Saints "to defend yourselves by exercising to the proper extent the few privileges left to you, among which are those of registration and voting. ... Let us guard well our franchise."[41]

With Mormon monogamists and monogamous wives and single men and women voting, John T. Caine was elected to fill the delegate's seat vacated by George Q. by a resounding vote of 19,692 to 4,621, thus frustrating Liberals, who assumed their candidate, Philip T. VanZile , would be elected if most Mormons did not vote. Even less amusing to Liberal Party adherents, Cannon returned to Washington to assist Caine.[42]

Frank and Mattie Cannon returned from San Francisco to Utah unannounced while George was there in June 1882. Logan Saints continued to harbor hard feelings for Frank since his quick departure. George Q. counseled Frank to go to Logan to "clear up, as far as possible, the disgrace which was still attached to his name." Abram Cannon accompanied him. Stake President William Preston instructed Frank to publicly confess his adultery in the ward where they had lived, to ask forgiveness, and to make matters right with Maud Baugh's parents. The local ward bishop told him the same thing. Frank was willing to talk to Maud's parents but did not believe a public confession was necessary. Abram agreed with the stake president and bishop. Frank was given three months to resolve the matter, and, if he did not, he would be excommunicated.[43]

The next month, Franklin D. Richards, who had been advised by George Q. on how to address the church discipline against Frank, traveled to Logan with his namesake. Afterward, Richards noted in his diary his prayer that he be able to "adjust" Frank's "unpleasant affair in

41. "An Address," *SLH*, Sep. 3, 1882, 3; GQC, Discourse, *JD*, Oct. 8, 1882, 272–73.
42. "The Election," *SLH*, Nov. 10, 1882, 5; GQCJ, Nov. 27, 1882.
43. AHCJ, June 29, 1882; KLC, "Wives and Other Women, 85–88.

accordance with principles of righteousness & salvation." George Q., who had editorialized in 1868 that "seducers" should be killed by the seduced woman's father, husband, or brother, now appears to have recommended that Frank not even be required to publicly confess his sin and not lose his church membership. The unhappiness of many in Logan over this matter remained for some time.[44]

In Washington, George not only helped Delegate Caine develop his political skills and contacts, he also continued to write for the *Juvenile Instructor* and to write and deliver discourses on how God would protect his people if they put their faith in him and that the Saints would ultimately prevail. After it was clear that Caine would be seated, George had a conversation with Caine, Franklin S. Richards, and David H. Peery, who had also been in Washington helping Caine. George thought it unnecessary for all three to remain to advise Caine and hoped that he might be able to go home. Caine "expressed himself strongly in favor of my staying." George talked to Caine "about sending for my wife" to join him, and one of his wives did soon join him. George already had "had in mind to have one of my wives to come down on a visit, if possible, to be with me while here; but just now it would expose me too much." George previously never took a wife with him on such a trip other than his "official" wife, Elizabeth. This one time, when he had one of his other wives join him in DC, he was coy about who it was, referring to her simply as "my wife," even in his journal. In December 1882, George Q. noted only that his son Abram had traveled to Ogden with "my wife" to help her on her way to DC. In his diary, Abram recorded that he "accompanied Aunt E." to Ogden after obtaining railroad passes Washington. This was likely his third wife, thirty-seven-year-old Eliza Tenney Cannon. George Q.'s care not to identify her in his journal evidences how concerned he was to be seen with a plural wife in public. George decided to send "my wife" home on January 5, 1884, just two weeks after she arrived. He regretted seeing her leave, "but deemed it imprudent for her to remain longer."[45]

44. HJGJ, Aug. 3, 1887; KLC, "Wives and Other Women," 87–88; [GQC], "Inviolability of Virtue," *DN*, February 26, 1868, 2.

45. GQCJ, Dec. 11, 14, 19–21, 24, 28, 30, 1882, Jan. 2–5, 11, 1883. George Q.'s journal suggests that he was mostly living with Eliza while in Salt Lake City before leaving for Washington. GQCJ, Nov. 1, 26, 1882, Jan. 18, 24, Mar 22, 1883.

While he was helping Caine in Washington to defend against even more punitive legislation that George Edmunds was working on, George Q. looked for the best advisors available. Thomas Kane suggested that the church retain Jeremiah S. Black, a powerful lawyer, judge, and prominent Pennsylvania Democrat who had served in James Buchanan's cabinet, first as secretary of state and then as attorney general, and who had fought radical Reconstruction. Black did not condone polygamy but did believe that its practice as a religious tenet was protected by the Constitution. As expected, Edmunds immediately began to propose even harsher measures against the Mormons. Black dug into the legal arguments against Edmunds's new proposals and worked closely with George Q. and the church's lawyers in Salt Lake City. Black convinced some Democrats that Edmunds' new bill violated traditional Democratic views, and he worked hard for appointment of friendly officials to the Utah Commission, as governor, and as judges. Some Democrats were unwilling to buck public opinion, however, and most of Black's efforts were futile. Nevertheless Black was properly credited with turning back Edmunds from obtaining passage of a new anti-polygamy law in 1883. George Q. liked Black's arguments and lobbying activities. After Black's sudden death in August 1883, George Q. extolled Black's activities and arguments and published a letter Black had written to the Utah Commission. As Cannon noted in the editorial, "We as a people have lost a staunch, courageous and able friend."[46]

On Christmas Day 1883, Kane died in Pittsburgh. He had been one of George Q.'s most important mentors, and this must have been a crushing blow to George after his expulsion from Congress, the death of Elizabeth, the adultery (or worse) of Frank, and the fear that everyone in America was against the Mormons. George must have been comforted by Elizabeth Kane's assurances that Kane's last thoughts were to send "the sweetest message you can make up to my Mormon friends—*to all my dear Mormon friends.*"[47]

---

46. Matthew J. Grow, *"Liberty to the Downtrodden": Thomas L. Kane, Romantic Reformer* (New Haven: Yale University Press, 2009), 280; GQCJ, Sep. 28, Dec. 20, 1882, Jan. 29, 31, Feb. 1, 1883; Jeremiah S. Black, *Federal Jurisdiction in the Territories* (Salt Lake City: Deseret News Press Co., 1883); GQC, Discourse, *JD*, 24:62–64, Mar. 18, 1883; [GQC], "Editorial Thoughts," *Juvenile Instructor* 18 (Sep. 15, 1883): 280–81; Bitton, *GQC*, 264–65.

47. As quoted in Grow, *Thomas L. Kane*, 282.

George Q. only spent a few weeks in Washington during the 1884 session of Congress to help Caine, but the two maintained a brisk correspondence, which included Cannon providing helpful advice. Shortly after George returned home, he and Franklin S. Richards discussed how helpful it would be to send a smart young man to work as a clerk to assist Caine. Joseph F. Smith proposed that Frank Cannon fill this role and Richards supported the proposal. George Q. "had a dread" of this possibility and worried about whether Frank might lapse into drinking or worse but evidently remained silent. Smith and Richards were so supportive that Frank was designated as Delegate Caine's new clerk and did an exceptional job, using this as the springboard of his political career.[48]

As George's three oldest sons—John, Frank, and Abram—grew to adulthood, they assumed increasingly important roles. Abram served an LDS mission in Great Britain, Germany, and Switzerland where he distinguished himself for hard work, intelligence, and responsibility. He was called to the First Council of the Seventy shortly after he returned from Europe in October 1882. John had recently returned from a mission in Switzerland. While on his mission, he was nominated to be an apostle, though his great-uncle, President John Taylor, did not appoint him. John was, however, made mission president for the last year of his time abroad. He then made a name for himself as a reporter for the *Deseret News* and as a member of the Utah territorial legislature. In October 1884, George was very happy when John was called to be the second counselor in the Presiding Bishopric. Thus, Elizabeth's two oldest sons were made general authorities of the LDS Church while in their mid-twenties.[49]

In July 1884, Caroline "Carlie" Partridge Young Croxall divorced her husband of almost sixteen years, Mark Croxall, a handsome and talented musician whose band was a favorite of Salt Lakers. Carlie, born in 1851, was a daughter of Brigham Young and Emily Dow Partridge.[50] On October 23, 1884, George Q., who knew Carlie

48. KLC, "'The Honor of American Citizenship': Frank J. Cannon's Contributions to Utah's Statehood," *Pioneer* 67 (no. 4, 2020): 39–40; GQCJ, Mar. 5, 7, 1884.

49. KLC, "Wives and Other Women," 75–76, 96; D. Michael Quinn, *Mormon Hierarchy: Extensions of Power* (Salt Lake City: Signature Books, 1997), 644–45, 648–49.

50. GQCJ, Oct. 23, 1884, Family Group Records of Mark Croxall and Caroline Young Croxall, www.familysearch.org (accessed Oct. 2021); Bitton, *GQC*, 268.

well, approached her at her half-brother Brigham Young Jr.'s house. George said to her, "I heard that [you] wanted to be sealed as a wife to me. I asked her if she would enter into an ordinance with me and become my legal wife. She consented." From their subsequent relationship, it is evident that George was very attracted to Carlie. He was also very fond of Brigham Young and the allure of becoming part of his family was irresistible. A few days after this second meeting, they agreed that George Q. would pick a date and prepare the "necessary things regarding the marriage ordinance and then meet up with her again." George thought Apostle Wilford Woodruff would be the perfect person to officiate.[51]

After this unusual whirlwind courtship, George Q. and Carlie were sealed by Woodruff, presumably in the Endowment House, on November 3, 1884, with only themselves as witnesses. George's journal is silent about the occasion. Later, the two were married in a civil ceremony under Utah law, whereby Carlie became his "legal" wife, meaning that his other four wives all remained polygamous wives. It is likely that his other wives, particularly second wife Sarah Jane, felt hurt that George chose to make wife number five his official wife. Carlie apparently stayed for the time being in the house in which she was then living and did not yet move to the Cannon farm.[52]

In the meantime, federal officers and judges in Utah were taking seriously the enforcement of the new Edmunds Act, although they initially failed to convict many of unlawful cohabitation. There were a few successful prosecutions in 1883 and 1884, such as the polygamy conviction of Rudger Clawson, who let his polygamous wife testify. Prosecutors William H. Dickson and Charles Varian thought that they needed evidence that a polygamous couple was having sexual contact to establish unlawful cohabitation and they went to great lengths to prove this. After George's brother, Angus M., the Salt Lake Stake president, was arrested on January 20, 1885, the prosecutors took a different tack. Now, they argued that they needed only to show that a Mormon man was dwelling with two or more women in the same or different households to prove unlawful cohabitation.

51. GQCJ, Oct. 23, 1884. George Q.'s journal entries regarding their conversations are in Hawaiian, which he used when he wanted to keep matters confidential.

52. Bitton, *GQC*, 268.

Judge Charles Zane agreed and his ruling was affirmed on appeal by the Utah Supreme Court and the United States Supreme Court.[53]

After this ruling, Mormon "cohabs" were relentlessly pursued and a flood of men were then arrested, tried, and convicted of unlawful cohabitation. Zane not only began imposing long prison sentences and fines on men for polygamy and unlawful cohabitation, he also began imprisoning witnesses who refused to testify and denying bail for the release of prisoners. Immediately after Angus's arrest, George became aware that deputy US marshals, referred to universally as "deps," intended to arrest him as well. Soon, not only were they searching for him, they were also stalking his wives and children in an attempt to find him.[54]

Federal prosecutors also developed the punitive concept of "segregating" offenses so that a polygamist charged with unlawful cohabitation could be separately convicted of cohabiting with different wives and also with the same wives during different periods of time. The Utah courts continued to segregate offenses until the US Supreme Court found it to be improper in 1887.[55]

From 1884 to 1895, just under 900 Mormon polygamists were convicted of crimes in Utah, mostly for unlawful cohabitation, a misdemeanor that carried the mildest fines and sentences (up to $300 and six months in prison per offense), a few for polygamy, a felony (up to $800 and five years in prison, though most sentences were three years or less), and a surprising number for adultery, which was added in 1887 and was punishable by up to three years in prison. One Poland Act provision made it easy to appeal convictions to the US Supreme Court. The high court issued a number of decisions during this period, a few beneficial to the Mormons but most strictly enforcing the law.[56]

---

53. Ken Driggs, "The Prosecutions Begin: Defining Cohabitation in 1885," *Dialogue* 21 (Spring 1988): "The New Departure of the Prosecution," *Deseret News*, May 6, 1885, 8; *U.S. v. Cannon*, 7 P. 369, 372–76, 380 (Utah Territory, 1885); *Cannon v. U.S.*, 116 U.S. 55, 71–75, 79 (1885).

54. GQCJ, Jan. 20, 1884.

55. Edwin Brown Firmage and Richard Collin Mangrum, *Zion in the Courts: A Legal History of the Church of Jesus Christ of Latter-day Saints, 1830–1900* (Urbana: University of Illinois Press, 1988), 179–83; *In re Snow*, 120 U.S. 274 (1887).

56. Edmunds Act, 22 Stat. 30b (1882), §§ 1, 3; Edmunds–Tucker Act, 24 Stat. 635 (1887), § 1, Poland Act, 18 Stat. 253 (1874), § 3.

Federal law enforcement officials all agreed that George Q. would be the plum Mormon to imprison for unlawful cohabitation or polygamy. He went from celebrity polygamist to fugitive on the "underground." He had his wives move from their homes on the farm. Martha moved to Manassa, Colorado, with her children where they lived for two years under the name of Lawrence. Eliza and Sarah Jane hid out with friends and family in Salt Lake City and environs. Carlie moved between Millcreek and Holladay (Salt Lake Valley) and even resided in San Francisco for a time, living under the name Madson.[57] It was not common knowledge that George had married Emily, and most people in Utah assumed that she was simply taking care of her deceased sister's children.

The person the deps most desperately wanted to arrest was George Q. Cannon, not his wives. The First Presidency established an elaborate mechanism to keep George Q., John Taylor, and other senior leaders in hiding. Secret panels were installed in houses and outbuildings. George Q. spent time living in a hideout in the Tithing Office across from Temple Square, where he would stay with a guard, and had a bedroom in an adjacent barn. Later, he moved into a room in his friend Hiram B. Clawson's house. Two fiercely loyal friends, Charles Wilcken and L. John Nuttall, moved the church leaders from one hiding place to another, usually at night, stayed aware of federal authorities' plans, and managed to keep George Q. and John Taylor from capture. Wilcken and Nuttall also arranged secret meetings of church leaders and even on occasion were able to find a way for Cannon or Taylor or one of the apostles to appear and speak at a stake conference. Second counselor Joseph F. Smith, who, like George, had completed a mission in the Sandwich Islands, moved there to avoid arrest. Over the next few years, it became increasingly difficult to live on the "underground." In August 1886, George recited some of the stresses caused by this: "There is so much talk and excitement in the city about the deputies making raids and such uneasiness is felt concerning our safety, that it was thought better for us to have a place selected to which we could go in case of a descent upon us."[58]

57. Rick Jay Fish, "Life on the Farm or Life on the Run: The George Q. Cannon Family During the Anti-Polygamy Raids," 15, as referred to in Bitton, *GQC*, 282.

58. GQCJ, June 2, 1885, Aug. 30, 1886; Bitton, *GQC*, 270–76, 280–82. Wilcken is mentioned in hundreds of journal entries and Nuttall not many less.

Cannon and Taylor hid out together for a time to make administration of the church from the underground more efficient, but after a near capture or two, they and their bodyguards decided to remain apart and communicate by messenger. The *Salt Lake Herald* opined that it was remarkable that neither had yet been apprehended.[59]

The year 1886 brought new kinds of intrigue to George Q. and his family. On February 9, Marshal E. A. Ireland printed a wanted poster, fixing a bounty of $500 for information leading to the arrest of Cannon and initiated a wide-scale raid searching for Cannon.[60] Local federal officials were intent on finding George Q. and charging him with the most serious offenses possible to crush the Mormon church into submission. Charles Penrose, editor of the *Deseret News*, described how Mormons perceived the lust for punishment of Cannon: "A great deal of nonsense is being uttered and published in regard to the case of President George Q. Cannon. If it were possible to enlarge the penalty which the law provides, so as to cover his particular case as it is viewed by his enemies, there is no doubt that he would be put to death or imprisoned for the term of his natural life. The gentleman is indicted for a simple misdemeanor."[61]

John Taylor made the decision to have George Q. move to Mexico for a time to avoid prosecution and to close on the purchase of property there as a refuge for polygamists.[62] In an elaborately planned trip, on February 10, 1886, with the help of his oldest son, John Q., George traveled by freight train to Ogden and then by carriage to Willard, Utah. On Friday, February 12, Cannon boarded an unattached Pullman sleeper car in the midst of friends including

---

59. GQCJ, Feb. 27, 1886; "$500 Reward, President Geo. Q. Cannon Yearned for, An Extensive Raid," *SLH*, Feb. 9, 1886, 8. Cannon's lengthy February 27 journal entry is his personal account of the events from this time period.

60. "$500.00 Reward! … for information leading to the arrest of George Q. Cannon …," wanted poster, Feb. 9, 1886, copy pasted into GQCJ, Feb. 9, 1886; "President Geo. Q. Cannon Yearned For," and "Dodging the Deputies," *SLT*, Feb. 9, 1886, 4. A year later, a better-known wanted poster was issued for the arrest of both George Q. and John Taylor, with a bounty of $500 for Cannon, $300 for Taylor, and $800 for both. A copy of that handbill is also pasted into Cannon's journal. GQCJ, Feb. 2, 3, 1887. A more detailed account of this episode is KLC, "'[J]umped from the overland train near Promontory': The Raid, Flight from Utah, Arrest, Escape, Re-Arrest, Arraignment, and Bail Jumping of George Q. Cannon, February-March 1886," unpublished paper.

61. [Charles W. Penrose], "Defeating Their Own Ends," *DN*, Feb. 16, 1886, 2.

62. GQCJ, Feb. 27, 1886.

Apostle Erastus Snow and Ogden mayor David Peery. The Pullman car was then attached to a west-bound Central Pacific train. Cannon intended to take the train to San Francisco, book sea passage down the California coast, and enter Mexico. To further avoid detection, George Q. shaved his beard and colored his hair and eyebrows dark.[63]

George worried from the time he boarded the train that too many people knew of his plan to travel by train to San Francisco and that he would be arrested. Despite attempts to keep his trip secret and to keep him out of sight, someone on the train learned of his presence and telegraphed Marshal E. A. Ireland in Salt Lake City on Saturday morning. Ireland sent a telegram to Humboldt County sheriff Frank Fellows informing him of the famous fugitive aboard the train. Fellows boarded the train in Winnemucca and started searching for Cannon. He had never met him but found one or two passengers who knew him, including US Senator William Morris Stewart of Nevada, who knew Cannon well. The train continued traveling west as Fellows entered the drawing room of the sleeper car. Senator Stewart told Fellows that he did not "see George Q. Cannon here." Fellows then asked Mayor Peery to look over those in the sleeper car. Peery responded that one of the passengers looked like Cannon but he could not be sure. Fellows saw the knowing glances that passed between Peery and Cannon, however, and realized he had his man. He immediately arrested Cannon. George Q. reportedly offered him a $1,000 bribe to let him go, but if it was offered, the sheriff refused. Fellows also wired Marshal Ireland, who soon set out for Nevada with a deputy. Sheriff Fellows stopped the train and he, Cannon, and others got off and soon boarded an east-bound freight train for Winnemucca. They stopped there for the night while they waited for the arrival of Ireland and his chief deputy, J. W. Greenman.[64]

63. AHCJ, Feb. 10, 1886; GQCJ, Feb. 27, 1886.

64. GQCJ, Feb. 27, 1886. Val Holley, Frank Cannon's biographer, assumes that the bribe was actually offered because Trumbo "later persuaded the Nevada legislature to pass a law forbidding prosecution of GQC for attempted bribery." Val Holley, *Frank J. Cannon: Saint, Senator, Scoundrel* (Salt Lake City: University of Utah Press, 2020), 51, 291n3. In a journal entry in 1891, Cannon flatly denied offering a bribe in Nevada while explaining why Trumbo had persuaded Nevada to create a statute of limitations for bribery charges. Cannon stated, "I had been accused of having tried to bribe an officer there, which was without the least foundation in truth; but [Nevada provided no statute of limitation for someone who] did not reside in the State … it would hang over [me] as long as [I] lived." GQCJ, Oct. 13, 1891.

The news of George's arrest hit Salt Lake City on Sunday morning, February 14, causing elation among some non-Mormons, alarm among the Saints. Many accounts followed over the following days. Everyone assumed that the offer of a $500 reward had resulted in Cannon's arrest.[65] The same day, Franklin S. Richards sent Cannon a dispatch by telegraph indicating that Cannon had the right to a bail hearing in Nevada. A Nevada magistrate fixed bail in the amount of $10,000. Cannon worked to arrange for the bail to be wired and Richards had the funds ready but George Q. ultimately decided not to pursue posting the bail bond when he learned Ireland was on his way to Winnemuccca. When Ireland and Greenman arrived the following day, Cannon boarded the next train to return to Utah with them. Frank J. Cannon and Alonzo Hyde also arrived on the same train as Ireland. Hyde told George Q. that "the brethren at Salt Lake [had formulated a plan] to stop the train and rescue me." Frank also told his father that he and Abram had devised a plan to rescue their father "if he so desired."[66]

Cannon thought the plan of having Mormons stop the train was ill-conceived and would put many people into legal peril, but he had no opportunity to communicate this to anyone. If it looked as if such a holdup might occur, he would get off the train and prevent it. On the other hand, a group waiting outside to help him escape might work if he could get off the train "unperceived" at one of many stops and join them. George had "full liberty" to visit the water closet, and he might be able to leave the train during one of his visits. The only other person in the car with him was Marshal Ireland, who was treating George well and was often asleep. Cannon kept watching railroad stops (usually at telegraph stations), but saw no one waiting to help him escape. Finally, as the train slowed pulling into Promontory, he saw "the light dawn in the East," and decided if he were to get off, now was the time. He went to the back of the car, intending to jump off because "the thought of the train stopped seemed to me so overpowering that I could not resist the inclination to get away."

65. "The Reward Earned! President Cannon Captured Yesterday," *SLH*, Feb. 14, 1886, 9; "George Q. Arrested, He Spent Last Night in Jail in Winnemucca," *SLT*, Feb. 14, 1886, 4.

66. "The Great Prisoner," *DN*, Feb. 17, 1886, 3; GQCJ, Feb. 27, 1886; AHCJ, Feb. 15, 1886.

The door was locked. He quickly went to the other end of the car, where a porter and a brakeman were standing. He waited until they "got out of the way," then walked out on the platform to see if he might jump off. The train had started and "by this time being under full headway," he decided not to jump because he would be injured. Just then, there was "a sudden lurch of the swiftly moving train" as it passed through a double curve which threw him "headlong" from the car. He fell on the frozen ground on the "side of the track in a dazed and badly wounded condition." He had planned to step off the train when it was moving slowly or stopped, not to be pitched out while the train was traveling at full speed.[67]

George Q.'s injuries were serious: his cheek was "dreadfully swollen and bleeding"; there was a "great cut in my eyebrow" that was bleeding so much that he thought he may have cut an artery; and he worried he may have fractured his skull. His nose was broken. His limbs were badly injured. No one had seen him fall, and he began staggering along the tracks. Eventually, Deputy Marshal Greenman, who had realized Cannon was no longer on the train, got off the train and walked back four miles, where he found George in the middle of the tracks. Greenman and Cannon walked back to the "house" in Promontory. Mrs. Sturtevant, proprietress of the house, cleaned George up and put him to bed.[68]

Ireland heard rumors of a "tumult" planned at the Ogden depot and asked George to send a dispatch "quieting anything of the kind," which he did. Ireland promised that no troops would be involved in returning him to Salt Lake and that the train would not leave before dawn. He did not inform George that Judge Orlando Powers, furious at Cannon's "jumping" off the train, had asked for military assistance, and that army troops from Fort Douglas were already on their way to Promontory. The train was not to leave until daylight, but once the westbound cars with about thirty troops and additional deputies arrived, Cannon's train left, long before daylight. Ireland promised that there would be no troops in the rail car with George, but "Captain Pinney," who took control of the train, ordered "eight

67. GQCJ, Feb. 27, 1886; Frank J. Cannon, draft letter clipped into GQCJ, Mar. 13, 1888. National news reports universally accused George Q. of jumping from the train. See "Cannon's Leap for Freedom," *NYT*, Feb. 17, 1886, 1.

68. GQCJ, Feb. 27, 1886.

to ten" soldiers, with guns loaded, to surround the bed on which the "semi conscious" George was lying,. The only familiar person permitted to sit with him was his son Frank. Two doctors, one who accompanied the troops and one from Ogden hired by Frank, examined him and sewed up his wounds with "iron wire," "having no silk and no silver that was small enough." As Cannon had promised, there was no "tumult" at Ogden.[69]

Shortly after reaching Salt Lake City on Tuesday, February 16, George Q. was transported to Ireland's office, where he lay on a mattress waiting to be arraigned. Franklin S. Richards reported to George that prosecutors intended to ask for $70,000 bail. Judge Zane ordered bail be set for $45,000, $25,000 for the first indictment for his violations of anti-polygamy laws before 1885 and $10,000 for each of two other claims, for Cannon's unlawful cohabitation with two wives since then. Today, $45,000 is roughly the equivalent of $1.5 million. If convicted of the three misdemeanors, he could be fined a total of $900 and be sentenced to prison for eighteen months. Four Mormon businessmen posted bail: John Sharp and Feramorz Little for the $25,000 bond, and Francis Armstrong and Horace Eldredge for the two $10,000 bonds.[70]

President John Taylor, afraid of Franklin S. Richards's view that federal authorities would find some way to keep Cannon in prison the rest of his life, and Charles Penrose's concerns that George Q. might be killed in prison, instructed George to jump bail. Taylor told George he had had a revelation how the bondsmen would be repaid, which made him comfortable making the decision to have Cannon leave. Cannon had a difficult time deciding not to appear and forfeit bail and did so only because the church president instructed him to. When his case was called on March 17, 1886, George was not present in the courtroom. Prosecutor William H. Dickson yelled, "Call the sureties!"[71]

George and Elizabeth's son, Abram, was sentenced to prison for unlawful cohabitation on March 17, 1886, the same day that his

69. GQCJ, Feb. 27, 1886.

70. GQCJ, Feb. 27, 1886.

71. GQCJ, Feb. 28, Mar. 2, 4, 11, 16, 17, 1886; "President Cannon's Case," *DN*, Mar. 17, 1886, 3. Taylor was shown in the revelation how Cannon's bondsmen could be repaid from the special trust fund that had been created in favor of the church president consisting of stock in the Bullion Beck & Champion silver mine. GQCJ, Feb. 28, 1886.

father was to have appeared for trial.[72] George Q. was unhappy that Abram had to serve a prison sentence for his polygamous activities, but was proud when Abram responded to a question at his trial from prosecutor William Dickson about whether Sarah Jenkins and Wilhelmina Cannon were his wives by saying, "They are, thank God."[73] George Q. was much less happy when Septimus Sears and Truman O. Angell Jr. "played a most craven part [by] agreeing to comply with the law and discard their plural wives."[74]

While George Q. was attempting to avoid arrest by traveling to Mexico, Dickson subpoenaed George's fourth wife, Martha Telle, to testify against her husband. Martha was clearly pregnant, and Dickson asked her about this, seeking evidence to charge George Q. with unlawful cohabitation. George's son Frank, Frank's cousin Angus M. Cannon Jr., and Frank's younger brother Hugh J., who was sixteen, were offended by Dickson's treatment of Martha. After the proceedings, Frank and Angus Jr., who had been drinking, approached Dickson at the restaurant in the Continental Hotel and asked him to come outside to talk to them. Frank yelled at Dickson, but Hugh was so angry with Dickson that he hit him on the side of the head. Frank told Hugh to run, which he did, and Frank and Angus Jr. were arrested, much to the annoyance of George, who knew that just such an incident would only make stressful times worse. At the same time Dickson was prosecuting George, he also charged Frank, Angus Jr., and Hugh with assault. Martha, who was threatened with prison until she testified against George (she made it clear that she would rather go to prison than testify about the father of her unborn child), took George's eventual advice to testify and was released from police custody.[75]

After he failed to appear in court and forfeited bail in March 1886, George Q. returned to the underground, hiding out from the

72. William C. Seifrit, "The Prison Experience of Abraham H. Cannon," *UHQ*, 53 (Summer 1985): 223–36.

73. Seifrit, "Prison Experience," 227.

74. GQCJ, Oct. 2, 1885. Rather than "discarding" his plural wife, Sears divorced his first wife and legally married his second wife, Isabel Whitney, who was Emmeline Wells's daughter. Septimus and Isabel left Salt Lake City after the divorce and marriage and were living in San Francisco when Louie Wells left Salt Lake to live with them amid the John Q. Cannon scandal described below.

75. "An Unfortunate Occurrence, District Attorney Dickson Assaulted by a 16-Year-Old Boy in the Continental Hotel," *DN*, Feb. 23, 1886, 3; GQCJ, Feb. 27, Mar. 23, 28, 1886; Holley, *Frank J. Cannon*, 58–63.

authorities. He worked as best he could with John Taylor to lead the church. He and Taylor maintained a close relationship, and Taylor relied on Cannon for counsel and advice. Some church leaders, particularly younger apostles like Moses Thatcher and Heber J. Grant, believed that Cannon may have sought to be the principal connection to Taylor to the exclusion of others and that he might have tried to exploit that relationship for his own benefit.

As if 1886 had not already been a horrible year in George Q.'s life, the fall brought more painful troubles in his family. George knew of his son Frank's problems, and occasionally threatened never to associate with him again, but he believed John Q. was faithful to his religious convictions and had high expectations and ambitions for his oldest son. Before George left on his mission to England in 1860, he blessed John and Abram that they would become important leaders in the Church "if [they would] only remain faithful to God."[76] Both John and Abram had, in fact, been made general authorities of the church while they were in their twenties. John in particular had been groomed for important callings—he studied shorthand so he could report Brigham Young's talks, studied classical languages, and served as his father's secretary in Congress in the late 1870s. He was a talented writer and became an editor at the *Deseret News*. He was elected to the Utah territorial legislature and was discussed as a possible replacement for John T. Caine as territorial delegate.[77] Heber J. Grant later mused: "There probably is not a young man in the whole church who has had more opportunities and advantages extended to him educationally, spiritually, and every other way than John Q. Cannon."[78] John was tall and handsome, liked and respected by most of his peers. He was also rumored to have drinking and gambling problems.

John had married Annie Wells in March 1880. He was called on a mission to Switzerland and was made mission president his last year. Annie joined him in Switzerland for a year. After they returned in 1884 John was called as a counselor to Presiding Bishop William Preston, who had been his brother Frank's stake president in Logan. The *Salt Lake*

76. KLC, "Wives and Other Women," 73.

77. KLC, "Wives and Other Women," 75–76.

78. KLC, "Wives and Other Women," 75; KLC, "The Tragic Matter of Louie Wells and John Q. Cannon," *JMH,* 35 (Spring 2009): 145–47; HJGJ, Sep. 7, 1886.

Tribune published an article that John Q. and Annie's younger sister, the popular and talented Louie Wells, had been married in a polygamous marriage. This was not true and John confronted and assaulted Joseph Lippman, the writer of the story, on East Temple Street.[79]

Two years later, in the fall of 1886, while George Q. remained on the underground, John Q. confessed to his brother Abram that he had had an extramarital relationship with Louie. John was consumed by guilt and was prepared to be punished for his sins. Abram's reaction was that the news "will nearly kill Father." Abram could not understand why John and Louie had not just married polygamously.[80] It is possible that John and Louie had, in fact, considered a plural union, and it appears that Annie was supportive. But John Taylor had decided that young leaders would not be permitted to marry polygamously for a time, and it is possible that Taylor and George Q. knew of other inappropriate acts by John, such as embezzling tithing funds, which would make him unworthy of the sacred right of plural marriage. Abram contacted his father, who could do nothing publicly because he continued to hide out from federal authorities. George told his brother, Salt Lake Stake president Angus M. Cannon, that John had had an adulterous affair with Louie Wells. George Q. instructed Angus to have John publicly confess and then to have the congregation excommunicate him at the regular church meeting in the Mormon Tabernacle that afternoon.[81]

John gave a heartfelt confession, Angus proposed that his nephew be excommunicated, and the congregation unanimously voted to expel John.[82] All of the local newspapers carried extensive reports of what happened.[83] Oddly, George then instructed Annie to divorce John, and, when she had obtained a legal divorce from LDS bishop and Salt Lake probate judge Elias Smith, John asked Louie to marry him. She responded she "would think of it," and the two

79. KLC, "Tragic Matter," 149–56.

80. KLC, "Tragic Matter," 161–62.

81. KLC, "Tragic Matter," 163.

82. AHCJ, Sep. 5, 1886; "Sunday's Sensation. John Q. Cannon's Excommunication," *Salt Lake Herald*, Sep. 8, 1886, 4; "Sunday Services," *DW*, Sep. 8, 1886, 533.

83. John Q. Cannon Cut Off," *Salt Lake Tribune*, Sep. 7, 1886, 4. The *Tribune* was happy at the fall from grace of the oldest son of the "Mormon Premier." "Some Conundrums," *SLT*, Oct. 10, 1886, 2.

were married shortly after by Abram Cannon. Louie was pregnant. Federal deputies then arrested John and charged him with polygamy, believing that he and Louie had been married in 1884. Louie, Annie, their mother, Emmeline Wells, and others were humiliated when they were forced to testify at a hearing against John. After that, Louie Wells Cannon moved to San Francisco to live with her sister and brother-in-law until after her baby was born. Her son was stillborn, and Louie died six weeks later from complications of childbirth.[84]

At Louie's funeral in May 1887, President Angus Cannon announced that George Q. had instructed him to disclose that Louie Wells had been John's adulterous partner, which drew an audible reaction from those attending the funeral and reportedly caused several women to faint. George noted in his diary that he had not instructed his brother to do this and that he had no idea why Angus would say such a thing. The disclosure caused long-term tensions between the Cannon and Wells families.[85]

Perhaps George's most serious indignity in 1887 was enactment of the Edmunds–Tucker Act on March 30, 1887. Senator George Edmunds had continued to pursue legislation designed to stop polygamy after Jeremiah Black's check on his proposed legislation in 1883. Now, under the guidance of Edmunds and Congressman John Randolph Tucker, the new law moved towards passage. The bill went further than the Edmunds Act. Among other provisions, it disincorporated the LDS Church, escheated most liquid church assets to the state, required those who wished to vote to take an anti-polygamy oath, abrogated the common law spousal privilege, disenfranchised women from voting, and replaced local judges such as probate judges with federal appointees.[86] The most important new concept of the Edmunds–Tucker bill was its focus on taking most of the LDS Church's property. The bill passed with large majorities and became law without the signature of President Grover Cleveland, even though he had reservations about its constitutionality.

---

84. KLC, "Tragic Matter," 179–83.

85. GQCJ, May 22, 1887; Ronald W. Walker, "Grant's Watershed: Succession in the Presidency, 1887–1889," *BYUS* 43 (Jan. 2004): 202–5.

86. Edmunds–Tucker Act, 24 Stat. 635 (1887).

CHAPTER SEVEN

THE MORMONS STRIKE BACK

1887–92

"I am perfectly convinced that public opinion has become so crystallized on what is called 'the Mormon question,' that it is idle to expect to modify ... it. I have never known anything in the course of my life that presented such a phenomenon."
—George Ticknor Curtis, January 1887

Before the Edmunds–Tucker bill passed, Utah territorial delegate John T. Caine and his assistants, Charles W. Penrose and Franklin S. Richards, drafted a resolution to delay the bill from becoming law for six months. Caine then persuaded William L. Scott, a Democrat from Pennsylvania with ties to the railroad lobbies, to sponsor the resolution.[1]

Penrose and Richards hoped to provide a sufficient period of time during which Utah (or at least Utah Mormons) could propose and vote for a constitution for the future state of Utah, which would include a provision making polygamous marriages criminal. They believed that this would counter the new federal law, whose "evils with which we are menaced and which are likely to come upon us under the operations of the [Edmunds] Tucker Bill should it become law."[2] With this provision, and assuming ratification by Utahns of such a constitution, they hoped that Grover Cleveland might even support statehood. Penrose and Richards believed once statehood was attained, church members could continue to practice polygamy

1. GQCJ, Jan. 24, 26, 1887; Charles Penrose and Franklin S. Richards to John Taylor, Feb. 16, 1887, copied into GQCJ, Feb. 19, 1887; Edward Leo Lyman, *Finally Statehood! Utah's Struggles, 1849–1896* (Salt Lake City: Signature Books, 2019), 153.

2. John Taylor and GQC to Penrose and Richards, Feb. 19, 1887, copied into GQCJ, Feb. 19, 1887.

extralegally. George Q. could not bring himself to agree to such a provision. He believed that Penrose and Richards were clever and two of the best writers in the territory, but that their scheme would not work and that the Mormons would be viewed as guilty of "Punic faith" (treachery or perfidy).[3]

Cannon and Taylor had recently heard from John W. Young, a son of Brigham Young who lived in New York City and had long been a lobbyist for the church, that he doubted Cleveland would support Utah statehood even if its new constitution banned polygamy. To Cannon and Taylor, "the plan of Penrose and Richards if it could be successfully accomplished might, perhaps, avert the evils which are impending [under the Edmunds–Tucker bill]; but it is chimerical. The public men of the nation would not accept it," for "nothing less than the complete destruction of our system of plural marriages will appease the popular demand."[4] The Scott Amendment had been defeated before the Edmunds–Tucker bill passed.

The Edmunds–Tucker Act escheated to the federal government (that is, the federal government took control and essential ownership of) most church property. Church leaders had suspected this was coming and had completed a series of changes to limit the damage. Separate business associations involving the Logan, Manti, and St. George temples were formed in 1886, and the temple properties were transferred to these entities. Local LDS wards and stakes were separately incorporated and church real property assets were transferred to these new entities to insulate the assets from being taken by the government. Some assets, particularly liquid assets such as securities, were also transferred to individual church leaders under "trust assignments." Just before the Edmunds–Tucker Act became

3. GQCJ, Jan. 24, 1887.

4. John Taylor and GQC to John T. Caine and John W. Young, Feb. 21, 1887, copied into GQCJ, Feb. 21, 1887. Modern legal historian Sarah Barringer Gordon agrees with Cannon. She wrote that the Edmunds–Tucker Act "took Congress, and the Supreme Court, further into the realm of coercion than they had ventured before. Put bluntly, the Edmunds–Tucker Act recognized the connections between faith, marriage, and property in Mormon culture; then it set out to destroy them. Victory, in this sense, was the creation of a legal community possible only with the destruction of an alternative one." Sarah Barringer Gordon, *The Mormon Question: Polygamy and Constitutional Conflict in Nineteenth Century America* (Chapel Hill, NC: University of North Carolina Press), 187.

law, John Taylor ordered tithing receipts transferred to local stakes.[5] Most of these transfers were probably fraudulent conveyances under common law and avoidable by the government because they were made with intent to hinder, delay, or defraud the federal government from obtaining assets escheated to it under the Edmunds–Tucker Act. This was not a typical debtor-creditor relationship, but it still fit in the general class of debts.[6] In their defense, church leaders were genuinely concerned that the property in the hands of the government would not retain its value and they tried to remedy this through creative transfers that kept property from being taken by the government.

At general conference in April (held in the Provo tabernacle), an "epistle" from the First Presidency, but almost entirely the work of George Q., was read.[7] The broad-ranging statement described many achievements and prospects of the church and its members. The Edmunds–Tucker Act was described under the heading "Legislative and Judicial Tyranny," which excoriated Congress for enacting legislation that "contained shameful unrepublican features, the evident purpose of which was to entirely destroy all the liberties of the majority of the people of Utah." The *Salt Lake Tribune* called this "last epistle" the "most turgid, stupid and perverse production that ever emanated from that body."[8]

Mormons took the offensive shortly after enactment of the Edmunds–Tucker Act. Charles Penrose, on leave from his job as *Deseret News* editor to work with John T. Caine, drafted a new constitution for Utah and a new convention was called. Section 8 of the new constitution provided that "bigamy and polygamy being considered incompatible with a republican form of government, each of them is hereby forbidden and declared a misdemeanor." The penalty for either of these crimes would be a maximum of $1,000 and a prison

5. Leonard J. Arrington, *Great Basin Kingdom: An Economic History of the Latter-day Saints, 1830–1900* (Cambridge: Harvard University Press, 1958), 360–64; GQCJ, Mar. 8, 1887.

6. Elizabeth Warren, Jay Lawrence Westbrook, Katherine Porter, and John A.E. Pottow, *The Law of Debtors and Creditors*, 7th ed. (New York, NY: Wolters Kluwer, 2014), 511–16; *Twyne's Case*, 3 Coke 806, 76 Eng. Rep. 809 (Star Chamber, 1601).

7. GQCJ, Apr. 4–5, 6, 1887.

8. "An Epistle of the First Presidency," *DN*, Apr. 8, 1887, 2; "The Last Epistle," *SLT*, Apr. 10, 1887, 2.

sentence between six months and three years. This section of the proposed state constitution could not be amended without Congress's approval and ratification.[9]

Cannon noted his support for the constitution because it provided for a political solution. His understanding was that Cleveland, his solicitor general, George A. Jenks, and a number of senior Democrats in Congress had approved these provisions.[10] Jenks even visited Utah during the convention in early July, supposedly to initiate some test lawsuits regarding escheatment of assets, but really to talk to Mormon leaders. While Jenks was in town, he provided important advice. He counselled LDS leaders to stop referring to polygamy in all their public addresses. To Jenks, the less said by Mormon leaders about their controversial marriage practice, the better. The *Salt Lake Tribune* and like-minded newspapers would have a much harder time engaging with LDS newspapers if those papers avoided discussing the subject. Better to be silent on controversial issues.[11] The *Tribune*, showing some anxiety, asserted that Jenks's visit showed an interest on the part of the Democratic administration in the admission of Utah and that he was in town to "manage the necessary negotiations" for statehood.[12] The *Tribune* argued sarcastically that of course Utah should be made a state so that the "benign rule [of our crowned King, John Taylor, with his counselors] may thenceforth be unquestioned that we may have the further rule of robbing and cutting the throats of all who dare to oppose any device or order of their chiefs."[13] The new constitution was overwhelmingly ratified by Utah voters.[14]

Cannon and Taylor remained in hiding on the underground, inhibiting their ability to lead the church. Second counselor Joseph F. Smith was also in hiding in the Sandwich Islands. Being required to hide out on the underground—sleeping when and where he could, staying in uncomfortable, sometimes hastily constructed hiding

9. "The Constitution," *DW*, July 13, 1887, 412; GQCJ, July 15, 1887.

10. GQCJ, June 15, 1887. Some expressed doubt about the seriousness with which Mormons took the anti-polygamy provisions. "Polygamy a Misdemeanor," *NYT*, July 6, 1887, 2; "The Utah Constitution. The Anti-Polygamy Clause Declared a Mormon Trick," *SLT*, July 7, 1887, 1.

11. AHCJ, July 8, 1887.

12. "Jenks's Visit to Utah" *SLT*, July 8, 1887, 1.

13. "Statehood, What Is Really Wanted," *SLT*, June 21, 1887, 2.

14. "Still Coming In," *SLH*, Aug. 4, 1887, 8.

places, and being forced to move from one to another with guards—did not help Taylor's failing health. On July 25, 1887, he passed away in the home of Thomas F. and Margaret Roueche in an isolated part of Kaysville, Utah, near the Great Salt Lake wetlands.[15] To George Q., his uncle, prophet, and father figure had been "killed by the cruelty of these people [the federal officials]," who had forced him to live on the underground for the past few years.[16]

Jenks's counsel was consistent with advice given by Alexander Badlam, a lobbyist for the railroads who had Mormon relatives and who consulted with church leaders on how to improve the public image of the church and its leaders. Badlam advised the *Deseret News* and *Salt Lake Herald* to stop engaging the *Tribune* whenever it criticized the church: Never "allow the name of the *Tribune* ... to appear in either of your papers." He also counselled them not to mention potential statehood for Utah at all: "Don't allow one word to be said in either of your papers in favor of statehood." Church leaders agreed to comply and instructed editorial writers at both papers to stop writing about the *Tribune* and statehood.[17]

Taylor's death created, as the deaths of Joseph Smith and Brigham Young had created before, a lack of clarity in church leadership. Upon Smith's death in 1844, many asserted the right to succeed him as leader of the church. Young led the largest group on the basis that he was president of the Quorum of Twelve Apostles. After Young's death in 1877, Taylor waited three years before reorganizing the First Presidency. Now, with Taylor's passing, Wilford Woodruff was the senior-most apostle, but at least a few other apostles thought that someone else should be made president. Some junior apostles believed that George Q. was attempting to manipulate matters to be named the leader of the church and even suggested that Joseph F. Smith had been sent to Hawai'i was part of Cannon's plan to succeed Taylor.[18] Because of his unusually close relationship, both personal and ecclesiastical, with Taylor, George Q. was in a natural position

15. Plaque on house, article from Lakeside News, 1000 Roueche Lane, Kaysville, Utah 84037, "Thomas Roueche Home, Kaysville, Utah," Ensign Peak Foundation, ensignpeak-foundation.org.

16. GQCJ, July 27, 1886.

17. Lyman, *Finally Statehood!* 181–82.

18. Walker, "Grant's Watershed," 206.

of taking leadership, but there is scant evidence he ever considered seeking the church presidency for himself. The whole process was complicated by most of the leaders not being able to appear in public, let alone meet together, and not having regular interaction to discuss important issues that could have calmed concerns. George Q. and Smith (who had recently returned from Hawai'i at Taylor and Cannon's request) took care of immediate matters.[19] With the dissolution of the First Presidency, the Quorum of Twelve Apostles asserted its leadership, with Wilford Woodruff in charge of that body.

Woodruff was aware that the tradition starting with Young in 1844 was that the senior-most apostle became the senior leader of the church. The question of whether George Q. should continue as a member of the First Presidency was a primary reason for the delay in the presidency's reorganization.[20]

Heber J. Grant, Moses Thatcher, and others were concerned about several matters concerning George's control of access to Taylor. They did not like the way George handled the matter with his son John and the Wells sisters, particularly instructing Annie to divorce John and then telling John to marry Louie. They were angered by the hurt George inflicted on Annie, Emmeline Wells, and other members of the Wells family by reportedly having his brother, Angus, disclose publicly (at Louie's funeral, no less) that Louie was John's partner in adultery, which deepened a rift already brewing between the families. George denied having asked Angus to make this disclosure at the funeral. This was all against the background of the untimely death of the beloved Louie. The Wells family was already furious with John Q., whom they closely associated with his father, over the humiliation of Annie, Louie, and Emmeline having to testify in a hearing against John. The animosity increased in the summer of 1888 when George rebaptized John and Wilford Woodruff restored John's temple blessings just a year after Louie's death.[21] George, in his typical direct way, confronted Daniel H. Wells about the difficulties between them. They had a "very long conversation

19. Walker, "Grant's Watershed," 198–99.

20. Walker, "Grant's Watershed," 202–21.

21. Walker, "Grant's Watershed," 202–6; KLC, "The Tragic Matter of Louie Wells and John Q. Cannon," *JMH,* 35 (Spring 2009): 168–75, 177–78, 183–88; GQCJ, May 22, 1887.

over John Q's case," in which Cannon explained certain aspects of the matter and, at least from George's perspective, removed "much prejudice and mis-information from [Daniel's] mind." The discussion ended, to George's understanding, with Wells "being perfectly satisfied with me and as having no feelings towards me."[22]

Another area of concern among some apostles involved a special trust held by Taylor consisting of a majority share of stock in the Bullion, Beck & Champion Mining Co. (Bullion Beck), which owned a silver mine in Eureka, Utah. John Beck had developed the mine and then sold a substantial amount of the stock to Taylor and Cannon, for which both borrowed quite heavily. The three agreed to take 60 percent of the stock each owned to fund a trust for the president of the church to use for the benefit of the church. They discussed using the money for the acquisition of the Kirtland, Ohio, temple and the construction of a temple in Jackson County, Missouri. Later, three church leaders from Cache Valley—Moses Thatcher, Marriner W. Merrill, and William B. Preston—invested smaller amounts in the company and mine, but with the same understanding that 60 percent of what they owned would be placed in the trust.[23] As Taylor grew increasingly ill, he and George worried about how to transfer the stock to the new church president. Given the circumstances of leaders living on the underground, Taylor and Cannon wanted to make sure to keep the trust in control of church leadership. They decided to transfer ownership to George Q. for him to use as he saw fit for the benefit of the church when Taylor died.[24]

This caused significant controversy. Several members of the Quorum of Twelve, including most vocally Moses Thatcher and Heber J. Grant, found such an arrangement to be entirely inappropriate. The funds should be controlled by the president of the church. Thatcher, Grant, and others harbored concerns that George wanted to be president, but they did not agree he should be.[25] A possible reason that Cannon was not as transparent about the Bullion Beck stock and the trust fund was that Taylor felt comfortable directing George Q.

22. GQCJ, Nov. 8, 1887.
23. GQCJ, June 24, 1887
24. Bitton, *GQC*, July 1, 1887; Walker, "Grant's Watershed," 207–8.
25. Walker, "Grant's Watershed," 206–8.

to jump bail and forfeit up to $45,000 on the bonds because Taylor decided it would be appropriate to use funds from the Bullion Beck trust to reimburse the sureties who posted the $45,000. The only two who had required reimbursement of their bonds were John Sharp and Feramorz Little, who had posted $25,000 security for the bail. Taylor repaid them the $25,000 from funds in the Bullion Beck trust.[26]

Further complications surrounded Bullion Beck. New parties, consisting of some of the railroad lobbyists and clients or friends of them, invested substantial sums in the mine. Litigation involving a neighboring mine lingered and created headaches for George Q., Hiram B. Clawson (who took over operation of the company), and others. Sometimes, when Cannon was talking to the lobbyists, they discussed not only improving the church's public image but also resolving disputes among Bullion Beck shareholders and company litigation.[27]

In the midst of controversy, Woodruff and Cannon continued to look for ways to enhance the public image of Mormons and their leaders, with the ultimate goal of attaining statehood. One of the clever initiatives that Cannon embarked on was convincing prominent urban newspapers and hundreds of smaller papers that received wire stories from the Associated Press (AP) to run articles favorable to the Mormons. In this Cannon enlisted the help of Clawson, an LDS bishop, an astute businessman, one of Cannon's closest friends, and a cousin of Isaac Trumbo. The Mormons needed to find a way to counteract the influence of the *Salt Lake Tribune*. For many years, the *Tribune*, principally through William Nelson, a longtime reporter and editor, maintained a close tie into the AP network through his old friend, William Henry Smith, the Chicago-based manager of the Western AP. Not only did Nelson stir things up against the Mormons in Salt Lake City through inflammatory reporting, many of his articles went out by telegraph over the AP to hundreds of newspapers every day. George Ticknor Curtis, a lawyer and constitutional historian who often practiced before the US Supreme Court and who believed that the campaign against

26. GQCJ, Mar. 21, 1892. Cannon was in the process in 1892 of seeking forgiveness of the $20,000, which had not been paid and recovering from the US government the full $25,000 of bonds which had been paid.

27. See, e.g., GQCJ, Nov. 22, 1884, Apr. 9, May 31, June 16, July 11, 26, Aug. 26, Sep. 1, 1885, Aug. 9, 24, 1886, May 5, Sep. 8, 1887, Apr. 27, May 15, 23, 1889.

Mormon polygamy violated the Constitution, "observed that he had never seen such a phenomenon as the journalistic furor over polygamy." Curtis later became a paid lawyer for the church, but his own personal legal views were favorable to the Saints.[28]

The railroad lobbyists, who had much greater access to journalists nationally than the *Salt Lake Tribune* had through the Nelson-Smith AP relationship, saw common interests between the railroads and the church. The railroad barons wanted US senators from Utah and other politicians who would be friendly to the railroads' interests, as well as friendly judges in the new state. The railroad owners also believed that the LDS Church would have influence in many Western states. Clawson met secretly with Badlam, Trumbo, and Leland Stanford, at the time a US senator. The agents of the railroads agreed to arrange positive coverage for the church by a number of large metropolitan newspapers and the AP in exchange for which the church would pay a substantial sum, estimated at $140,000. Such bribery was a cost of doing business at the time. Stanford agreed to provide lobbyists for the effort if the church made agreed-upon payments to newspapers and newspaper syndicates and even to help with those if the church were "drained" of resources. The church appropriated $100,000.[29]

In the meantime, Penrose was asked to take additional time from his position as *Deseret News* editor to go to New York City to learn if he could get favorable articles published in newspapers there. He would also determine if John W. Young's contacts in New York were useful. Penrose placed some articles but soon realized that Young's "contacts" were not helpful. On the other hand, Young's "rapport" with the Democratic Grover Cleveland administration appeared to be genuine.[30]

The lobbyists reiterated that the *Deseret News* and the *Salt Lake Herald* needed to stop arguing with the *Tribune* and to stop mentioning statehood. Church leaders agreed. It took some time, but by

28. George T. Curtis to Franklin S. Richards, Jan. 23, 1887, copy in GQCJ, Feb. 5, 1887; Lyman, *Finally Statehood!* 168; GQCJ, Apr. 27, 1887; O. N. Malmquist, *The First 100 Years, A History of the Salt Lake Tribune, 1871–1971* (Salt Lake City: Utah State Historical Society, 1971), 244–46.

29. Lyman, *Finally Statehood!* 176–79; GQCJ, May 26, 1887

30. Lyman, *Finally Statehood!* 179–80.

late summer 1887 with payments being made and stories prepared, newspapers which had been critical of the Mormons and of Utah statehood began running favorable articles about the church and Utah. As the year wore on, even some papers in New York City were publishing friendly stories and sending correspondents to Utah for personal interviews. By the end of 1887, Isaac Trumbo noted that everything looked better than they had hoped.[31]

As the Edmunds–Tucker law began to take effect, the Utah Commission was expanded and two new commissioners were appointed. US Marshal Frank H. Dyer was appointed as receiver to take charge of escheated assets and "seized the church president's office, locked the desks, and took the keys."[32] Some church leaders feared that the Mormon whom federal deputies most relentlessly sought to arrest, George Q. Cannon, "would be convicted on so many counts that he would be held in prison indefinitely— that he might, in fact, end his days there."[33]

Cannon was not willing to turn himself in as long as it was likely that he would be tried by someone like Judge Charles Zane, who had earned a reputation as being harsh in his sentencing of "cohabs" (and who had imposed $45,000 in bonds for George Q. in 1886). Several lobbyists were working to "get Judge Zane removed." Harvey D. Talcott, a prominent lawyer in San Francisco, was universally recommended in 1887, but Zane was not removed. In 1888 George Q. told his son Frank to look for a new judge in New York City. Frank visited Abraham S. Hewitt, mayor of New York and a good friend of George Q., and asked for recommendations. Hewitt suggested Elliot Sandford, a prominent New York attorney who was a "fine man, great legal ability, courageous, of undoubted integrity." Hewitt arranged an introduction, Frank made an eloquent plea, and Sandford, with the support of his wife, Sarah, agreed to be considered.[34]

Frank then went to Washington, DC, and talked his way into seeing another acquaintance of his father, Navy secretary William C.

31. Lyman, *Finally Statehood!* 181–91.

32. Bitton, GQC, 290.

33. Stewart L. Grow, "A Study of the Utah Commission, 1882–1896," PhD diss., University of Utah, 1954; "An Epistle of the First Presidency," DN, Apr. 8, 1887, 2; Cannon and O'Higgins, *Under the Prophet*, 44.

34. GQCJ, May 25, 1887; KLC, "'The Honor of American Citizenship,' Frank J. Cannon's Contributions to Utah's Statehood," *Pioneer* 67 (no. 4, 2020), 40–41.

Whitney. Frank persuaded Whitney to help him obtain an interview with Grover Cleveland. Frank told the president that his—Cleveland's—reelection chances would be improved if he could get LDS leaders to come out of hiding and face prosecution and imprisonment. Frank indicated that, beginning with George Q., leaders would do this if they knew the judges would treat them fairly. Cleveland responded that he had appointed friendly officials and it had had no impact, leading him to conclude that the only way to get the Mormons to "break" was to impose increasingly harsh measures. Frank disagreed and explained why. Over the next few weeks, Frank met with Cleveland several times and convinced him to replace Zane as chief judge with Eliot Sandford. Shortly after Sandford took office, church lawyer Franklin S. Richards and Frank J. Cannon negotiated the terms for George's indictment, surrender, trial, sentence, and incarceration with new prosecutor George S. Peters and with Judge Sandford. Those terms included fair treatment with no favors, none of George's wives would be called to testify, George would turn himself in, he would be tried on two counts of unlawful cohabitation, and he would receive a full sentence. With the agreement set, George Q. surrendered. He was arrested, pled guilty, was convicted of two counts of unlawful cohabitation, fined $400, sentenced to 175 days in prison, and incarcerated all on the same day, September 17, 1888. Utah's most wanted man was now behind bars in the territorial penitentiary (the "pen").[35] Abram Cannon understood that the *Tribune* Ring were "blue with rage" because they thought the sentence was unduly lenient.[36]

In prison, George was a model inmate. He had many visitors, including members of Congress, all of whom brought him reading material. He shared these with his fellow Mormon inmates, or "cohabs," as they were called. He also received fruits, vegetables, oysters, and sweets, and he shared most of these with other cohabs as well as with the guards. He finished, with the help of a son or two, his biography of Joseph Smith. He taught Sunday school classes on the sabbath. He interacted genially with the cohabs, guards, and the

35. KLC, "'The Honor of American Citizenship,'" 42–43; GQCJ, Sep. 12, 1888; *WWJ*, Sep. 18, 1888; Bitton, *GQC*, 291–92.

36. AHCJ, Sep. 18, 1888; "'That Hero and Martyr,'" *Salt Lake Tribune*, Sep. 19, 1888, 2.

warden, who was Orson Pratt's son, Arthur, though this Pratt had left the LDS Church many years before. George Q. also planned photo shoots intended to tie into the church's plan to improve its image and to hint that it might be willing to give up polygamy on the right terms. George's six months in the pen is mostly remembered because of the photographs that were taken by Charles R. Savage.[37]

The first two days of photographs were taken in the chilly November air in 1888. Many of the images taken on November 13 and 15 have survived, all with different Mormon inmates, except for one, George Q. Cannon. Cannon is at the center of almost all of the photographs, either sitting or standing. Similar images were taken in January 1889. In the best-known of the prison photos, George Q. sits in the middle surrounded by fourteen other prisoners and two guards. For some reason, he is holding flowers and looking off into the distance. The other prisoners in the photo are the fourteen Mormon bishops who were in the pen at the time. They were from different parts of Utah: St. George, Cedar City, Richfield, Provo, Salt Lake City, Ogden, Cache Valley, and many places in between. On close examination, Cannon and a majority of the bishops are wearing formal shirts and ties under their prison stripes.[38]

What is the significance of George Q. sitting in formal wear under prison stripes with fourteen bishops? Cannon was communicating that Mormon leaders were willing to accept the punishment that the country decided to impose. They should now be treated reasonably as the details of the Saints' reintegration into American society were worked out. As George remembered on the third anniversary of his incarceration: "The Lord revealed to me with great plainness my duty, and pointed out with certainty the results that would follow my action, if I would do as He directed. … As I said, the Lord had revealed to me that if I would do this, it would be easier and better for all concerned, and it would tend to create a change of sentiment." The formal wear under the prison stripes communicated another message: these devout Latter-day Saints were dressed well

37. KLC, "The Penitentiary Photographs of George Q. Cannon as Propaganda," presentation, Mormon History Association conference, June 2022, Logan, Utah; GQC, *The Life of Joseph Smith, The Prophet* (Salt Lake City: Juvenile Instructor Office, 1888).

38. KLC, "Penitentiary Photographs of George Q. Cannon."

under their prison uniforms to show that they were proud, civilized, even cultured, and very much American. Their dress was intended to counteract the perception of broader America that they were, as one scholar refers to them, "barbarians within the gates."[39] Most of the remaining photographs taken by Savage pictured one of the bishops shown in the "mother" photograph with other cohabs from the same part of Utah as the bishop.[40]

All of this—Cannon's submission to prosecution and incarceration and the scores of different photographs—was part of a choreographed propaganda message, intended for both gentiles and Mormons. Cannon's submission to punishment provided a clear message: the church was ready to negotiate if the terms were reasonable. Sandford, who likely did not know why the most powerful Mormon in the world had surrendered to authorities, was chosen as someone who would be reasonable in his sentencing.

As he had shown many times, George had a humorous streak, and one of the photographs that has always confused historians is one in which his hair and beard are dark (in all the other photographs his hair and beard are white). Cannon colored his hair and beard for this image just as he did when he was trying to escape Utah by train in 1886. The cohabs in this photograph are from northern Utah, near where the train traveled before he was arrested. George seems to have been amusing himself—he had come so close to escaping in February 1886.[41]

Shortly after he was released on February 20, 1889, George Q. gave a memorable talk in the Tabernacle. He expressed how delighted he was to be out of prison and with the Saints, but he also noted how happy he had been in the pen, with fellow believers being punished for something they all believed in. Cannon concluded by stating emphatically, "We need not fear; I tell you there is no cause or room for fear. God is with us; the glorious army of martyrs who have died for the truth in the past ages are looking down upon us."[42]

Mormon lobbyists had improved the public image of the church

39. Stephen Eliot Smith, "Barbarians within the Gates: Congressional Debates on Mormon Polygamy, 1850–1879," *Journal of Church and State* 51 (Autumn 2009): 587–616.

40. KLC, "Penitentiary Photographs of George Q. Cannon."

41. KLC, "Penitentiary Photographs of George Q. Cannon."

42. GQC, Discourse, Feb. 24, 1889, Stuy, *CD*, 5:203.

by placing positive articles in major newspapers and the AP syndicate, as well as with periodic strategically-placed bribes, sometimes from the church, sometimes from Central Pacific lobbyists.[43] One can only imagine how frustrated William Nelson, regular Salt Lake contributor to the AP, must have become as his articles were published less and positive articles about the Saints appeared more frequently. Not surprisingly, the positive press improved public views of the Mormons. At the same time, the work of Frank J. Cannon and others with Democratic Grover Cleveland's administration had resulted in friendlier judges and better relations with the federal government.[44]

About the same time George Q. and his fellow cohabs were having their photographs taken in November 1888, Republican Benjamin Harrison defeated Cleveland in the presidential election of 1888. The Republicans also achieved a majority in the House of Representatives. Immediately after the election, the Senate was split evenly between Republicans and Democrats with thirty-seven senators each, but the admission of four new states, all of which sent Republican senators to Washington, resulted in a majority of Republicans in the US Senate by the end of 1889. All the good relations that the Mormons had developed with Democrats in 1887 and 1888 seemed to be lost in early 1889 with the new Republican administration and Congress. They also had no choice but to find ways to make peace with the Republicans if they wanted to attain statehood.[45]

By April 1889, Wilford Woodruff had complete confidence in George Q. and his abilities. Much as Brigham Young and John Taylor had said of George Q. previously, now-church president Woodruff told George's son, Abram, that his father had "the biggest brain and best mind of any man in the Kingdom, without exception," and he had come to rely on Cannon to advise him on political, business, and ecclesiastical matters.[46] George had once again made himself indispensable to a church president. On April 5, Woodruff announced that he had been inspired to reorganize the First Presidency, with himself as president, George Q. as first counselor, and

43. Lyman, *Finally Statehood!* 202–3. Mormon leaders apparently tended to "bribe" only journalists—they generally did not bribe politicians.

44. KLC, "'Honor of American Citizenship,'" 40–41.

45. Bitton, *GQC*, 297–99.

46. AHCJ, Feb. 22, 1889

Joseph F. Smith as second counselor. At the quorum meeting just before the conference session, Apostle Moses Thatcher agreed to sustain George as first counselor but regretted that he had not received a manifestation from the Lord that George should be in the presidency and hoped to receive such a manifestation in the future. Apostle Heber J. Grant noted in his diary that he intended to say that he sustained Cannon as a counselor but "did not have perfect confidence in his [Cannon's] methods as I wished I had," but did not after Woodruff discouraged all further discussion. The reorganization of the First Presidency was sustained in conference.[47]

Not long after general conference in April 1889 ended, Woodruff, Cannon, and Hiram B. Clawson traveled to San Francisco, mostly for political meetings but also for George Q. to see Frank, who was ill and had gone with Mattie to California in the hope of regaining his health. Carlie was also there with some of their children taking a vacation. Amid extensive sightseeing for several days with family, the group met with W. W. Stow, a wealthy friend of the church. Stow introduced the Mormons to Judge Morris Estee, who had presided at the Republican convention in Chicago a year before, and two of the Central Pacific's "Big Four," Collis Huntington and Leland Stanford. Estee indicated that he had become interested in the issues faced by the Mormons through Isaac Trumbo. It soon became clear that creating alliances with Estee, Stanford, Huntington, and their lobbyists would become important to improving relations between LDS leaders and Republicans in Washington.[48]

As pressure against polygamy increased, Woodruff directed that no new plural marriages be solemnized in the United States. Cannon later noted in his journal that he "was not fully prepared to endorse these remarks" as "it is an exceedingly grave question, and it is the first time that anything of this kind has ever been uttered, to my knowledge, by one holding the keys."[49] Federal authorities continued to watch for prominent Mormons visiting polygamous wives so they could be arrested. Thus, though George helped plan a surprise party for his second wife Sarah Jane's fiftieth birthday on September 11,

47. Grant Diary, Apr. 5, 1889; Bitton, *GQC*, 298.
48. GQCJ, Apr. 17, 18–24, 1889; Bitton, *GQC*, 299.
49. GQCJ, Sep. 11, 1889, Bitton, *GQC*, 300.

1889, he wrote her "a brief outline of his feelings" and congratulated her on the celebration of an important birthday, the risk of being arrested was too great for him to actually attend the party.[50]

In October 1889, three new apostles were called. Among the three was Abraham H. Cannon, second son of George Q. and Elizabeth, who had served as one of the First Council of Seventy for the past seven years. George noted in his diary that he "felt much embarrassed about Abraham being named," because he did not want anyone to think that he had suggested or promoted the calling. All agreed that "the Spirit of God bore testimony to us that these were the men whom He had chosen," and with that, George consented to Abram being advanced. Abram was relieved when his father told him he had had nothing to do with the appointment. Woodruff told the conference that names had been proposed by the Quorum of the Twelve, that he had prayed about those presented by the apostles, and that "the Spirit of the Lord manifested to me those whom we should appoint." George Q. was no doubt pleased, after the problems of his two oldest sons, John and Frank, to see Abram admitted to the apostolate.[51]

One of the new Utah judges who began serving in 1889 was Thomas J. Anderson. He created headlines and reminded the Mormons of Judge McKean. Anderson attracted the ire of Mormon leaders when he ruled that LDS immigrant John Moore would not be granted US citizenship until the judge could ascertain whether Mormons took an oath against the US government in the temple endowment ceremony. Hearings were scheduled for Anderson to take evidence on the question. Ironically, Woodruff, George Q., and Smith were in Alberta, Canada, at the time scouting out possible foreign locations where church members could continue to practice polygamy. Anderson ultimately concluded that devout Mormons were required to take a temple oath with a higher loyalty to church than to country, placing in doubt whether members would be able to vote, even if they did not practice polygamy.[52]

---

50. GQCJ, Sep. 11, 1889.

51. GQCJ, Oct. 1, 3, 6, 1889; AHCJ, Oct. 7, 1889; Bitton, *GQC*, 300.

52. "The Latest, Mormons Cannot Become Citizens, Anderson's Decision," *SLH*, Dec. 1, 1889.

In response, the First Presidency issued an official declaration signed by all members of the First Presidency and Quorum of Twelve Apostles. The declaration, which for once was not drafted by George Q. (but by Charles Penrose) denied and denounced allegations of "blood atonement" and further asserted that the church "does not claim to be an independent, temporal kingdom of God, ... aiming to overthrow the United States or any other civil government" or demand a higher loyalty to the church than the state. The declaration stated that church members would be "subject unto the powers that be until Christ comes, whose right it is to reign." When Penrose's initial draft was reviewed, George Q. indicated that he could not sign it because it made denials which he could not make. He had received his temple endowments in Nauvoo, Illinois, in late 1845, "at a time when our blood was warm concerning the cruel martyrdom of Joseph and Hyrum [Smith] and the murder and expulsion of our people, and I viewed covenants which I had made as binding upon me." The endowment had since been modified, and younger men could deny "things which I could not truthfully and conscientiously deny." The decision was made to narrow the denials, to take references to Anderson out of the official declaration, and to deny the things which Anderson had specifically ruled on. The declaration as published ended by repeating a favorite theme of George: if Latter-day Saints were excluded from voting "solely because they are members of the Mormon church," this would represent an "impolitic, unrepublican and dangerous encroachment on the civil and religious liberty of all."[53] As historian Thomas G. Alexander has shown, the declaration prepared the way for Mormon accommodation with the citizens of the United States.[54]

The year 1890 turned out to be an unusually important one in the history of the LDS Church. The year began with George Q. once again traveling to Washington, DC, to lobby for acceptable solutions to the Mormons' plight. Always the savvy politician, Cannon met first with Democrats and reminded them that the Saints would

53. "Where They Stand, Important Manifesto of the Church Authorities," *SLH*, Dec. 15, 1889; GQCJ, Dec. 6, 1889.

54. Thomas G. Alexander, *Things in Heaven and Earth: The Life and Times of Wilford Woodruff, a Mormon Prophet* (Salt Lake City: Signature Books, 1991), 258; Bitton, *GQC*, 301–2.

one day soon have significant political clout in a number of western states, hinting that if the Democrats did not find a way to support the church, LDS leaders would have to turn to Republicans. In the next few months, two US Supreme Court decisions created significant questions about whether Mormons could continue to practice polygamy. The first came in February 1890, in *Davis v. Beeson* (133 U.S. 333 [1890]), in which the court upheld the constitutionality of the Idaho test oath, which forbade believing Mormons and, on the facts of the case, even former Mormons) from voting. George told a reporter for the *St. Louis Globe-Democrat* that most Mormons could take the Idaho test oath "honestly" because, unlike him, most were not "ultras" who believed that God had commanded men to take plural wives through a revelation. Other church members, particularly younger ones, believed that practicing polygamy was "permissive."[55] Three months later, the Supreme Court issued *Late Corporation of the Church of Jesus Christ of Latter-day Saints v. United States*, in which the high court by a 6-3 decision upheld the constitutionality of the Edmunds–Tucker Act (136 U.S. 1 [1890]).

Fortified by these important appellate decisions, Congress began considering the Cullom-Struble bill, which would have essentially disenfranchised all Mormons—polygamists and monogamists—from voting or taking meaningful part in other political or civic activities in all territories in the United States.[56] The First Presidency asked George Q. to return secretly to Washington, DC, to oversee efforts to keep the new bill from becoming law. Recognizing his son Frank's political gifts, George had him join him. He correctly believed that Frank, a young Latter-day Saint who was not a polygamist and who had publicly declared himself to be a Republican, would be able to help stop the bill. In May 1890, George provided Frank with a list of important congressional leaders who might help him set an agenda to defeat the bill.[57]

Guided by his father, the younger Cannon met with a series of prominent politicians, including Colorado senator Henry Teller, a

55. "Prest. Geo. Q. Cannon, His Talk with a St. Louis Globe-Democrat Man," *SLH*, Feb. 23, 1890, clipping *St. Louis Globe-Democrat* (article dated Feb. 9, 1890).

56. KLC, "'Honor of American Citizenship,'" 43.

57. KLC, "'Honor of American Citizenship,'" 40–41.

Democrat and a friend of the Saints. Impressed by Frank, Teller counseled him to testify before the Senate and House committees considering the bill and to make clear that Frank was a Republican. Teller also told Frank to introduce himself around Washington. Frank next contacted Benjamin Harrison's secretary of state James G. Blaine. Judge Morris Estee had already explained to Blaine why Utah's admission as a state would benefit Republicans.[58]

Frank considered Blaine the preeminent American statesman and understood how helpful Blaine could be. Blaine advised Frank to tell his own personal story as a young, independent thinking, non-polygamist who could provide a personal story of the impact the harsh proposed bill would have on young Mormons unlikely to become polygamists and who had independent political views. Ever the tactician, Blaine also counseled Frank to emphasize that the Mormons would someday be a significant political force in the West and that Republicans could lose the Mormon vote before ever gaining it. As Frank was leaving, Blaine said, "'The Lord giveth, ... and the Lord taketh away.' Wouldn't it be possible for your people to find some way—without disobedience to the commands of God—to bring yourselves into harmony of the law and the institutions of this country? We may succeed, this time, in preventing your disfranchisement; but nothing permanent can be done until you 'get into line.'"[59]

Frank informed his father of the advice he had received from Teller and Blaine. George consulted with Wilford Woodruff and informed Frank that the church president "thinks he sees some light.... You are authorized to say that something will be done." Frank then followed Blaine's advice and confidentially informed several powerful Republican senators that "the Mormon Church was about to make a concession concerning the doctrine of polygamy."[60]

After his preparation with key senators, Frank testified before the relevant committees. Friends of George in Congress praised Frank's "very fine argument," which "had a remarkable effect upon the Committee." One Democratic senator from Kentucky described Frank's

58. KLC, "'Honor of American Citizenship,'" 43; GQCJ, May 23, 1890.

59. KLC, "'Honor of American Citizenship,'" 43; Cannon and O'Higgins, *Under the Prophet in Utah*, 87.

60. KLC, "'Honor of American Citizenship,'" 43–44.

testimony as "unanswerable." The bill was defeated. As Frank later wrote, "Aided by Mr. Blaine's powerful friendship, we were saved 'for a time.'" When Frank returned to Salt Lake City, he pushed his father to ensure that the church made the concessions on polygamy that Frank had pledged would be made. George Q. assured him that concessions were already being prepared.[61]

The immigration issue addressed in Anderson's decision in December 1889 was a problem that needed to be addressed. George Q. met territorial delegate John T. Caine in New York and together they consulted with the commissioner of immigration, who had served in Congress with Caine. The inspector of immigration had just visited Utah and "been stuffed by our enemies with all the current lies" about Mormon immigrants. Cannon and Caine responded to questions, noting that the Mormons did not want them "to overlook any violation of law but to treat the people fairly and without prejudice." The immigration officials agreed that "no prejudice should prevail in the treatment of immigrants."[62]

Immigration officials were not the only ones considering restrictions on Mormon immigrants. Learning that Congress was considering a bill to curtail LDS immigration, George Q. directed Hiram Clawson and Isaac Trumbo to visit Representative William D. Owen, the Republican chair of the Committee on Immigration. Owen acknowledged that his committee was considering legislation to exclude all Latter-day Saints from coming to the U.S. Trumbo argued persuasively to the congressman that Mormons constituted a growing political bloc in the West and that there could be political ramifications if Mormon converts in other countries were not allowed to immigrate. Owen responded that these political issues could change everything. He promised to send Trumbo drafts of legislation for review. Cannon noted in his journal what an important effect political considerations had on politicians.[63]

Back in Utah, controversy was boiling around the continued existence of the Mormon-controlled People's Party. George Q. outlined

61. KLC, "'Honor of American Citizenship'"; Cannon and O'Higgins, *Under the Prophet in Utah*, 94, 113.

62. GQCJ, May 31, 1890.

63. GQCJ, June 11, 1890; Bitton, *GQC*, 306–7

options for his fellow leaders. If the Mormons all started to vote for Republicans, they faced the likely reaction that they were unreliable. If they voted straight Democratic, Republicans would be angered and would continue to push to disenfranchise all Mormons. The better approach presented by Cannon was to permit church members to vote as they chose. As the First Presidency traveled, they began to tell local church leaders that Republicans had helped block anti-Mormon legislation. This countered a natural inclination among Mormons of the time to support Democrats (because almost all anti-polygamy legislation had been sponsored by Republicans). Frank Cannon and his friend Ben E. Rich led a movement out of the People's Party into the Republican Party, which hastened the formal demise of the People's Party in June 1891.[64]

The Utah Commission began questioning some church members about whether polygamous marriages were still being performed in temples. The commission's intent appeared to be to assert that illegal activity was taking place in temples, and on that basis they could be closed.[65] Woodruff and George Q. traveled to San Francisco in early September 1890, where they met with Morris Estee. The Supreme Court had remanded certain issues from the *Late Church of Jesus Christ of Latter-day Saints* case related to the receivership and use of funds, and Cannon and Woodruff were concerned that the Utah Supreme Court was close to ruling.[66] Estee made clear that, while Mormons had made inroads into the negative public image that most Americans held of them, 65 million Americans would never accept polygamy as a marital practice. Estee told them that they needed to announce they would "lay aside" polygamy. George Q. resisted this point and explained how difficult it would be. Estee pressed, acknowledging the difficulty but making clear that it was something that "must be done sooner or later."[67]

Just as Woodruff and Cannon returned to Salt Lake City in September 1890, the Utah Commission announced that it had

64. KLC, "'Honor of American Citizenship,'" 44–45; Bitton, *GQC*, 307–10.

65. GQCJ, Sep. 1, 1890; Bitton, *GQC*, 311.

66. GQCJ, Sep. 11, 1890; Edwin Brown Firmage and Richard Collin Mangrum, *Zion in the Courts: A Legal History of the Church of Jesus Christ of Latter-day Saints, 1830–1900* (Urbana: University of Illinois Press, 1988), 258

67. GQCJ, Sep. 11–12, 1890.

found evidence that forty-five polygamous marriages had been performed in the past year. The commission had solid evidence only as to one marriage, and George wanted to deny the report. Woodruff was more incensed, viewing this as simply the latest attempt to "malign us before the country" and to prompt passage of bills pending in Congress before it adjourned.[68] Woodruff immediately dictated a "manifesto" to First Presidency secretary George Gibbs. Cannon liked the draft but thought it needed revision. They called George Reynolds, Charles Penrose, and John R. Winder to prepare it for publication. The three men revised it and brought back a new draft. George Q. made "emendations" to the new version. The First Presidency then met with several apostles, who suggested further alterations. George's journal contains Woodruff's original draft, the published version, and Cannon's "emendations." Most of the ideas in the Manifesto are Woodruff's, but most of the actual language is the product of Reynolds, Penrose, and Winder.[69]

On September 24, 1890, Woodruff issued his now-famous "declaration"—almost always referred to as the Manifesto—which amounted to the formal abandonment of plural marriage by the LDS Church. The next day, Woodruff recorded in his journal that he had arrived at a point in his life where he was "under the necessity of acting for the Temporal Salvation of the Church. The United States Government has taken a Stand & passed Laws to destroy the Latter day Saints upon the Subject of poligamy [*sic*] or Patriarchal order of Marriage. And after Praying to the Lord & feeling inspired by his spirit," he had issued the Manifesto.[70]

It was hoped that the issuance of the Manifesto would be sufficient, but on the opening day of the church's semi-annual general conference, territorial delegate John Caine sent a telegram indicating that the secretary of the interior had told the leaders that he would not accept the Manifesto "without its acceptance by the Conference as authoritative." The decision was quickly made to seek church-wide ratification of the Manifesto the next day in general conference.[71]

68. GQCJ, Sep. 22–23, 1890.
69. GQCJ, Sep. 23–24, 1890; Bitton, *GQC*, 312–13.
70. *WWJ*, Sep. 25, 1890, spelling corrected.
71. AHCJ, Oct. 5, 1890.

The *Tribune* also noticed the absence of approval the first day. It took the oversight to mean "that it was a trick intended for one meaning to Gentiles and one to the Mormons."[72] The next day, the Manifesto was presented for approval in the church's conference attendees. After Bishop Orson F. Whitney read the text of the Manifesto, Lorenzo Snow, president of the Twelve Apostles, moved that the declaration be accepted as being issued by the only person in the world who could do so, President Wilford Woodruff. Some reports suggest that the vote of those assembled in the Tabernacle, while unanimous, was not uniformly enthusiastic. B. H. Roberts, a member of the Seventy, reportedly refused to raise his hand to sustain the issuance of the Manifesto. "It seemed to me the awfulest moment in my life, my arm was like lead when the motion was put, I could not vote for it, and did not."[73] George Q. then spoke, first reading Doctrine & Covenants 124:49, which states that when a commandment is given and everyone attempts to perform it but "enemies" hinder them, the work will no longer be required. He then rehearsed everything the Saints had done to live plural marriage and the history of the anti-polygamy laws. Church members had sought to live the principle "with all their might" but had been hindered from performing the work.[74]

The Manifesto does not specifically state that it was based on a revelation from God. Not surprisingly, many critics doubted the sincerity of the declaration. On the other hand, many who had been harsh towards Mormons over polygamy assumed the sincerity of the LDS leaders and anticipated reconciliation between Saints and gentiles in Utah. Woodruff occasionally spoke candidly thereafter about the Lord showing him "by vision and revelation exactly what would take place if we did not stop this practice." What he saw in the vision was the destruction of the temples and the abatement of temple ordinances.[75]

On October 13, 1890, George Q. met with Charles Varian, US District Attorney for the Territory of Utah, who had aggressively prosecuted polygamy and unlawful cohabitation cases for several

72. "That Manifesto," *SLT*, Oct. 5, 1890, 4.

73. Ronald W. Walker, "B. H. Roberts and the Woodruff Manifesto," *BYUS* 22 (Summer 1982): 364.

74. GQC, "Remarks," *CD*, 2:129 (Oct. 6, 1890).

75. "Remarks," *DW*, Nov. 14, 1891, 658–60.

years. Cannon asked "if there could not be some understanding reached on this question of unlawful cohabitation." Cannon hoped for leniency for polygamous couples long married. Varian asked George whether there had ever been court rulings that prevented polygamous husbands from providing material support for their wives and families. Cannon had hoped for more than this, believing that husbands and fathers should be able to visit their wives and children. Varian's answer was both reasonable and telling: where would lines be drawn? If something looked like criminal activity, how could it be countenanced by the law? Nonetheless, Varian asked that the church "formulate a plan … that would embody our wishes" and to submit it for consideration.[76] It does not appear that any plan was ever submitted for approval.

George knew that ending polygamy, or, at least, prohibiting new marriages, was an important step toward ending the crisis that the Mormons faced. Knowledgeable people like Varian knew that ancillary issues, such as continued relationships between existing polygamous couples and their children, would continue to create tensions. Another important issue that rankled US leaders and many Americans was the political hegemony practiced by the Mormons.

It was widely known in the United States that Latter-day Saints voted in political unison, which many found un-American. Ironically, many non-Mormons in Utah also voted together as supporters of the Liberal Party. Some younger Mormons had become Republicans and were campaigning for dissolution of the People's and Liberal Parties and for the joining of former members of these parties into the Republican and Democratic Parties. Younger LDS leaders such as Abram Cannon (likely at his father's urging) began considering ways to ensure that Mormons joined the two national parties, if possible, on a relatively equivalent basis. As Abram wrote in his diary and told his fellow apostles, it was difficult "going on the stump so as to convince the people that a man could be a Republican and still be a Saint."[77]

George Q. had learned how to dance to many political tunes. As the possibility of statehood for Utah improved, he worried that

76. GQCJ, Oct. 13, 1890.
77. AHCJ, July 9, 1891.

Republicans would not support it if they believed that Utah would become largely Democratic. When Republican President Benjamin Harrison visited Salt Lake City in May 1891, knowledgeable locals assumed that the Ring and Liberals would get the lion's share of Harrison's attention. The Liberals had generally been associated with the Republican Party. Cannon was determined to show that Mormons were fully invested in opening the City of the Saints to Harrison. Buildings were decorated with welcoming banners and Mormons joined in celebrating Harrison's visit. The two ranking LDS Church members, Woodruff and Cannon, sat within a few feet of Harrison at the celebration in Liberty Park.[78]

Just a month later, as young Saints had been leaving the People's Party for the Republican and Democratic Parties, the decision was made to disband the People's Party. Some critics worried that this was a ruse to break up gentiles into the two national parties and dilute the power of the unified Liberal Party. It soon became clear, however, that Mormons were becoming both Democrats and Republicans. This political realignment made it more difficult for the Liberal Party to last. It also folded, in December 1893, with members leaving to become Republicans and Democrats.[79]

Shortly after Harrison's visit to Salt Lake City, the entire First Presidency traveled to San Francisco to meet again with Morris Estee, who had been helpful in advising them earlier on certain issues without remuneration. Now the presidency decided to retain him formally to lobby for the recovery of the escheated church property, prepare a bill for Utah's statehood, and provide other political services. Estee immediately mapped out a plan. George Q. felt it would be better not to advertise Estee's lobbying so that it would not harm him in his own political and business pursuits.[80]

Results of Estee's efforts were mixed. The Irrigation Congress, with participants from around the West, met in Salt Lake City. Woodruff and George Q. sat on the dais. Both were invited to speak. Cannon gave a speech about the settlement of the Salt Lake Valley and the immediate commencement of irrigation. Cannon contrasted

78. GQCJ, May 9, 1891.
79. KLC, "'Honor of American Citizenship,'" 44–45.
80. GQCJ, June 23–25, 1891.

being honored by the Irrigation Congress with being incarcerated in the territorial penitentiary three years earlier. C. C. Goodwin, editor of the *Tribune*, proposed condemning Mormon policies but ended up being the only one to vote for his own resolution. Behind the scenes, Isaac Trumbo had helped to undermine Goodwin's, and others', efforts to make the Mormons look bad.[81]

At about the same time, the still-powerful Utah Commission issued a new report alleging that the church was continuing to encourage polygamous marriages and political dominance. Charles Penrose, B. H. Roberts, and John Caine countered the allegations at October's general conference and a series of resolutions were approved denying the allegations.[82]

Church leaders had little choice other than to stop authorizing new polygamous marriages, but other important issues remained. What about long-married polygamous couples with many children and grandchildren? What were they to do? Split up, essentially (or actually) divorcing each other? Did the wives and children move to Mexico or Canada or Colorado? Did the husbands keep supporting polygamous families and only occasionally spend time with children of their plural wives? Or did the couples find ways to carefully and perhaps infrequently spend time together? George hoped that, as tensions eased and new marriages ceased, there would be more leniency for existing couples and that they could discreetly continue marriage relationships.[83] A few years later, as it became clear that some well-connected Mormons had begun to solemnize new polygamous marriages usually, though not always, outside the United States (in Mexico and Canada), there was a fresh avalanche of bad publicity and condemnation of then-president Joseph F. Smith, whose plural wives had borne fifteen children between September 24, 1890 and 1906.[84]

Perhaps because he had been subjected to intense personal scrutiny and criticism in the 1870s and '80s (and, ultimately, to almost six

---

81. GQCJ , Sep. 16, 1891; Bitton, *GQC*, 322.

82. GQCJ, Oct. 5, 1891; Stuy, *CD*, 2:269–75; Bitton, *GQC*, 321.

83. "General Conference—President George Q. Cannon," *DW*, Apr. 11, 1891, 506; Edward Leo Lyman, *Political Deliverance: The Mormon Quest for Utah Statehood* (Urbana: University of Illinois Press, 1986), 141; Bitton, *GQC*, 323.

84. KLC, "'And Now It Is the Mormons': The 'Magazine Crusade' against the Mormons, 1910–1911," *Dialogue* 46 (Spring 2013): 1–63.

months in prison), George Q. was particularly careful to live openly only with his "legal" wife, Carlie. A few years after Elizabeth, his first wife, died, George Q. had married Carlie, his last and youngest wife (who also was the daughter of George's mentor, Brigham Young). George's other four wives remained polygamous wives. Carlie was a perfect hostess and young enough to bear children (although Eliza Tenney and Martha Telle also bore children after George Q. married Carlie). He avoided too close of contact with his other wives, although he would dine in the school building on the Cannon family compound near modern-day 900 West Street and California Avenue in Salt Lake City, where all of his wives had houses, and sit with Carlie while his other wives ate at separate tables.[85] In 1889, George Q. and Carlie finished a Victorian mansion at the northern end of the lane along which all of the wives' homes were constructed.[86]

Most of George's plural wives must have felt some indignation that George passed over all of them and married Carlie as his official legal wife and built her a finer home than the others had. They must also have chafed and felt hurt by the favoritism he first showed Elizabeth and later Carlie. The most likely one to be hurt was Sarah Jane, the second wife, who might have expected her husband to marry her legally when Elizabeth died in January 1882. Long after he became bitter about the Mormon Church, Frank noted how his mother suffered in polygamy, including as a second wife.[87] George Q. seems to have maintained close personal relationships with all of his wives, conferred with each wife about their children together, and loved all of his children. All of his wives knew how close he was to Brigham Young and likely were not surprised that he and Carlie were married legally. She was the youngest wife, had the celebrity status and social graces one might expect of being Brigham Young's daughter, and had the energy to host social events and keep up with George. As

85. Bitton, *GQC*, 323.

86. See "Pioneer Stories," Sons of Utah Pioneers, suponline.org (accessed Sep. 2021). Carlie's mansion still stands on the corner of Tenth West and California Street, though its ornate Victorian roof burned in a fire in 1938. The fancy roof, the best feature of the house, was replaced with a simple low-gabled roof.

87. Frank J. Cannon, "Pulling Mormonism's Poisoned Fang, Polygamy," *New York Tribune*, Mar. 21, 1915, as quoted in Val Holley, *Frank J. Cannon, Saint, Senator, Scoundrel* (Salt Lake City: University of Utah Press, 2020), 10–11.

the legal wife through much of the 1880s and all of the 1890s, Carlie could be seen in public with George, who risked being arrested if he were caught in public with one of his polygamous wives.[88]

On February 13, 1891, federal deputies seized the "Big House" on South Temple as property owned by the church and, therefore, subject to escheatment. George was indignant; he believed he still owned the elegant Second Empire mansion where he and his family had lived before they moved to the farm. In fact, as he may have forgotten, he had transferred ownership of the Big House to the church in 1878 in satisfaction of all his debts to the church.[89]

The church worked to have property taken by the federal government returned. The US Supreme Court ordered further proceedings by the Utah territorial supreme court to address the issue of what should be done with the escheated church property pursuant to the Edmunds–Tucker Act and order of the Utah Commission.[90] In June 1891, District Attorney Varian moved for the appointment of a "master in chancery" in the "church cases." Franklin S. Richards, on behalf of the church, suggested George Sutherland, future US Supreme Court justice, while Varian submitted Judge Charles F. Loofbourow, a transplanted Iowa judge, to act in this capacity because he "was well qualified for the position, as he had never been identified with the church cases."[91] On the other hand, Loofbourow was actively involved in Liberal Party activities, including with Varian, and it did not look as though Loufbourow would have an entirely impartial view. On July 1, 1891, the territorial supreme court appointed Loofbourow as the master in chancery.[92] The *Salt Lake Times* referred to Loofbourow as "one of the brightest minds in the territorial galaxy."[93]

---

88. Bitton, *GQC*, 373–401.

89. GQC to Eliza T. Cannon, Apr. 17, 1878, as quoted and cited in Bitton, *GQC*, 392.

90. Firmage and Mangrum, *Zion in the Courts*, 258.

91. "The Master in Chancery, Under the Escheat Mandate Is to Be Judge Loofbourow," *SLT*, July 2, 1891, 5.

92. "Master in Chancery"; "The Church Case," *DW*, July 11, 1891, 85–86. Chancery or equity courts are distinguished from common law courts because, in appropriate matters, they are permitted to apply principles of "equity" (fairness) rather than law and avoid the potentially harsh results of law.

93. "The Session Ends. The Appointment of a Master Ends an Eventful Day's Doings Before the Supreme Court Justices," *Salt Lake Times*, July 2, 1891, 5.

In August, church leaders discussed among themselves and with church attorney Richards how they should respond to questions before the master in chancery. Abram Cannon expected that, in spite of proposed attempts to avoid the direct question of whether the church had really abandoned polygamy, the circumstances would require the leaders to "say something in regard to the Manifesto and our future intentions in regard to polygamy, and hence it is expected that we will prove that the latter is really abandoned." Abram wrote in his diary that "we all believe that this suspension [of polygamy] is merely temporary, and that God will open the way for his divine revelation to be established, but judging from a human standpoint plural marriage is forever stopped."[94] By early October, as hearings before the master in chancery drew near, "it was thought best for the brethren to meet alone and unite upon their testimony, and then to meet William Dickson, Franklin S. Richards and LeGrand Young to receive their suggestions in regard to the desired testimony."[95] The principal lawyers for the government were Varian and Joseph L. Rawlins, who had grown up Mormon and whose father was a prominent Mormon bishop but who had not associated with the church for many years.[96]

Beginning on October 19, 1891, Loobourow heard arguments, listened to different "schemes" proposed for use of the escheated assets and funds held by the receiver, and watched as a variety of witnesses testified. The first witness, George Q., testified mostly about the origin and uses to which the church put assets and funds before they were escheated.[97] Wilford Woodruff testified that the practice of plural marriage by the church was definitely abandoned by the Manifesto under the inspiration of God and that there was no expectation that it would be renewed so long as present conditions remained. He testified that the effect of the Manifesto was that polygamous living in violation of the law as well as new polygamous marriages were forbidden – in response to a question from

94. AHCJ, Aug. 20, 1891

95. AHCJ, Oct. 2, 1891; Oct. 12, 1891. Dickson, one of the lawyers representing the church in the escheatment cases, had successfully prosecuted hundreds of unlawful cohabitation cases in the 1880s (and was assaulted by Frank and Hugh Cannon in 1886).

96. B.H. Roberts, *CHC*, 6:225; "The Church Cases," *DW*, Oct. 24, 1891, 577.

97. "The Church Cases," *DW*, Oct. 24, 1891, 576–77.

William Dickson, now representing the church, he stated that "he intended the Manifesto to cause men who had plural wives to cease associating with them." He also asserted that the prohibition of polygamy was universal, that is, in the United States and elsewhere, in all countries of the world. Finally, he said that anyone violating the prohibition of polygamous marriages or polygamous living was subject to excommunication.[98]

The next morning, George Q. was recalled as a witness and testified that he agreed with Woodruff on all points, including that a member violating church rules regarding polygamy "would be in danger of being severed from the Church." He added, however, that God had not changed the principle of polygamy because "truth is unchangeable," but God had given permission to cease the practice. Cannon stated that he had suffered "pretty severe ordeals" for polygamy but that "unless there was some interposition of Providence, the force of public opinion, becoming intensified as the years roll by, would eventually compel us to cease its practice, or we would be crushed."[99] Joseph F. Smith, Lorenzo Snow, and Apostle Anthon H. Lund then all testified in turn that Woodruff was inspired to issue the Manifesto and that they supported the church president.[100]

The proceedings before the master of chancery regarding the escheated assets continued for months. More important, however, were the statements made under oath by the LDS Church's highest ranking officials in late October about the Manifesto and its effect of ceasing plural marriage throughout the world, prohibiting new plural marriages, outlawing cohabitation between previously married polygamous couples, and threatening those who failed to follow these rules with excommunication. Three weeks after the testimony of the leaders, Woodruff explained to his fellow church leaders in a meeting of the Quorum of Twelve Apostles that "he was placed in such a position on the witness stand that he could not answer other than he did; yet any man who deserts and neglects his wives or children because of the Manifesto, should be handled on his fellowship. Our talk resolved itself into this that men must be careful to avoid

98. "Church Cases," *DW*, Oct 24, 1891, 577–79.
99. "Church Cases," *DW*, Oct 24, 1891, 579–80.
100. "Church Cases," *DW*, Oct 24, 1891, 580–81.

exposing themselves to arrest or conviction for violation of the law, and yet they must not break their covenants with their wives."[101]

At another meeting of the Twelve in January 1892, Woodruff confided that "he did not sleep a wink after his testimony in the court before the Master of Chancery, ... and felt very much chagrined at what he had said there. Did not intend to forsake his wives and had sworn that he would not and that the Lord would not require it."[102] Thus, not only would a man not be excommunicated for continuing to support and cohabit with his plural wives, his fellowship in the church would be put in jeopardy if he were to desert or neglect his wives or children. Lorenzo Snow also felt sheepish about his testimony. Woodruff, George Q., and Snow testified as they did in order to obtain statehood for Utah.

101. AHCJ, Nov. 12, 1891. Abram Cannon quoted Woodruff in the journal entry.

102. D. Michael Quinn, "Contexts of 'The Smoot Case': Polygamy Among the Mormons, 1890–1907" (Quinn Contexts), 11, unpublished manuscript in my possession.

CHAPTER EIGHT

STATEHOOD

1892-96

"Statehood bill signed. Your people are free, and this ends our labor."
—James S. Clarkson, Isaac Trumbo, and Hiram B. Clawson, July 17, 1894

With polygamy officially suspended by Wilford Woodruff's 1890 Manifesto and the breakup of Mormon political unity with the termination of the People's Party and encouragement to church members to join the national political parties, the two major obstacles to the Latter-day Saints and their church becoming part of mainstream America were removed. Proceedings before the master of chancery required church leaders to interpret the Manifesto broadly. The public relations campaign waged by the church with the help of the railroad lobby improved the country's perceptions of Mormons. With these changes, Utah was on the verge of statehood, but additional steps were needed.

In mid-1891, George Q., Isaac Trumbo, Hiram B. Clawson, Morris Estee, and others began working secretly on a proposal for general amnesty for polygamists.[1] In October 1891, as members of the First Presidency were preparing for their testimony before the master of chancery, Estee sent George a petition he had prepared to be signed by willing gentiles in Utah proposing that Congress grant amnesty to Mormon polygamists because they were now willing to obey the law.[2] One non-Mormon who expressed his willingness to sign such a petition, and even to seek signatures from others in Utah

1. GQCJ, June 11, 1891.
2. AHCJ, Oct. 15, 1891.

and surrounding states, was C. C. Goodwin, editor of the *Salt Lake Tribune*.[3] Goodwin was perspicacious enough to realize that Utah would soon be a state controlled largely by Mormons.

On December 19, the First Presidency formally submitted a petition for amnesty to Benjamin Harrison through Utah's governor, Arthur Thomas. The petition noted that the doctrine of "polygamy, or celestial marriage" had been publicly promulgated by Brigham Young forty years earlier and was "taught and impressed upon the Latter-day Saints" until recently. "Our people are devout and sincere, and they accepted the doctrine and many personally embraced and practiced polygamy." Many "endured arrest, trial, fines and imprisonment, and the immeasurable suffering borne by the faithful, no language can describe." President Woodruff, through revelation received after he cried to God "in anguish and prayer," "received the permission to advise the members of the" church "that the law commanding polygamy was henceforth suspended." The Manifesto was then accepted by thousands of church members "as the future rule of their lives" and they had since followed this rule. Now, "to be at peace with the government and in harmony with their fellow citizens who are not of their faith," the Saints "have voluntarily put aside … a sacred principle." Based on this, the church leaders asked for amnesty for the Saints and pledged "our faith and honor for their future."[4]

In March 1892, George travelled to Washington, DC, with Trumbo and Clawson to complete negotiations for amnesty. Because Cannon believed that amnesty was likely, he spent most of his time seeking forgiveness of $20,000 in bail bonds that were forfeited when he failed to appear for trial on March 17, 1886. When George Q. was first arraigned on February 17, 1886, Judge Zane ordered $25,000 bail for him to be released, partly based on William Dickson's allegation that Cannon had tried to bribe an officer in Winnemucca.[5] Commissioner E. B. Critchlow had then ordered bail of $10,000 on each of two earlier unlawful cohabitation charges which were still pending against Cannon, making the total bonds necessary to be posted

3. GQCJ, Oct. 27, 1891.

4. GQCJ, Dec. 19, 1891.

5. "The Great Prisoner, Brought to the City under Military Guard, Bailed out in the Sum of $45,000," *DN*, Feb. 17, 1886, 3.

$45,000. This was provided by four sureties. Some $25,000 (of the $45,000) were collected from John Sharp and Feramorz Little when the bond was ordered forfeited, and Sharp and Little were reimbursed from John Taylor's dedicated trust of Bullion Beck stock. Cannon's lawyers contested the obligation to pay the remaining $20,000 under the circumstances of the case, and their dispute eventually made it to the US Supreme Court in 1889. The court postponed addressing the issue several times as the Manifesto was issued and proceedings over the escheated property progressed.[6]

Cannon noted in his journal that he had never worked harder to seek forgiveness of the $20,000 because he would otherwise have to pay the amount plus interest and costs (totaling over $30,000). Cannon could not afford to pay these amounts because he was deeply in debt on guarantees and business loans. It was unclear whether the Department of the Treasury or the Justice Department had the authority to remit the bonds, and the issue was complicated because forfeiture of the bonds was the subject of a pending Supreme Court appeal. Cannon shuttled back and forth between the two departments for five or six days and was finally able to receive forgiveness of the $20,000.[7]

The forfeited bonds had one last political ramification. In October 1892, a spirited campaign for territorial delegate to Congress was being waged by George's son Frank, who was running as a Republican, and Democrat Joseph L. Rawlins, who had been one of George's lawyers in 1886. Rawlins told a political rally in Provo that "it is said that for this sum [the $20,000] Mr. [George Q.] Cannon bargained away the votes of the Mormon people"—that is, that he had promised Republican votes from Mormons in exchange for forgiveness of the bonds. Rawlins recalled that, when George Q. had been brought in from the train to be arraigned, he (Rawlins) had been called to the "courtroom one morning to aid 'the illustrious apostle, lying on his back, his face covered with gore.'"[8] Offended

6. GQCJ, Mar. 21, 1892.

7. GQCJ, Jan. 15, 1892; Mar. 22–Apr. 2, 1892. In January, in an act showing the easing of tensions, three members of the Utah Commission helped Cannon seek forgiveness of the bonds.

8. "General Items," *SLT*, Nov. 3, 1892, 4. The Republican *Tribune*, which supported Frank, noted: "It is rather scurvy for an attorney to make a jibe of the woe of his client,

by what Rawlins was reported to have said, George sent him a letter asking if he had actually made those comments and, if not, to give Cannon his version of what he actually said.[9]

George Q. had had to negotiate forgiveness of the bonds quickly in Washington, DC, because he needed to be present for the church's general conference beginning on April 6, 1892, when the capstone of the Salt Lake Temple would be laid.[10] Acting as a high profile spiritual leader of his church was the central focus of George's life. He had an unwavering devotion to the LDS Church and spent more of his time studying his religion, attending meetings large and small, preparing talks, and defending it in spoken and written word, than anything else. George saw his political, business, and professional activities as adjuncts to his service as First Counselor in the First Presidency. The completion of the Salt Lake Temple was something that he had looked forward to since its construction was announced in 1853, when he was a missionary in the Sandwich Islands.

Members of the church had looked forward to the completion the Salt Lake Temple for four decades and, though the St. George, Logan, and Manti temples had been operating for some years, the Endowment House, which was located on Temple Square and in which certain ordinances for living church members were solemnized, had been demolished in November 1889 as a gesture of good will on the polygamy issue. George and most of the Mormons along the Wasatch Front awaited anxiously completion of the Salt Lake Temple.[11] Construction of the temple was announced on April 6, 1853, exactly forty years before the planned dedication of the temple on April 6, 1893. The laying of the capstone on April 6, 1892, signaled completion was one year away. The national financial Panic of 1893 complicated completion because it made donations difficult. Through dedication, hard work, engineering acumen, and pleas for donations from Woodruff, George, and other church leaders, church members had labored together to raise their defining edifice. The

---

and Mr. Rawlins must have been driven to desperation or he wouldn't have at this date made his client's sorry plight the jest of a jeering political assemblage."

9. Copy of letter from GQC to Joseph L. Rawlins, dated Nov. 3, 1892, in GQCJ, Nov. 3. 1892.

10. GQCJ, Mar. 22–Apr. 2, 1892

11. *JH*, Apr. 6, 1892; GQCJ, Apr. 3–6, 1892.

exterior of the stately building was largely completed, and pioneer photographers were already taking the best nineteenth-century bird's eye view images of Salt Lake City from the wooden scaffolding surrounding all of the six towers of the temple. While the exterior was in good shape, much was left to be done inside. George had spearheaded financing to further the arts education in 1890–91 of John Hafen, Lorus Pratt, Edwin Evans, and Herman Haag at the Academie Julien in Paris. These "art missionaries," together with Danquart Weggeland, were called to complete the wall murals in ordinance rooms in the temple with skills they had honed in Paris.[12] Most of the interior rooms in the temple were finished for the dedication, but George and the artists decided to take a relatively "leisurely" approach to completing the decoration of the ordinance rooms to make sure they were done right and "in such a way that it would give us pleasure in years to come, and if it was necessary to dedicate the Temple without it that we could do so, and leave this to be done afterwards."[13]

Politics were changing rapidly in Utah after the dissolution in May 1891 of the People's Party, which was made up almost entirely of Mormons and typically voted as a bloc. The closest gentile analogue was the Liberal Party. Liberals generally were also involved in the national Republican Party. In the summer of 1892, factions of the Liberal Republicans and new Republicans, represented by Frank Cannon and other former People's Party members as well as many non-Mormons who did not like the Liberal Party, sought credentials at the national convention in Minneapolis. George and Estee, the prominent California Republican lawyer on retainer to the church, plotted to have the national party recognize the non-Liberal delegation. The national party initially recognized the new Republicans, with Frank Cannon and O. J. Salisbury, a prominent non-Mormon businessman, as the two delegates to the convention. This led the Liberals to complain loudly and bitterly, and, ultimately, a compromise

12. GQCJ, June 20, 1890, Apr. 12, 21, Aug. 5, Oct. 20, Dec. 2, 13, 1892, Jan. 12, 1893. Martha Elizabeth Bradley and Lowell M. Durham Jr., "John Hafen and the Art Missionaries," *JMH* 12 (1985): 91–105.

13. GQCJ, Aug. 5, 1892.

was reached between the Liberal Republicans and the new group of Republicans, and both delegations were seated at the convention.[14]

Frank, George's mercurial second son, was urged by Weber County Republicans to seek nomination to run for territorial delegate in 1892. Frank and half-brother Abram, a member of the Quorum of Twelve Apostles, approached the First Presidency for advice about Frank seeking the nomination. Both Woodruff and Joseph F. Smith supported him in running. Woodruff asked George his view. "Personally, ... I did not want Frank to run. I would rather he was not put forward that way," George responded, likely worried about Frank's checkered past becoming an issue in the race and also concerned that people would assume he was behind Frank's candidacy.[15]

Frank was nominated by the Republicans' territorial convention on September 17, 1892, narrowly defeating George Sutherland, future congressman, US senator, and US Supreme Court justice.[16] George was concerned that people would see Frank as the "nominee of the Church party" and that George would be accused of using his influence to have Frank nominated. George was chagrined but relieved that most opposing Frank were leading Mormons, while it appeared "that there were more Gentiles [who] voted for him than Latter-day saints."[17] The Democrats nominated Joseph L. Rawlins, an impressive young attorney and lapsed Mormon who a few weeks later raised George Q.'s ire during the campaign.. The Liberals nominated their final territory-wide candidate, C. E. Allen.[18]

A few days after Frank was nominated, George Q. received a telegram from Isaac Trumbo that had critical implications for Utah's statehood. Trumbo asked Cannon and Hiram B. Clawson to come to the old Plaza Hotel in New York City to meet with Thomas H. Carter, chair of the National Republican Committee, and James

---

14. GQCJ, May 26, 1892; Val Holley, *Frank J. Cannon: Saint, Senator, Scoundrel* (Salt Lake City: University of Utah Press, 2020), 122–26.

15. GQCJ, Sep. 13, 1892. Frank was not a church authority and would have had no obligation to seek approval as senior church leaders may have had. The brothers were simply asking for advice.

16. Holley, *Frank J. Cannon*, 128.

17. GQCJ, Sep. 16, 1892.

18. "The Cause at Logan, Further Particulars of the Great Ovation," *SLH*, Oct. 16, 1892, 3; "Liberals Choose a Candidate, C. E. Allen Will Work Hard for Congress," *Ogden Standard*, Oct. 13, 1892, 1.

S. Clarkson, chair of the party's executive committee. Trumbo also asked that they "have Judge Zane send me telegram showing that the Utah [Commission] report on Polygamy is false, that [there has been] no case of polygamy since the issuance of the Manifesto by the Mormon Church." George met immediately with Woodruff and Smith, and Cannon and Clawson left by the first train at 8:00 a.m. the next morning.[19]

Cannon "spoke very freely" with the Republican leaders about "the situation in Utah." Eventually, he needed to speak confidentially with them and had Trumbo and Clawson leave the room. He told them that he had been approached in Salt Lake City by one "who stood high in Democratic counsels"—this was George L. Miller, a wealthy, prominent newspaper owner and entrepreneur in Omaha. Miller had asked Cannon to help the Democrats secure the Mormon vote in various intermountain states to ensure Grover Cleveland's election in 1892 because of the "dreadful consequences that would follow Republican success" and the benefit to the Mormons and Utah's statehood desires if the Democrats were elected. He said that he was telling them this to show how much the Democrats were willing to promise for the support of the Mormons. George had responded to Miller that he was willing to help however he could in an honorable way if it was for "the liberty of Utah." Cannon related that he had also told Miller that the LDS Church believed it was "important to our interest that there should be a Republican party in Utah" to which Miller said, "But subordinate, of course, to the Democratic party." Cannon replied that it would depend on how the people were helped.

George Q. told Carter and Clarkson that the church had been "loyal in our work to the Republican party" by seeking to "restrain the spread of Democracy among our people and to give the Republicans every chance to ... advocate their doctrines." Cannon felt directed by

19. Telegram, Isaac Trumbo to GQC, Sep. 23, 1892, copied in GQCJ, Sep. 23, 1892; "What Became the First, Short-Lived, Plaza Hotel," Ephemeral New York, ephemeralnewyork.wordpress.com, accessed Sep. 2021. The Utah Commission believed it had found evidence of new plural marriages. See chap. 7. Cannon noted in his journal that this trip would prevent him from conducting the marriage of his daughter Amelia to William H. Chamberlin, which was disappointing to him, his daughter, and the family. GQCJ, Sep. 23, 1892.

"the Spirit of the Lord" in the discussion. The next day, Cannon impressed on Carter and Clarkson "the importance of doing what they could for our people" because the Mormons would stand with them, unlike Republicans such as *Salt Lake Tribune* co-owner Patrick H. Lannan "and men of his character" who accomplish their "nefarious plans" by obtaining aid from the national Republicans.

Before Cannon and Clawson left for home for October 1892's general conference, an agreement was struck. The First Presidency would work to ensure that Republicans would be able to compete with Democrats on a level field and that Mormons and Republican leaders would pressure Benjamin Harrison to keep his promise to grant amnesty to Mormon polygamists and to appoint a federal marshal and other federal officials in Utah who would treat the Saints fairly.[20] James Clarkson, a powerful national Republican leader, had an important impact on Utah's becoming a state, and this significant meeting between him and George Q. was a key part of the role he played.

The election for territorial delegate in 1892 turned out to be a dirty affair. Democrats and Frank Cannon detractors were outraged when Joseph F. Smith, an ardent Republican, and Frank's friend Ben E. Rich, who chaired the territorial Republican party, published a pamphlet called *Nuggets of Truth*, featuring a front cover portrait of church founder Joseph Smith and a back cover photograph of Frank Cannon. Smith had also obtained and made public a certificate from Frank's bishop that he was "in good standing" with the church, apparently in response to rumors of Frank's drinking and frequenting prostitutes and the church discipline court held in Logan against him in 1882. Not surprisingly, Democrats were quick to point out Frank's shortcomings. One who was particularly critical of Frank was William Seegmiller, the stake president in Sevier County, the speaker of the house of the territorial legislature, and perhaps central Utah's most prominent citizen. When Seegmiller began making pejorative comments about Frank, George wrote to Seegmiller asking him to identify his sources for alleging that Frank "is a common seducer, an immoral man, a bad egg, a man unworthy

20. GQCJ, Sep. 28–30, Oct. 1, 1892.

of association with respectable people; he has seduced the wives of three missionaries while they were absent."[21] Seegmiller declined to "communicate the names of informers" "at present," though they would step forward for a church investigation into Frank's actions at an appropriate time. He responded that it would be a "calamity" if Frank were elected and promised to "do all that I can consistently to prevent his election."[22]

Although he was painfully familiar with Frank's transgressions, George considered withdrawing church fellowship from Seegmiller for his spreading rumors about Frank and for refusing to tell George the sources of those rumors.[23] Seegmiller had committed a major mistake—he had spoken critically of one of George's children.[24]

Seegmiller noted in a postscript to his letter how saddened he was at the news of David H. Cannon's death while serving as a missionary in Silesia and extended his deep sympathies.[25] David was a younger son of Elizabeth and may have been George Q.'s favorite child. George was upset about David's death on October 17, 1892, and his strong reaction to Seegmiller's allegations against Frank may have been exacerbated by the tragic news.[26]

Frank Cannon was defeated in the final election in November 1892 in a plurality vote. Democrat Grover Cleveland was elected to a non-consecutive term as US president, Democrats took narrow control of the Senate and maintained their large majority in the House.[27] It remained to be seen whether Utah would attain statehood with Democrats back in control just after an important alliance had been struck between Republican leaders and the church's First Presidency.

While Frank was losing the territorial delegate election of 1892, his father and two of his brothers negotiated the lease of the *Deseret News*. George Q., several of his sons, and his nephew, George Cannon Lambert, had operated the largest publishing house in Utah,

21. Letter, GQC to William Seegmiller, Oct. 17, 1892, copy included in GQCJ, Oct. 26, 1892.

22. Letter, William Seegmiller to GQC, Oct. 22, 1892, copy in GQCJ, Oct. 26, 1892.

23. AHCJ, Oct. 25, 1892.

24. AHCJ, Oct. 25, 1892; Holley, *Frank J. Cannon*, 131; GQCJ, Oct. 26, 1892, Apr. 5, 1893.

25. Seegmiller to GQC, Oct. 22, 1892;

26. GQCJ, Oct. 12, 17, 1892.

27. See www.senate.gov/history/partydiv.htm, 53rd Congress.

generally known as the Juvenile Instructor Office, for decades.[28] John Q. had been a reporter for the *News*. Now the Cannons took over editorial and operational control of the newspaper. John, who had been living in Ogden and sometimes working with his brother Frank since his own excommunication over his affair with Louie Wells, returned to Salt Lake City to be editor while Abram became the business manager. George noted in his journal that "the brethren ... seemed to think it absolutely necessary that something of this kind be done in order that there may be a change. The business has fallen into a rut ... and it is thought that this will do so."[29] This did not meet with universal approval. Heber J. Grant later stated in a meeting of the Quorum of the Twelve that "it was an outrage ... that the Church's official paper should be edited by John Q. Cannon."[30]

In January 1893, President Benjamin Harrison finally issued the long-hoped-for amnesty for Mormon polygamists. George believed that Harrison's "timidity" came from a concern that the strict Presbyterian would "shock the country by issuing a pardon for such offenses as unlawful cohabitation, adultery, and polygamy—terms which our enemies have used to make our conduct as odious as possible."[31] It was no surprise that Harrison waited until after he lost his bid for reelection. The amnesty issued by Harrison required polygamists to follow the law going forward, which meant not only that no new marriages could be solemnized but that long-married polygamous couples could no longer cohabit. The amnesty only covered those who followed the law from the time of the Manifesto in 1890 on. Joseph F. Smith, after he became church president in 1901, was famously convicted in 1906 of unlawful cohabitation under the Edmunds–Tucker Act.[32]

George Q. and many other senior church leaders had serious qualms about ending polygamy, not only in regards to continuing

28. Craig S. Smith, "Utah Book Publishing in the 1880s: The Juvenile Instructor Office and the Cannons," unpublished paper in my possession.

29. GQCJ, Sep. 12, Oct. 14, 1892; AHCJ, Sep. 8–9, Oct. 1, 1892.

30. HJGJ, Jan. 4, 1898.

31. GQCJ, Mar. 22–Apr. 2, 1892. Estee was particularly "dissatisfied" with Harrison, who had promised to issue the amnesty many times and Estee even offered to write it for him. GQCJ, May 26, 1892.

32. "Joseph F. Smith Pleaded Guilty before Judge Ritchie," *Salt Lake Tribune*, Nov. 24, 1906, 1.

marital relations between polygamous couples but to banning new plural marriages. Cannon once characterized himself as an "ultra" on the issue of plural marriage—meaning that he absolutely believed in it and was loath to see it end.[33] There was a fair amount of confusion among lay church members about the end of polygamy. Most polygamous couples continued to cohabit, and some new plural marriages continued to be performed, mostly in Mexico. An apostle was generally resident in the Mexican colonies, and either he or the local Mexican stake president performed the approved marriages. On the other hand, in 1890 and 1891, both George and Woodruff were sufficiently worried that information about new marriages would leak that they refused to approve certain requested marriages, even if performed in Mexico.[34] In April 1891, Woodruff told the First Presidency and Quorum of the Twelve that "the principle of plural marriage will yet be restored to this Church, but how or when I cannot say."[35] In August 1892, a polygamous marriage was performed in a Mormon village in Canada, with authorization by Woodruff. In the same month, a couple was married polygamously in Mexico following a procedure created by George. The couple received a discreetly written "note of recognition" signed by George Q. or Smith in the First Presidency's office and a similar "letter of authorization" regarding the same man signed by a First Presidency member was separately mailed to the marriage officiator. Only after this double authorization was received by the officiator would the illegal but secretly sanctioned ceremony be performed.[36]

During this period, George even suggested at a meeting of the First Presidency and Twelve the possibility of utilizing the Old Testament practice of concubinage. If a Mormon man could not

33. "Prest. Geo. Q. Cannon," *SLH*, Feb. 23, 1890, clipping *St. Louis Globe-Democrat* article dated Feb. 9, 1890.

34. D. Michael Quinn, "LDS Officials Involved with New Plural Marriages from September 1890 to February 1907" (Quinn Appendix), in Michael Harold Paulos and Konden Smith Hansen, eds., *The Reed Smoot Hearings: The Investigation of a Mormon Senator* and *the Transformation of an American Religion* (Logan: Utah State University, 2021), 248–50.

35. AHCJ, Apr. 2, 1891.

36. Quinn Appendix, 250; D. Michael Quinn, "Contexts of 'The Smoot Case': Polygamy Among the Mormons, 1890–1907" (Quinn Contexts), 12, unpublished manuscript in my possession.

marry polygamously, perhaps he could be given permission to take a concubine (i.e., a common-law "wife" in the eyes of the church), covenant to strictly "observe the law of marriage," raise children with her, and be sealed to her after one of them died. In the meantime, they would not marry and thus not violate federal law against polygamy. Woodruff and Lorenzo Snow both supported the suggestion. However, the problems in such a plan must have become apparent as there is no evidence of Mormon men actually "taking" concubines.[37]

Writing in 1911, Smith told Utah Senator and Apostle Reed Smoot to inform President Theodore Roosevelt that

> President [George Q.] Cannon was the first to conceive the idea that we could consistently countenance polygamy beyond confines of the Republic where we have no chartered law against it, and consequently he authorized the solemnization of polygamy in Mexico and Canada after the manifesto of 1890, and the men occupying presiding positions who became polygamists since the manifesto did it in good faith.[38]

In December 1897, the First Presidency and Quorum of the Twelve made clear that marriage sealings could be solemnized outside a temple by reiterating "that the sealing of a couple outside of a temple as husband and wife for time and eternity[,] by one holding the requisite authority [the President of the church, or any one deputed by him] is as valid as when performed in the House of the Lord, even when either or both of the parties have not been previously endowed."[39]

In early 1893, George traveled once again to Washington to lobby for the repayment by the US government of the "other" $25,000 in bail bonds which had been forfeited to the government in 1886. After intense lobbying and obtaining the support of Charles Foster, the secretary of treasury, for the federal government to repay the $25,000, Senator William Morris Stewart of Nevada introduced a bill to refund Cannon, and on March 4, 1893, Congress approved

37. GQCJ, Apr. 7, 1894; B. Carmon Hardy, *Solemn Covenant: The Mormon Polygamous Passage* (Urbana: University of Illinois Press, 1992), 214–15.

38. JFS to Reed Smoot, Apr. 1, 1911, telegram, as quoted in Victor W. Jorgensen and B. Carmon Hardy, "The Taylor Cowley Affair and the Watershed of Mormon History," *UHQ* 48 (Winter 1980): 36.

39. Quoted in Quinn Contexts, 4.

repayment in an appropriation bill.[40] Thus the entire $45,000 bond was forgiven or repaid.

While George was in Washington, he had a "satisfactory" meeting on March 11 with Grover Cleveland, who was back in the White House after a four-year hiatus. Cannon told Cleveland that the Mormons had "every disposition … to conform to the law" but that it was difficult for men and women who had been married "for time and all eternity" to be apart—"a man could not visit a plural wife without exposing himself to a charge of unlawful cohabitation … men had been sent to prison merely for visiting the houses of their families." George was looking to the president to give some indication that the government would go easy on polygamists. "Fair-minded, judicious men" needed to be appointed to federal positions in Utah. Cleveland asked about Judge Zane, and Cannon responded that Zane had "been exceedingly harsh and severe" before but that he had accepted the Manifesto as "sincere and had changed his attitude entirely." Now, he was "very much respected by the Saints." Cleveland said that that had always been his view of Zane and was pleased that he was reconciled with the Saints.[41]

An economic downturn in agriculture had begun in Utah in 1887. The LDS Church faced significant financial hardship from this decline because many of its properties were agricultural. The loss of these and other properties to the federal government under the Edmunds–Tucker Act aggravated the problem. Church members paid less in tithing because they worried that the government would confiscate the funds. With the escheatment of this property to the government, the church and its businesses borrowed heavily to maintain operations, increasing expenditures even further. The Utah Sugar Company was created during this period to cultivate and process sugar beets. The church recognized the unusual opportunity the development of a sugar beet industry constituted.[42]

---

40. "Forfeiture of Cannon's Bond, the Documents Produced in the Case, and Reasons for Refunding," *Ogden Standard*, Feb. 14, 1893, 4; "Cannon's Bail Bond, Senator Stewart Introduces a Bill to Refund the Amount to Geo. Q.," *SLH*, Feb. 14, 1893, 1; "Cannon's Forfeited Bond," *SLH*, Mar. 4, 1893, 1; "President Cannon's Bond," *DN*, Mar. 6, 1893, 4.

41. GQCJ, Mar. 11, 1893.

42. Matthew C. Godfrey, *Religion, Politics, and Sugar: The Mormon Church, the Federal Government, and the Utah-Idaho Sugar Company, 1907–1921* (Logan: Utah State University Press, 2007), 19–41.

These financial problems were exacerbated by the Panic of 1893, which was a broader economic depression that affected every sector of the national economy and created political upheaval. Mormon leaders sought recovery of its property whose value had been reduced not only by the recession but also by mismanagement and neglect of the federal receiver. At the same time, the church was rushing to complete the Salt Lake Temple by April 6, 1893, which resulted in the greater expenditure of scarce resources. Only through sacrifice (and the incurrence of $1 million in debt) was the temple sufficiently completed for its April 6, 1893, dedication.[43]

For George Q., temple work had been central to his life since his first experience in Nauvoo, even though through most of his life there was no temple in which to perform the saving ordinances. George brought forty-five of his immediate family members to the dedication of the Salt Lake Temple where they joined thousands of others on Temple Square to celebrate the completion of this edifice to LDS spirituality and worship.[44]

As the Panic of 1893 deepened and the church had not yet not received back its escheated property, church leaders looked for financial sources to help them navigate economic privation. Apostle Heber J. Grant, a successful businessman, went east to raise funds for the church. He secured a loan for $100,000 but failed to find any more funding. Grant encouraged Cannon to visit England to see if he could find lenders there willing to loan money to the church. George's personal financial condition was precarious, and he probably hoped he could find a lender who might make a personal loan to him as well.[45]

George Q. took Carlie and his fifteen-year-old son Sylvester (Elizabeth's son) across the Atlantic, landing in Liverpool on June 27, 1893. They spent a day visiting the mission office at 42 Islington, where George and Elizabeth had lived thirty years earlier, and touring different neighborhoods in the city where George was born. They then traveled to London and met with John W. Young,

43. Leonard J. Arrington, *Great Basin Kingdom: An Economic History of the Latter-day Saints, 1830–1900* (Cambridge, MA: Harvard University Press, 1958), 389–401.

44. GQCJ, Apr. 6, 1893.

45. Ronald W. Walker, "Crisis in Zion: Heber J. Grant and the Panic of 1893," *Sunstone* 5 (Jan.–Feb. 1980), 26–34; GQCJ, June 17, 1893; Bitton, *GQC*, 339–40.

who had recently moved there from New York City. When they arrived, George received a dispatch from home that stated, "Situation desperate, growing worse. Help absolutely necessary; can John W. Young cable 50,000 immediately?" That night, they went to the performance of the play *Niobe.* In the next days they visited Covent Garden, the National Gallery, an amusement park with a treacherous ride called the "Toboggan Slide," Westminster Abbey, Madame Tussaud's, the Tower of London, and other places of interest.[46] Even in dreary times, George found time to enjoy cultural events and experiences with his family.[47]

George had a cordial meeting with Lord Rosebery, the Prime Minister of the United Kingdom. Cannon had gotten to know him as Archibald Primrose, who was already the Earl of Rosebery, when he visited Utah in 1873 at age twenty-six, inquisitive about the culture and history of the Mormons. Shortly after, Cannon and Primrose had also spent time together in Washington, where George Q. was serving in Congress. Lord Rosebery had married Hannah de Rothschild, the only child of Mayer de Rothschild (who had died years earlier, making Hannah one of the wealthiest women in England). George hoped to speak to the Rothschilds about loans for the church and himself.

As they talked, George was disappointed to realize that Lord Rosebery "did not display the interest which he formerly had in us and our affairs." In response to the possibility of the LDS Church receiving a loan, the prime minister told George that he had "but little to do with financial affairs," but did give George a "kind letter" of introduction to his wife's cousin, Baron de Rothschild. Shortly thereafter, Baron Rothschild and two of his brothers met with Cannon. The Rothschilds knew nothing of Utah or the Mormons and made clear that they could not offer a loan to the LDS Church. They did, however give Cannon a positive letter of introduction to a merchant banking firm, Panmure Gordon. After an extensive interview with Henry Panmure Gordon, "it became clear to me that as affairs are in this city it is useless for us to try and get money here

46. Telegram to GQC, quoted in GQCJ, June 29, 1893; GQCJ, June 30, July 1, 3, 7, 1893.

47. GQCJ, June 29–30, July 1, 3, 1893

with which to release ourselves." The church had neither the credit nor the collateral to attract a loan. George spent a sleepless night realizing he had failed to raise any money for the church.[48]

George Q., always a royals watcher, saw the Duke of York, later King George V, his new wife, Princess Mary of Teck, and watched Queen Victoria and Edward, Prince of Wales, in "the famous Gold coach drawn by eight cream colored Hanoverian horses." He and Carlie and John W. Young (who was Carlie's half-brother) had obtained seats along the procession route from Westminster Abbey to St. James Palace. To top things off, George spent a day in the Isle of Man, though he did not record meeting any relatives or remembering boyhood sounds and smells of the island as he had in 1861.[49]

George Q. was deeply committed to family. He loved all of his wives and found ways to maintain good relationships with them. He adored his children and grandchildren and spent as much time with them as his busy schedule permitted, sometimes taking one or more on trips. He was close to his brothers and sisters and extended family members. He was candid and when someone criticized any member of his family, he would respond directly and usually defensively. He was charming enough to soften his bluntness, but he confronted difficult matters head-on. He has surviving correspondence with most of his wives, and was cordial and affectionate in tone in all of his letters. His letters are full of useful information and helpful questions. He was not perfect and favored Elizabeth and her children and Carlie over his other wives and children. Somehow, the households got along quite well and the children of all the wives retained lasting pleasant memories of living together on the farm.

George continued to fret about serious financial concerns when he returned home in November 1893, but soon he went to California and met with James S. Clarkson (national Republican secretary) and Isaac Trumbo. They discussed funding the nascent sugar industry in Utah and a potential new project, building a railroad line from Salt Lake to Los Angeles. Morris Estee prepared an agreement under which Clarkson and Trumbo would raise the necessary funding,

48. GQCJ, July 3, 4, 9, 1893. Panmure Gordon continues as a prominent London merchant bank in the twenty-first century.

49. GQCJ, July 6, 10, 1893.

provide rails, and be principals, but the church would control the road. Some church leaders, including Heber Grant, worried that Collis P. Huntington, a competing railroad magnate, would be angered by the church's entry into railroad development and might oppose Utah statehood. Cannon believed that large projects would employ many church members and improve the economy and should not affect statehood.[50] Consistent with his actions he included a pitch in his October 1893 conference address for the success of sugar beet crops and sugar production in Utah.[51]

On January 10, 1894, after a tortured process involving many judicial decisions, the First Presidency collected from the federal receiver a payment of $438,174.39 in cash, all still surviving furniture owned by the church which had been confiscated, and 4,732 shares of Deseret Telegraph Company. Historian Leonard Arrington believed that the receivers and courts had liquidated much of the property escheated to the government at bargain sale prices or worse in an attempt to "get the church out of business."[52] The much needed funds ran out quickly because, as Cannon noted, "our debts are much greater than we can meet."[53] The church would not receive back the real property escheated to the government until June 1896. LDS leaders would have to find alternative ways for the church to pay its debts than relying on the funds paid by the receiver.[54]

The matter of approval of Utah's statehood was moving forward in Washington, DC. Democratic delegate Joseph L. Rawlins filed a statehood bill. Rawlins worked hard with Democrats to ensure their support, and his predecessor, John T. Caine, came to Washington to help. Trumbo, James Clarkson, Estee, and Alex Badlam all worked behind the scenes to convince Republican lawmakers to approve statehood. Through intense lobbying and a series of political twists and turns, the enabling act for Utah statehood was passed by the House of Representatives in December 1893 with only a handful of nay votes and by the Senate in July 1894 with broad bipartisan support. Grover Cleveland signed Utah's enabling act on July 17, 1894.

50. GQCJ, Nov. 29, 1893; Bitton, *GQC*, 345–46;.

51. GQC, Discourse, *CD*, 3:358–59, Oct. 6, 1893.

52. Arrington, *Great Basin Kingdom*, 378.

53. GQCJ, Jan. 13, 15–16, 1894.

54. Arrington, *Great Basin Kingdom*, 378.

The enabling act provided that US senators would not be elected from Utah until 1896, largely to facilitate both parties having a chance to elect officials from their party.[55] George worked closely (though confidentially) with Republican lobbyists and politicians, but was fully aware of work on the Democratic side that moved Congress from enacting unusually harsh laws against polygamy and Mormons to bringing Utah into the union. The principal reason for the broad support among Republicans and Democrats was that most understood that the LDS Church would soon be a major political force not only in Utah but throughout the Intermountain West.[56] Some of those not from Utah who had been most instrumental in helping Utah expected that their efforts would be rewarded by election to high political office or creation of important business connections. Particularly on the Republican side, certain individuals had been especially instrumental. Trumbo, for example, expected to be elected as one of Utah's first US senators, moved to Salt Lake City, and rented the Gardo House as his home from which to campaign. Most Utahns, Mormon and non-Mormon alike, in the end supported Utah statehood and elected Utahns to Congress.[57]

At the same time he was working for statehood, George supported the development of a hydroelectric project on the Ogden River by a company called the Pioneer Electric Company, and soon the First Presidency also indicated its support. The largest project contemplated by Cannon and the church was construction of several railroad lines, including one from Salt Lake City to Coalville (where George obtained a lease on one coal mine and options on others) to have access to coal, which was thought necessary to build a railroad westward to Los Angeles. In January 1894, George Q. once again headed east looking for capital to finance the ventures.[58]

In New York City, he met financier George Purbeck, who had

55. "Utah's Day Is Dawning," *SLH*, Dec. 14, 1893, 1; "For Utah," *SLT*, July 11, 1894, 1; "Utah to Become a State," *NYT*, July 18, 1894, 9; "Why Statehood Is Delayed," *Ogden Standard*, July 13, 1894, 2.

56. Edward Leo Lyman, *Finally Statehood! Utah's Struggles, 1849–1896* (Salt Lake City: Signature Books, 2019), 320–21.

57. Edward Leo Lyman has written the most cogent and complete descriptions and analysis of Utah statehood in a series of articles and books. See generally Lyman, *Finally Statehood!* and *Political Deliverance*.

58. GQCJ, Jan. 16, 1894; Bitton, *GQC*, 346–48.

already discussed the ambitious plans with Frank Cannon. Purbeck indicated he could sell the $300,000 in bonds already authorized for a Utah-to-California railroad, the Coalville line, and the Pioneer Electric hydroelectric plans for 15 percent interest. This ruffled Republican lobbyists Trumbo and Clarkson, who thought they would raise the capital and manage some or all of these projects. The problem was that Trumbo and Clarkson had not been able to show any capital commitments that did not require cash already in hand. In discussions in Salt Lake City between Clarkson and Trumbo on the one hand and Cannon and other senior church leaders on the other, it came to light that Clarkson and Trumbo had been promising participation in future profits to help persuade investors and politicians to support the Mormons. If Cannon and other leaders had failed to disclose negotiations with people like George Purbeck, Clarkson and Trumbo had been similarly quiet about using promises of future returns to further interests. The business issues were interrelated with the statehood efforts in which Clarkson and Trumbo had been engaged.[59]

George challenged the claims of Trumbo and Clarkson that they were entitled to raise the funds and participate as managers in the planned large projects. To Cannon, no one had been more appreciative of the work that Trumbo and Clarkson had undertaken to bring Utah into the Union, but he did not believe they were entitled to all the spoils of potential financial success that the church might enjoy with the new projects. Cannon's reaction was that the promises that Trumbo and Clarkson had been making gave him a sense of "oppression still greater than I have been suffering from." How could the Mormons involved in the transactions "ever repay these mortgages which are now upon us—obligations that are indefinite and so extensive that they cover the life of man." George Q. had his son Frank write a response to Clarkson "and his associates" which Clarkson subsequently called "one of the most cruel letters that he had ever received."[60]

The November 1894 territorial delegate election was critically important because it would give the winner the upper hand in seeking

59. GQCJ, Aug. 1, Sep. 11, 17–18, 24, 1894, and letters copied therein; Bitton, *GQC*, 348–51.

60. GQCJ, Aug. 1, Sep. 11, 17–18, 24, 1894.

election to the US Senate in 1896 once Utah became a state. Joseph Rawlins ran for reelection on the Democratic ticket and Frank Cannon once again was nominated by the Republicans, though with less controversy than in 1892. Frank won the final election by a margin of about 1,500 votes.[61]

After the election, the *New York Times* published an extraordinary front page article with the headline, "Sold to Republicans, Utah Auctioned Off by George Q. Cannon, an Ecclesiastical 'Pull,'" which set off serious disputes in Utah. The front page article appeared on February 13, 1895, and devoted three full columns on page one and four more columns on page two. In it, the *Times* accused George of using his personal and ecclesiastical influence to help the Republicans win, not just the territorial delegate race in Utah but US senate races in a number of western states. The article was framed as the result of investigative reporting by the *Times*, though George was confident that it was actually written by a Utah Mormon with inside connections in the church who did not like him. The article predicted that within a short period of time, the Mormon vote would tip the balance in US senate races in Idaho, Wyoming, Nevada, and Arizona (once it was admitted as a state). The article also predicted that Cannon's sellout to the Republican Party would result in even greater personal political clout than he already held and would also benefit his Republican contacts (and essentially co-conspirators) Clarkson and Joe Manley, who were national Republican leaders. Cannon had been the power behind the throne in the LDS Church for decades, but his influence was so subtle—"so impersonal, so indirect, that rarely any public indication of the exertion of his influence is discernable" and no one had been able to understand that he had sold the church and Utah territory to the Republicans. The article hit a touchy subject when it claimed that George's family had "become noted in local finances, and [successful] in political directions." Though the article asserted that Cannon received $3,000 a year from the church, this was not enough to support his extensive family, so "his name is found associated with the largest enterprises in the Territory. He is a miner, a merchant, a real estate owner, a banker, a

61. "Republicans on Top in Utah," *SLT*, Nov. 7, 1894, 1; GQCJ, Nov. 6–7, 1894; Bitton, *GQC*, 353.

railroad proprietor, a manufacturer, a farmer, a publisher, an editor, an ecclesiast, the owner of coal fields, a cattle raiser, a promoter of power, and other enterprises, and withal a politician." According to the *Times*, he also exercised his influence through three of his sons who were "the editor of the leading Mormon newspaper, The Evening News. Another, [the territorial delegate to Congress] … , and still another[,] a member of the Twelve apostles."[62]

George was offended and hurt by the allegations, many of which were facially accurate. But it was the implications and conclusions (and details) that Cannon found especially troubling. It was also galling that the *Times* had asserted that he had sold Utah out to moneyed parties represented by Clarkson and Manley, a close associate of James G. Blaine. Only months before Cannon had asserted that Clarkson and Trumbo had done what Cannon was now accused of—working to use Utah's resources for their own gain—and had made clear he would not allow that. George was incensed at nepotism assertions, something that always rankled him. He had worked for Utah statehood for a majority of Utahns and hoped it would help all Utahns.

The article was reprinted in both the *Salt Lake Tribune* and the *Salt Lake Herald*, though the *Times* later claimed, inaccurately, that the "power of the Mormon Church … was exerted … to prevent republication of the revelations made by The Times."[63] Publication in Utah meant that more locals had ready access to the startling allegations. George Q. responded a week later in the *Salt Lake Herald*, which was reprinted in the *Times*, and Frank Cannon responded to the *Times* directly two weeks after the original publication. George took issue with all of the important points—having sold out Utah to the Republicans, using his influence to further the positions of his sons and brothers, receiving a salary from the LDS Church, and working with Republican operatives to develop businesses and industries in Utah for his own benefit in exchange for ensuring

62. "Sold to Republicans," *NYT*, Feb. 13, 1895, 1, 2. Another *Times* article published later in the year summarized the earlier piece but attributed far less malice to Cannon. "The Sale of Utah," *NYT*, Oct. 15, 1895, 4.

63. "Attack George Q. Cannon, Papers Charge that He Traded Church Votes, Allegations of Fraud," *SLT*, Feb. 14, 1895, 1; "Asserts that Utah Was Sold, New York Times on the Territory and Some of Its People, Geo. Q. Cannon Attacked," *SLH*, Feb. 18, 1895, 1; "The Sale of Utah," *NYT*, Oct. 15, 1895, 4.

Republican victories.[64] Frank argued that he and fellow Republicans had won the 1894 elections fair and square and there was no "sell-out." He also upbraided the anonymous correspondent, who "abuses without reason and accuses without truth."[65]

The Democratic *Salt Lake Herald* thought the assassination of George Q.'s character was "false," "cowardly," "foul," and "vile," but that there was no benefit to Democrats in such an attack. It also concluded that the *Times* article had been intended to prevent large money transactions in which Cannon was involved to benefit Utah.[66] The Republican *Salt Lake Tribune*, on the other hand, decided it was nothing but a partisan tempest in a teapot: "considerable curiosity is expressed here as to the object of these assaults upon Utah men and Utah interests. That the purpose is political is plain: that it comes from local Democrats in Salt Lake City is equally apparent."[67]

The original *Times* article did prompt some Democratic complaints in Washington, DC, in addition to trying to make George Q. look bad. Denouncing Cannon was important to a campaign to try to ensure that he would not be one of Utah's senators after statehood. Now the enabling act for Utah would soon make the territory a state, renewing the question about whether George would be elected as a senator and, if he was, whether he would be permitted by Congress to take the seat. In an April 1895 article, the *Times* asserted that Utah's two senators would be George and whichever gentile he chose as the second.[68]

As the furor over the *Times* articles raged, George continued to search for funds either loaned or invested to pay the expenses of the business initiatives he was pursuing, which included rail, sugar, salt, hydroelectric power, Saltair (a pleasure resort on the banks of

64. "Mr. Cannon's Flat Denials," *SLH*, Feb. 20, 1895, 1; reprinted as "George Q. Cannon's Statement, He Replies to the Charge that He Had Sold the State to Republicans," *NYT*, Feb. 26, 1895, 9.

65. "Republicanism in Utah, Charges Against George Q. Cannon Energetically Denied, Son to the Rescue of the Father, Frank J. Cannon Insists that Utah Was Not Sold to Republicans, but Went to Them Legitimately," *NYT*, Feb. 26, 1895, 9.

66. "Attack on President Cannon," *SLH*, Feb. 18, 1895, 3; "N.Y. Times and Hon. G. Q. Cannon," *SLH*, Feb. 20, 1895, 4.

67. "Another Times Attack," *SLT*, Mar. 9, 1895, 1.

68. "The Utah Senatorships, George Q. Cannon Wants One, His Son Longs for the Other," *NYT*, Apr. 10, 1895, 13.

the Great Salt Lake), colonization, and mining interests. The First Presidency was happy to learn from Clarkson that he was proposing an alliance between the First Presidency and his group by inviting the church to invest $100,000 in Clarkson's purchase of a controlling share in a Chicago newspaper, the *Inter Ocean.* George Q. traveled with Carlie to Chicago to meet with Clarkson, and he was willing to put up his personal "Big House" property as collateral, but was taken aback when Clarkson asked him to sign a promissory note that provided that he, Woodruff, and Joseph F. Smith owed Clarkson $100,000. Cannon erupted, telling Clarkson that the church leaders were willing to invest and would without question if they had ready funds, but they would not acknowledge that they or their church owed a debt to Clarkson.[69]

George Q. and Carlie continued to New York City so he could continue to look for loans to help with his personal financial difficulties as well as to look for investments or loans to fund companies he was involved with. When they arrived, Cannon found a telegram from someone he did not identify in his journal informing him that prosecutors in Utah, under directions from "Washington," "will immediately commence proceedings against leading men," referring to unlawful cohabitation. George headed for Washington the next day and met with Attorney General Richard Olney, who assured him that no instructions had been given to prosecute "cohabs." He also met with the director of US Marshals, who indicated that he would do all he could to "keep things quiet." He sought out the secretaries of agriculture and the Navy to seek a personal audience with President Cleveland, who squeezed him into his schedule.[70]

Cannon told Cleveland, who had read the *Times* articles, how hard he had worked to comply with the Edmunds–Tucker Act and had had to fully modify his living arrangements. Cleveland indicated that he understood. George left hoping that there would be no new surge of prosecutions against polygamists for living with their wives.[71]

69. GQCJ, Mar. 22, 1895. As noted above, George Q. had told his family in 1878 that he had transferred the Big House on South Temple to the church in satisfaction of debts he owed. Apparently, he continued to be treated as owner of the house. GQC to Eliza Tenney Cannon, Apr. 18, 1878, cited and quoted in Bitton, *GQC,* 390–91.

70. GQCJ, Mar. 23, 25, 1895.

71. GQCJ, Mar. 23, 25, 1895.

With statehood only months away, Utah was holding its constitutional convention when Cannon returned in May 1895. Female suffrage under Utah law was a leading issue at the moment. Women had held the right to vote in Utah between 1870, when the territorial legislature had granted it, and 1887, when woman's suffrage had been removed in Utah by the Edmunds–Tucker Act. Now, sometimes contrarian LDS general authority B. H. Roberts opposed including woman's suffrage in the new state constitution, though he did not oppose enacting it by statute after statehood. Local and national suffragists insisted that women enjoy the right of suffrage in the new state. The Constitutional Convention agreed, and delegates voted overwhelmingly to restore women's voting rights.[72] For his part, George Q. supported women's suffrage and sat on the stand between national suffrage leaders Susan B. Anthony and the Reverend Anna Shaw at the convention.[73]

The final proposed constitution drafted by the convention restored woman's suffrage and met the requirements of the enabling act by "perfectly tolerat[ing]" religious sentiment and prohibiting molestation of a person or his or her property on account of religious worship, with the important exception that "polygamous or plural marriages are forever prohibited."[74] The proposed constitution was overwhelmingly approved on November 6, 1895, in the general election.[75]

In the summer of 1895, George Q. counseled Woodruff to take a trip to the west coast to help with his sleeplessness. Woodruff invited his two counselors to go with him. George and Carlie had so much fun steaming down the Columbia River, spending time in Portland, and taking a voyage through the Puget Sound that they discussed the possibility of continuing up into Alaska, and soon George wired Abram to arrange for the oldest children still at home to join him and Carlie in Victoria. Four daughters and one son, children of Elizabeth, Sarah Jane, Martha, and Carlie, joined them and the entire group steamed up the coast to Alaska on the *Wellefrah*, stopped in Sitka and

72. John Sillito, *B. H. Roberts: A Life in the Public Arena* (Salt Lake City: Signature Books, 2021), 211–27; Bitton, *GQC*, 357–58.

73. GQCJ, May 12, 1895; Bitton, *GQC*, 357–58.

74. "Utah's Star Is Now Shining, 'The Queen of the West' at Last Takes Her Place Among the Sisterhood of States," *SLH*, Jan. 5, 1896, 1.

75. "It's Settled," *SLT*, Nov. 7, 1895, 1.

Juneau, and thoroughly enjoyed the spectacular scenery. George did not often get to spend two-week vacations with his children.[76]

The political campaign of 1895, where the first full member of Congress from Utah was elected and where officeholders would be running a state rather than a territory, was very partisan. Division of People's Party and Liberal Party adherents into the national parties in the early 1890s complicated matters for church leaders. Whereas Mormons had previously voted essentially as a bloc, now they were pitted against each other. Most inclined to the Democratic Party for various reasons, including that most of the anti-polygamy legislation had been sponsored and pursued aggressively by Republicans. Church leaders wanted to have credibility and maintain party contacts between the church members and the two major parties.

LDS Seventy B. H. Roberts ran unsuccessfully for the US House as a Democrat, being beaten by Republican (and former Liberal) C. E. Allen. Apostle Moses Thatcher was nominated by the Democratic Party for the US Senate, though at the time, prior to enactment of the Seventeenth Amendment to the Constitution, senators were chosen by the state legislature. In Thatcher's case, his nomination occurred after Utah became a state. Neither Roberts nor Thatcher had asked the First Presidency for permission to run. Joseph F. Smith, an ardent Republican, viewed it as a serious omission and indirectly attacked the two church leaders in a conference address in October. It was an interesting question whether the First Presidency would have approved their candidacies given Smith's Republican partisanship and Cannon's close alliance over the prior few years with national Republican leaders, but Smith viewed Thatcher and Roberts' failure to ask permission as a serious matter. Democratic leaders cried foul, which pressured Smith to explain his remarks.[77]

George had spoken on the subject several times over the past few years, generally taking the position that senior church leaders should not run for office or even take an active role in partisan politics. This was somewhat ironic, given that he had served for ten years as Utah territory's delegate to Congress, but that service occurred during a time when church and political party coalesced in the People's

76. GQCJ, June 25–July 9, 1895; Bitton, *GQC*, 360.
77. Bitton, *GQC*, 362–63.

Party. Shortly before the 1895 election, President Woodruff advised church leaders not to run for office "without first counseling with the Presidency of the Church, or with his quorum, on its propriety, and getting permission to do so."[78] Surprisingly, in the end, the Republicans swept the elections. Roberts, who continued to be popular in spite of his opposition to woman's suffrage, came closest to winning but lost by about 1,000 votes.[79] Thatcher was not a contender for the Senate because membership of the new Utah state legislature was heavily Republican.

The conditions to statehood had been met. Utah Commissioner J. R. Letcher attested that the electorate had approved the new constitution, and US Attorney General Judson Harmon approved the constitution. On the morning of Saturday, January 4, 1896, President Cleveland signed the proclamation officially admitting Utah as a state.[80]

A telegraphic "flash" was sent to Utah and citizens of the newest state. The formal inaugural celebration was held on Monday, January 6, 1896, when a grand parade chaired and planned by John Q. Cannon was staged. The parade, which was viewed by over 30,000 people, included a platoon of police, the marshal, an army band, two battalions of US infantry, carriages carrying dignitaries—including the new governor, Heber M. Wells, Wilford Woodruff and Presbyterian minister T.C. Iliff, former territorial delegates John T. Caine, Joseph L. Rawlins, and George Q. Cannon—veterans of various wars, and a number of secret societies. The parade ended at the Tabernacle, which had attached to its ceiling an immense US flag with forty-five stars. An expanded Tabernacle Choir with 1,000 voices sang the "Star Spangled Banner." Woodruff was not well enough to offer the opening prayer, so George read Woodruff's prayer. A festive ball was held in the Salt Lake Theatre, to which George invited all five of his wives. It became apparent that the women's dresses, though different in style and taste, were all cut from the same fine bolt of cloth that George Q. had brought back with him from New

78. Jean B. White, "Utah State Elections, 1895–1899" (PhD diss., University of Utah, 1968), 89–91; Bitton, *GQC*, 363.

79. "It's Settled," *SLT*, Nov. 7, 1895, 1.

80. "Utah State," *SLT*, Jan. 5, 1896, 1.

York. A woman at the ball reportedly commented how "quaint" it was for Cannon to dress them all alike.[81]

Many people were responsible for statehood. Rawlins shepherded the enabling act through both houses of Congress (with surprisingly bipartisan support) and final approval by President Cleveland. Clawson, John W. Young, Badlam, Estee, Clarkson, and Trumbo all contributed to creating the environment in which statehood was attractive both to Democrats and Republicans. Statehood never would have been attained without Woodruff's Manifesto. Frank Cannon helped in Washington at a critical time in 1889 to change the political climate in Utah. Many former Liberal Party members helped by supporting statehood. But the father of Utah statehood, the ultimate puppeteer making the critical strategic decisions, employing the necessary advisors, traveling to the most important meetings, and keeping everyone on task was George Q. Cannon.

After Utah became a state, one critical matter remained. All state and federal offices from Utah had been determined by the 1895 elections except Utah's first two US senators. Before enactment of the Seventeenth Amendment in 1913, Senators were elected by state legislatures. The common wisdom in Utah had been for several years that one of the first senators would be a Mormon and the other a gentile. Frank Cannon had given notice that he was running for the "Mormon" seat by not running for US congressman in November 1895. A number of others were vying for the non-Mormon seat, including Trumbo, Goodwin, and Arthur Brown. In 1895, the *New York Times* had assumed that George would be elected and essentially choose who the non-Mormon senator would be.

The initial US senate elections in Utah were political theater. Moses Thatcher and Joseph Rawlins, the Democratic candidates, were not viable candidates because both houses of Utah state's initial legislature had large Republican majorities. On the Republican side, Frank Cannon had been viewed as the leading Mormon candidate for some time. The most likely competitor for the Mormon vote, however, was his father. The most interesting part of the race was for the "gentile" seat. Trumbo, who had moved to Utah, was thought

81. Bitton, *GQC*, 367; "Inaugural Parade," "Inaugural Exercises," *SLH*, Jan 7, 1896, 1. In this context, "quaint" probably meant "odd."

to be the leading candidate until he earned George's mistrust. This was reinforced when nationally prominent Republican Joseph H. Manley privately confided to George that Trumbo "would be an unsuitable person to represent our State in the Senate."[82] Goodwin, editor of the *Tribune*, was considered to be the other leading gentile candidate for a time. It is likely that George and other Mormon leaders never felt entirely comfortable with Goodwin given his harsh criticisms throughout the 1880s. National Republican leader Clarkson characterized Goodwin's historical interactions with Latter-day Saints as conducted "with the conscience of butchers and the fury of enemies." Clarkson would have looked bad if his chosen candidate, Trumbo, had not won and Goodwin had.[83]

George always insisted, in his journal and elsewhere, that he was not a candidate for the US Senate. This despite his usually being picked as the "shadow" senator when Utah had applied for statehood over the past thirty-four years; he was also always the one who would have been chosen if Utah had become a state earlier. No one, from the *New York Times* to many LDS leaders, believed George's denials, although Frank Cannon's biographer believes that George wanted to be elected to the Senate "only as the outcome of an immaculate campaign," that is, without getting his hands dirty and having God open the way for his election.[84] George did not campaign. He defended Frank as deserving of the office. Importantly, both Abram Cannon and Joseph F. Smith had been opposed to George's running for office. But when the prophet, Wilford Woodruff, announced to the First Presidency and five apostles on December 26, 1895, just three weeks before the election, that the Lord wanted him to be senator, Cannon half-heartedly took up the cause. No doubt George was both flattered and, perhaps, saw a way to pursue something he had always wanted.[85] Frank was unwilling to step aside and made clear that he would work to keep the legislative supporters who were pledged to vote for him.

George knew better than anyone that his election would cause

82. GQCJ, Oct. 25, 1895.

83. James S. Clarkson to Wilford Woodruff, Dec. 14, 1895, as quoted in Holley, *Frank J. Cannon*, 153.

84. Holley, *Frank J. Cannon*, 151.

85. AHCJ, Dec. 26, 1895

controversy. Even if the former Liberals who had fought his election to Congress were now largely passive, polygamy was still wildly unpopular in America, and everyone knew that George had five wives and many children. He had also been at the center of Mormon political dominance. It is likely that he would have faced the same scrutiny that B. H. Roberts faced when he won but was not seated in the US House of Representatives in 1898. George knew that he would risk a continuation of the controversies from his earlier ten years as territorial delegate. There was only one reason that George would be willing to be considered for a senate seat—namely, if God's prophet decided that should happen. George always followed the prophet.[86]

When it came time for the legislature to prepare to vote, the First Presidency appointed trusted men to poll the politicos on the question of whether George Q. could be elected. Abram Cannon, Angus Cannon, and John Henry Smith investigated and concluded that George would not be elected but that his name might be proposed in the state legislature's Republican caucus. "It became evident to Presidents Woodruff and Smith that if my name were allowed to go before the caucus it might lead to an adverse vote being cast against me and might bring discredit upon me." Further investigation confirmed that Frank had sufficient legislators lined up to be elected. The First Presidency agreed that George should publish a "card" (that is, a note or letter) announcing that he was not a candidate and could not accept the office.[87]

As expected, Frank was elected. Non-Mormon attorney Arthur Brown, who had some supporters and had recently received financial and political support from Collis P. Huntington, was elected as the other senator. As expected, one Mormon senator and one non-Mormon, though neither man particularly distinguished himself and neither was reelected.[88]

86. GQCJ, Dec. 26, 1895.

87. GQCJ, Jan. 14, 1895; "President Cannon and the Utah Senatorship," *DN*, Jan 14, 1896, 4. A copy of George Q.'s "card" is also copied into his journal.

88. Lyman, *Finally Statehood!* 352.

CHAPTER NINE

INTO A NEW CENTURY

1896-1900

> *"There are two things required of us as apostles, a perfect union among ourselves, and a perfect union with the First Presidency. … Bro. Geo. Q. Cannon was doing some things that we could not approve of. This makes no difference as it is our duty to sustain him."*
> —*Lorenzo Snow, January 4, 1898*

With the Salt Lake Temple finished, Utah statehood attained, and a problematic US senate candidacy (largely) avoided, one would have thought that George Q., at age sixty-nine, would slow down and enjoy life more with his five wives, his thirty-four living children (biological and adopted), and his many grandchildren. Though he sometimes tried, he never succeeded and continued to have ecclesiastical, business, civic, and journalistic obligations which kept him a busy man.

The hectic pace of Cannon's life was astonishing. The church, businesses, his immediate family and larger extended family, civic organizations, political activities, alongside his own regimen of keeping current on the news, composing talks and writing editorials and articles, studying the scriptures, attending plays and engaging in other cultural activities, keeping a detailed personal diary, and maintaining a busy, broad correspondence required considerable energy and stamina.[1]

One of the first important matters George had to face after Utah statehood was the issue of church leaders running for office. Controversy had been ignited during the 1895 campaign when B. H.

1. The *New York Times* once described Cannon as "reading a dozen newspapers in half an hour" in a restaurant in New York City. "Sold to Republicans," *NYT*, Feb. 13, 1895, 1.

Roberts and Moses Thatcher ran for major federal office as Democrats without asking permission from the First Presidency. George Q. half-heartedly sought election as a senator at the insistence of President Woodruff but had withdrawn before the election (at least partly because he would not have been elected). A public perception arose that Republicans could obtain approval but Democrats might not be able to. Church leaders needed to clarify the matter with a formal explanation of why high ranking officers of the church who were supposed to devote all or much of their time to their ecclesiastical duties needed to seek permission to run for office and why this did not represent political dominance or control by the church.

On April 6, 1896, the First Presidency issued what has come to be known as the political manifesto. It was signed by the entire First Presidency, ten members of the Quorum of the Twelve, all seven Presidents of the Seventy, the Church Patriarch, and the Presiding Bishopric. The two apostles who did not sign the documents were Anthon H. Lund, who was away serving as president of the European Mission, and Moses Thatcher, who refused to sign.[2] The absence of Lund's signature was explained in a note in the official published version of the manifesto, but the absence of Thatcher's was not.

The document was dictated entirely by George the morning that he introduced it to the general authorities and has many hallmarks of both his writing style and his process of presentation. As Cannon biographer Davis Bitton noted, the political manifesto may not have been entirely accurate in its recitation of history but "was a significant statement of the condition that must now obtain."[3] The rhetoric is somewhat defensive and combative and characterizes a number of denials of "charges" regarding the relationship of church and state in strong terms, including that "any charge that has been made to the contrary is utterly false."[4] According to the document, church leaders had earlier served in political positions from necessity and senior authorities had never intended "to do anything looking to a union

2. "To the Saints," *DW*, Apr. 11, 1896, 532–34; "Thatcher Is Dropped … Address to the Saints," *SLT*, Apr. 7, 1896, 1; "Thatcher's Position," *SLT*, Apr. 7, 1896, 1; "New Manifesto Issued, Was Submitted at the General Conference Yesterday, Created a Great Stir," *SLH*, Apr. 7, 1896, 1.

3. Bitton, *GQC*, 404.

4. GQCJ, Apr. 5, 1896.

of Church and State" or to curtail the personal liberty of officers or members of the church, though the First Presidency did counsel church members "to be wise and prudent in the political steps they were about to take." The end of the People's Party and the division of church members into national parties ushered in an "era of peace and good-will," but "efficient and popular men," including LDS leaders, felt pressure to participate and run for office. Some men consulted with church authorities "before accepting the political honors tendered"; others did not, engendering "ill feeling" and misunderstanding toward some leaders, and occasionally "accusations of bad faith." This was at odds with the rule which "has been understood from the very beginning of the Church" that "it would be an improper thing to accept political office or enter into any vocation that would distract or remove [full-time church leaders] from the religious duties resting upon them, without first consulting and obtaining the approval of their associates and those who preside over them."[5]

It appears that George Q. had not solicited input on his draft document before the evening of April 5, 1896. When he presented the draft manifesto to ten members of the Quorum of Twelve that evening, he was "very much gratified to think that it met the feelings of the brethren as well as it did; for it was a very hastily dictated document." Only one minor change was made, to change the word "officers" to "leading officials." Early the next morning, all of the general authorities were invited to consider approving the political manifesto. As George noted in his journal, "All of us signed it, leaving a place for Brother Moses Thatcher to sign it in the regular order." B. H. Roberts, who had run for Congress the previous year without asking approval, signed the manifesto "with a great deal of cordiality." Cannon hoped that Thatcher, "seeing the names of his fellow servants, would sign it without any question."[6]

Thatcher was not at the meeting because of illness. Lorenzo Snow and Brigham Young Jr. delivered the document to him for his approval. Early in the afternoon of April 6, Thatcher responded with a short letter to Snow and Young that was gracious, noting that he endorsed much of the document (though he could not endorse other

5. "To the Saints," *DW*, Apr. 11, 1896, 533.
6. GQCJ, Apr. 6, 1896.

portions "without stultification") but that, in his "weakened state," he could not sign it. He hoped that the Lord would enable him "to define his views and acts as running along those of honor, integrity, and truth." For now, he "humbly asked" that his brethren act according to the Holy Spirit's "dictation."[7]

Snow and Young reported that Thatcher seemed "very clear in his mind," that he read the document himself with a "great deal of care," and evidently "possesses his faculties fully." His letter declining to sign the manifesto was "adroitly written." George and his fellow leaders "felt grieved and disappointed" because they hoped he would join them in adopting the political manifesto, but, given Thatcher's refusal, the First Presidency and Twelve decided not to present his name as one of the Twelve and this "was noticed and created something of a sensation" among conference goers. After the "authorities were presented," George Q. felt impressed to speak and did so "with a great of deal of power, ... the main theme ... was to call on the people to have confidence in us, and not to indulge in suspicions and doubt concerning us and our conduct; that we were honest, true men and that our lives were before them in proof of this; ... I dwelt on the evils that result from the indulgence in distrust, jealousy, and suspicion."[8]

One complicating piece of George's actions was that he and Thatcher had sometimes been at odds with each other for eight or nine years. Thatcher had been most vociferous in arguing that Cannon had acted improperly with respect to the dedicated Bullion Beck stock and had apparently convinced others, including Heber J. Grant and Presiding Bishop William Preston, to share his suspicions. Thatcher, Grant, and John Henry Smith also asserted that George had restricted access to LDS president John Taylor while many of the general authorities were on the underground, had failed to involve the apostles in important decisions, and had secretly plotted to become the new church president after Taylor's death.[9] In addition, George's view of Thatcher, as he recorded in his journal a few days later, was that he had been out of fellowship with

7. GQCJ, Apr. 6, 1896.

8. GQCJ, Apr. 6, 1896.

9. Edward Leo Lyman, "The Alienation of an Apostle from His Quorum: The Moses Thatcher Case," *Dialogue* 18 (Summer 1985): 67–71; Ronald W. Walker, "Grant's Watershed: Succession in the Presidency, 1887–89," *BYUS* 43 (Winter 2004): 207, 210–19.

other church leaders "for years" and his refusal to sign the political manifesto was simply the last straw. Cannon felt frustrated by the controversy surrounding the omission of Thatcher's name from the Twelve and believed that, if everyone knew how Thatcher had been acting, they would agree with Cannon. To Cannon, his fellow apostles had shown charity when dealing with Thatcher, partly because of his sickness and the opium habit he had developed while trying to alleviate his pain.[10] Personalities and hard feelings aside, Thatcher later disclosed that his principal objection to the political manifesto was narrow: he believed that it could be interpreted to bind virtually any man who held the priesthood and was thus too broad.[11]

Though no objection to the political manifesto was raised by the authorities who approved it, a number of younger leaders, including Heber Grant, were frustrated by Cannon's habit of being secretive and not seeking input from the Twelve. A few days before conference, George Q. had told all of the apostles that church finances should all be under the direct control of the Trustee-in-Trust (the church president), not under the Presiding Bishopric, which was an Aaronic Priesthood body. He also told them that he believed full-time church leaders should not be paid salaries, though they should be permitted to have expenses paid.[12] Grant worried that Cannon had exercised too much control over church finances during John Taylor's administration and viewed his proposals as further attempts to dominate in this area. These concerns primarily related to financial issues, but his proposal of the political manifesto without warning likely deepened the mistrust of some.

On April 8, 1896, just after the close of general conference, George received an unexpected invitation to accompany Union Pacific (U.P.) officials to Omaha. William H. Bancroft, the superintendent of the mountain division of the U.P. who was stationed in Salt Lake City, sent him a note that the U.P.'s general manager, Edward Dickinson, was traveling through town with Cornelius Vanderbilt II and that Cannon was invited to go with Dickinson and Vanderbilt to Omaha

10. GQCJ, Apr. 14, 1896.

11. Kenneth W. Godfrey, "Moses Thatcher in the Dock: His Trials, The Aftermath, and His Last Days," *JMH* 24 (Spring 1998): 58–64.

12. GQCJ, Mar. 27, Apr. 2, 1896; HJGJ, Apr. 2, 1896.

to meet with S.H.H. Clark, who was running the company. George had been informed a few weeks earlier that he was being proposed as a director of the U.P., which was in federal receivership proceedings. He did not think he had time to go to Omaha, but his son Abram promised to take care of everything in Salt Lake City and told him this was an opportunity he could not pass up "to talk railroad matters with these people." "These people" turned out to be Dickinson, Vanderbilt, the majority owner of the vast Vanderbilt railroad empire, Chauncey Depew, president of the Vanderbilt-owned New York Central and Hudson River Railroad and general counsel of all the Vanderbilt railroads, and others. Along the way, Vanderbilt and Depew treated George warmly, and he no doubt sought to learn as much as he could from them about developing a railroad.

In Omaha, Cannon had a long, high-stakes discussion with Clark, former president of the U.P. and at this time one of the receivers running the U.P., and W. R. Kelly, counsel for the U.P. receivers. They discussed the possibility that the U.P., through its subsidiary, the Oregon Short Line (OSL), would entertain selling its right of way through Nevada to the Salt Lake & Los Angeles Railway Co. (SLLA), whose president was George Q.[13] Clark told Cannon that he did not want to split the OSL up but, once the U.P. was out of receivership, it might consider selling the entire OSL system to Cannon's company. Both Clark and Kelly thought it would be better to wait until the U.P. was reorganized to attempt to consummate such a transaction and that it made no sense for Cannon to visit the East to raise money for the Salt Lake City to Los Angeles railroad at the present time.[14]

After his return to Salt Lake City, George attended a board meeting of Pioneer Electric, which was developing a hydroelectric plant on the Ogden River at the mouth of Ogden Canyon. C. K. Bannister, chief engineer of the company, proposed that George Q. receive a salary of $5,000 per year as president and treasurer of the company, which he had not discussed with Cannon. Wilford Woodruff and

13. The railway business created by GQC and associates to develop a line between Salt Lake City and Los Angeles had at least two names: the Utah Company and the Salt Lake & Los Angeles Railway Company. It is difficult to distinguish between the two in GQC's journal, and I refer to the business as the SLLA

14. GQCJ, Apr. 8–12,1896.

Joseph F. Smith were also members of the board. Woodruff and all directors other than Smith voted to approve the salary. Smith voted no, arguing that the company was not yet profitable. Indicative of the financial stresses he was experiencing, Cannon responded that he had never requested compensation for any position he had held but that, at the present time, he needed remuneration and thought it appropriate when serving in a commercial enterprise to be paid. Moreover, he could not continue to act in this capacity unless he were compensated. Cannon said he considered "his services cheap at that price, with my age and experience and the work I had done already." George felt "hurt" by Smith's no vote and hoped that Smith's action would not affect how he felt about him.[15]

That night, George and Carlie hosted a dinner with guests they had invited—several non-Mormon couples from St. Louis who were in town, Brigham Young Jr. and one of his wives, Lizzie, and Abram and two of his wives, Mina and Mamie.[16] Polygamous Latter-day Saints were already feeling more comfortable about appearing in public with their plural wives. It also offered a foreshadowing of an important decision by George and Abram that caused considerable controversy in coming years.

In late April 1896, George Q. traveled east for the U.P. shareholders' meeting where he would stand for election to the U.P.'s board. He took Carlie, Abram's third wife (and Carlie's niece), Mary Eliza (Mamie), and George and Carlie's daughter, Anne. On the trip, the group visited four of his sons, William, Lewis, Sylvester, and Willard, who were studying at universities in Philadelphia and Boston. They also engaged with son Frank (who was also part of the management of the SLLA) in negotiations regarding the purchase of the OSL's "Utah and Nevada property." Geoge Q. was elected as a director of the U.P. at a stockholder's meeting in Boston.[17]

George Q. came away from the negotiations with Clark and the OSL officials with a preliminary plan under which the SLLA would purchase OSL's Utah and Nevada properties for which OSL would take first mortgage bonds in payment, and SLLA would purchase

15. GQCJ, Apr. 15, 1896.
16. GQCJ, Apr. 15, 1896.
17. GQCJ, Apr. 26–29, 1896.

fifty miles of steel, also for first mortgage bonds. The transactions were not without risk, as Frank informed brother Abram in an internal memorandum. If all went well, however, George, Abram, and Frank might become wealthy. If the new railroad did not work out, they could all be even deeper in debt than they already were.[18]

Just as things seemed to be going well, catastrophe struck. Abram, who had been spending most of his time on railroad matters, died unexpectedly in July 1896. He was only thirty-seven. As if this were not enough, it soon became evident to insiders that Abram had married an additional polygamous wife shortly before his death. As Abram was a member of the Twelve, this would be viewed as a serious breach of the church's pledges to abandon polygamy.

George Q. and Elizabeth Cannon's son David had died at age twenty-one while serving a mission in Germany on October 17, 1892. Prior to his mission, he had courted a young woman named Lillian Hamlin. George had been impressed the year before by Lillian's valedictory address at Brigham Young Academy's graduation ceremony. He noted that she gave the address "with fine elocutionary effect, and the language was very beautiful."[19] David and Lillian had intended to marry, but he did not want to tie her down while he was in Germany in case something were to happen to him.

After David died, his sister Mary Alice tearfully told her father that she would willingly have her husband, cousin Lewis M. Cannon, marry Lillian for "time," that is, for the time of earthly lives, while Lillian would be "sealed" to David for eternity; all so that children born to Lillian would be David's eternal offspring. George was concerned that "such a thing would [not] be possible under the present circumstances"—in other words, in the midst of the continuing controversies over plural marriage—but also thought that one of David's brothers, not a cousin, should "perform such a duty."[20] Frank Cannon, David's half-brother, reportedly volunteered to marry Lillian, but George knew of Frank's problems and would

18. GQCJ, Apr. 29, 1896, draft letter, Frank J. Cannon to Abraham H. Cannon, May 3, 1896, included.

19. GQCJ, June 10, 1891; Bitton, *GQC*, 334.

20. GQCJ, Dec. 11, 1892. Lewis M. Cannon, Mary Alice's husband, did later marry Lillian Hamlin as a plural wife in December 1901, after Abram died. Family group records of Lewis M. Cannon and Lillian Hamlin. See familysearch.org (accessed July 2020).

never have permitted him to father eternal children for David.[21] In October 1894, George talked to Abram "about taking some good girl and raising up seed to my brother David." Because Abram already had three wives, such a marriage would be a polygamous marriage. Several days later, Abram suggested a specific "good girl" to marry for time (with David to be her eternal spouse): his cousin Ann M. Cannon (Annie). David and Annie had been close friends as well as cousins. Wilford Woodruff, Joseph F. Smith, and Annie's father, Angus M., all agreed it was a good idea. Woodruff and Smith stated that they would approve such a polygamous marriage if it were performed in the LDS Mexican colonies. Angus approached Annie about the possibility, but she was not interested.[22] The idea stuck with George Q. and Abram—perhaps Lillian Hamlin would agree to be sealed to David for eternity and to Abram for time and Lillian and Abram's children would belong to David in eternity.

Lillian was agreeable. On June 17, 1896, Abram's second wife, Wilhelmina "Mina" Cannon, who was also Abram's first cousin, visited her father-in-law and uncle, George Q. Cannon, and was livid. Mina had just heard that Lillian was willing to be sealed to David for eternity and to her husband, Abram, for time. George explained "very plainly and kindly" to Mina that Lillian's "affections seem to be centred on David" and that she would be sealed to him for eternity. In fact, it appears that Lillian had already been sealed to David with Abram acting as proxy that very morning in the Salt Lake Temple in a ceremony officiated by Joseph F. Smith and that, in the process of that eternal sealing, Lillian and Abram had been married for time. The two left the next day on a combination honeymoon and business trip to California with Smith and his wife, Edna.[23]

Abram became sick shortly after he returned to Salt Lake City

21. George F. Gibbs, Affidavit dated Jan. 10, 1912, as cited in D. Michael Quinn, "LDS Church Authority and New Plural Marriages, 1890–1904," *Dialogue* 18 (Spring 1985): 78. The affidavit was provided by Gibbs, a secretary to the First Presidency, long after the marriage, in the midst of responding to Frank J. Cannon's explosive new book, *Under the Prophet in Utah*, so its veracity is questionable.

22. AHCJ, Oct. 19, 24, 1894.

23. GQCJ, June 17, 1896; Quinn, "LDS Church Authority," 83–84. The Cannon family tradition is that Smith married the couple on a steamship between San Pedro harbor and Santa Catalina Island. Quinn's argument that the two were married by Smith in the Salt Lake Temple as part of the proxy marriage to David is more consistent with the evidence.

about July 1. By July 6, he could not speak aloud and had difficulty breathing. He passed away on July 19, 1896, apparently from cerebral meningitis. The entire family was grief-stricken. George Q. and others attributed it to Abram "overtaxing" himself by working too hard.[24] The marriage of Abram and Lillian was an open secret at least from the time Lillian was seen, dressed in black, among the immediate family mourners at the family viewing. Lillian bore a daughter, Marba (Abram spelled backwards), eight months later in Philadelphia, where she had no doubt gone to avoid the notoriety surrounding her marriage and pregnancy.[25]

The Abram-Lillian marriage is likely be the single most infamous of all post-Manifesto polygamous marriages and was the subject of a good deal of testimony in the US Senate's investigation of Reed Smoot's election beginning in 1904. For George Q. and other family members, it was, however, inextricably connected to Abram's tragic early death.[26]

The respect of the community for Abram was evident in his funeral in the Tabernacle, the thousands who lined the route of the 200-carriage-long cortege, and the dramatic burial site with Abram's friend, Richard W. Young, who rode a "black charger" and acted as the "marshal of the day" keeping the site clear for family members from the thousands crowding in around the grave.[27]

At another recent funeral, George had expressed his view that "the exposure to public gaze of the remains [at a viewing] is violative of the spirit." He did not believe that the remains of "deceased friends" should be exposed to the "vulgar gaze of mixed crowds." George Q. was particularly concerned that "many persons," presumably non-church members, would go to a funeral "for no other purpose than to have the opportunity of looking at the Temple clothing in which the deceased

24. GQCJ, July 4, 19, 1896; "A Victim of Overwork," *SLT*, July 20, 1896, 1; Richard S. Van Wagoner, *Mormon Polygamy: A History* (Salt Lake City: Signature Books, 1986), 170.

25. Family Group Records, Abraham H. Cannon and Lillian Hamlin, familysearch.org (accessed Dec. 2020).

26. U.S. Senate, Committee of Privileges and Elections, *Proceedings ... in the Matter of the Protests against the Right of Hon. Reed Smoot, a Senator from the State of Utah, to Hold His Seat, 4 vols., 59th Cong., 1st sess., S. Rept. No. 486* (Washington, D.C.: Government Printing Office, 1904–6) (hereafter Smoot Hearings), 1:1068, 1082–83 (testimony of Angus M. Cannon, Jr.).

27. "The Last Sad Rites," *Salt Lake Herald*, July 17, 1896, 1.

is clad." Consistent with his father's view, Abram's body did not lie in state, and only immediate family members and "intimate friends" were permitted to view his "features" in a small open-casket viewing at the residence of Abram's first wife, Sarah, before the funeral.[28]

Abram's death was a deep blow to his father. In Bitton's words, Abram was "not as brash as John Q. or as flamboyant as Frank," but he was steady, talented, devoted, and hard-working; he and his father had worked closely for decades in church service, banks, mining companies, publishing companies, railroads, and the *Deseret News*.[29] The two had an unusually close relationship in a family with many close relationships.

Devastated, George Q. went on an extended trip down the Pacific coast with Carlie and Wilford Woodruff and his wife Emma, and the Woodruffs' son, Asahel. George needed a break from the hectic schedule he had been following and to deal with the death of his son. Woodruff, who was eighty-nine years old, also needed some relaxation. They took the train to Portland, then went by steamer down the Columbia River and the Pacific coast to San Francisco, where they stayed in the city's finest hotel, the Palace. For once, George Q. did not suffer from seasickness. The group took a carriage ride through the Presidio and Golden Gate Park, stopping at the conservatory to admire the flowers. George loved seeing the *Victoria Regia* lily in bloom. He noted "the very great" change between his sojourn in the city publishing the Hawaiian Book of Mormon and the *Western Standard* and his current visit. They spent the next afternoon in the magnificent new Victorian Cliff House overlooking the Sutro baths and Pacific Ocean and "had a fine view of the sea lions" on Seal Beach.[30] George also visited Judge Morris Estee, who was "very careful in his expressions about people" but told George that the church was smart not to support Isaac Trumbo for Senate in 1896 because "Trumbo would have done us no credit in that office."[31]

The party next traveled to Monterey, where they stayed in the Hotel Del Monte, the stunning Victorian hotel and grounds built

28. GQCJ Mar. 26, 27, 1896; "Viewing the Dead," *DW*, July 25, 1896, 167.
29. Bitton, *GQC*, 407.
30. GQCJ, Aug. 19–20, 1896
31. GQCJ, Aug. 21, 1896.

and owned by Central Pacific principal, Charles Crocker. On August 24, the Cannons and Woodruffs took a carriage ride "through the Pacific Drive," which began and ended at the front door of the hotel.[32] This same road is now called the Seventeen Mile Drive. George, Wilford, and Asahel spent the first afternoon fishing on Monterey Bay, leaving George with a terrible sunburn. The hotel was "brilliantly lit up with electric lights and 500 chinese lanterns," making the scene "dazzlingly brilliant, and it might be described as a fairy land." "In all my travels," George Q. wrote, "I have never seen a more beautiful place than this."[33]

The party returned to San Francisco, then took the train south. Reaching San Diego, they took a ferry across to Coronado Island, where they checked into the almost-new Hotel Del Coronado, which George described as a "magnificent house, and the surf beats almost to the edge of the building." The group went out to the pier and posed for photographs fishing from the wharf and sitting in front of the iconic hotel. They then went fishing on a "naptha launch." In six hours, the party of the Cannons, Woodruffs, and several missionaries, caught over 600 pounds of fish. Woodruff enjoyed the sport fishing "as eagerly as a boy." The press had been following the Mormon leaders' vacation. George received a telephone message from former Utah governor Eli Murray, who had issued a certificate of election to Allen Campbell in 1881 in the face of an overwhelming vote in favor of Cannon and had lobbied in Washington, DC, for Campbell to be seated. Though Cannon visited the former governor, who "welcomed me with some warmth," he again showed his long memory for those who had opposed him when he recorded that Murray "did not apologize for the great wrong he had done me and through me to the people of Utah," although Murray's manner "clearly conveyed the idea that he desired my forgiveness." George could not help but note how "the Lord has spared me to see a great change take place and to have deadly enemies bow to me to seek my friendship and good will. I refer particularly to four men—Gen. Maxwell, Mr. R. N. Baskin, Mr. Allen G. Campbell, and now ex-Governor Murray."[34]

32. *WWJ*, Aug. 24, 1896.
33. GQCJ, Aug. 25–27, 1896.
34. GQCJ, Aug. 29, 30, 1896.

The group then headed north, stopping at Los Angeles, where they stayed a night in the Hollenbeck Hotel in downtown Los Angeles, toured Pasadena, and stayed two days on Santa Catalina Island. Woodruff again had a wonderful time deep sea fishing. The Cannons and the Woodruffs had a memorable month on the Pacific Coast, staying in the three nicest hotels in California and visiting many church missionaries and members. George met with old friends and political acquaintances and remembered old grudges, but he enjoyed rest and relaxation. They headed back to Utah in sleeping cars through Sacramento because no rail line had yet been built between Los Angeles and Salt Lake City.[35]

Though members of the First Presidency, led by Cannon, had sanctioned a small number of new plural marriages after 1890, usually performed in LDS colonies in Mexico and Canada after Utah's statehood, the number of such unions grew and several hundred polygamous sealings were performed.[36] Neither George Q. nor anyone else gave public discourses supporting plural marriage or the performance of new polygamous marriages or even of cohabitation with polygamous spouses married many years before, and Cannon was careful not to reside with any of his wives other than Carlie. But the controversial practice did continue and was approved by the highest ranking leaders in the church on a limited basis. The continuation of such marriages drew national attention when it came to light during the investigation of Apostle Reed Smoot's election as US senator in 1903 and continued to attract attention as the *Salt Lake Tribune* published lists of these marriages and, in the 1910s, as Frank Cannon and others wrote and lectured on post-Manifesto polygamy.[37]

---

35. GQCJ, Sep. 1–5, 1896.

36. D. Michael Quinn, "LDS Officials Involved with New Plural Marriages from September 1890 to February 1907," in Michael Harold Paulos and Konden Smith Hansen, eds., *The Reed Smoot Hearings: The Investigation of a Mormon Senator* and *the Transformation of an American Religion* (Logan: Utah State University, 2021), 245–88; Smoot hearings, 1:110–12, 127, 184, 476, 479 (Joseph F. Smith), 1:1060–64, 106–67, 1082–83 (Angus M. Cannon Jr.), 2:67 (John Henry Hamlin), 2:97–98 (Josiah Hickman), 2:141–46 (Wilhelmina Cannon Ellis), 2:307 (John Henry Smith).

37. KLC, "Do I Hear an Echo? The Continuing Trial of the Mormon Church after Smoot's Retention," in *Reed Smoot Hearings*, 129–52; KLC, "'The Modern Mormon Kingdom': Frank J. Cannon's National Campaign against Mormonism, 1910–1918," *JMH* 37 (Fall 2011): 60–114; KLC, "'And Now It Is the Mormons': The 'Magazine Crusade' Against the Mormons, 1910–1911," *Dialogue* 46 (Spring 2013): 1–63.

In late 1896, as state elections neared and as Senator Arthur Brown's term was set to end, the First Presidency and Quorum of Twelve Apostles unanimously decided that George Q. should seek Brown's seat "if everything worked right."[38] In November, however, the First Presidency and Twelve concluded that it would not be wise "to present the name of President George Q. Cannon for fear of a failure to elect him."[39] It could be that allegations of new polygamy would have resulted in renewed criticism of the church and many of the protests of George from his time in Congress might have been revived. In the same meeting the senior leaders discussed Moses Thatcher, and all were "satisfied that he was a great apostate & was doing all against the church he could."[40]

In November, William Jennings Bryan won most western states and his coattails helped Utah Democrats take the House and Senate. One of the Democrats who won a seat in the state senate was Dr. Martha "Mattie" Hughes Cannon, fourth wife of George Q.'s brother, Angus. Mattie and Angus had both run for state senate with three Democrats and three Republicans vying for three at-large seats. Mattie ran as a Democrat and won a seat; Angus ran as a Republican and lost. Mattie thus became the first woman in the United States to be elected as a state senator.[41]

In January 1897, Moses Thatcher had the highest number of votes from legislators for US senate on the first ballot, though not enough to win. Three men, all Democrats, vied for the honor: Thatcher, Henry Henderson, and former territorial delegate Joseph Rawlins. Though Cannon favored Henderson—he would never support Thatcher—he understood that he could not win. Rawlins's people made clear that "his attitude toward the Church and towards us individually [was] very favorable." Cannon mused in his journal that "if the Henderson men who belong to the Church will act with Rawlins men, and then two Republican members, who are our brethren, vote for him, Rawlins can be elected." That is precisely what

38. Brigham Young Jr., Diary, Oct. 15, 1896, as cited and quoted in Bitton, *GQC*, 415–16.

39. *WWJ*, Nov. 26, 1896. Spelling and punctuation corrected.

40. *WWJ*, Nov. 26, 1896.

41. Constance L. Lieber, *Dr. Martha Hughes Cannon: Suffragist, Senator, Plural Wife* (Salt Lake City: Signature Books, 2022).

happened by a razor-thin margin, on the fifty-third ballot, though Cannon was careful not to support any candidate publicly, realizing that his voice would only help Thatcher.[42]

Abram Cannon's death had repercussions for George Q. in financial ways. Abram was working to purchase and rehabilitate a bank called the Utah Loan & Trust Co. of Ogden. After he passed away, a committee led by Franklin S. Richards encouraged George to take Abram's place to calm depositors and protect Abram's estate. The estate would be harmed in two ways if the bank failed: Abram's large stock holdings would be rendered worthless and his estate would be liable to the bank on his $40,000 note. George was too busy with other business matters and declined, even with the risk that failure would be bad for Abram's estate and hard on his widows and children.[43]

Both George and the church were in desperate straits of indebtedness. Another business that Abram had been managing was the Cannon-Grant Company, an investment firm in which George Q. and Heber J. Grant held ownership interests. George had guaranteed $65,000 in this firm, though Abram had been the principal person obligated on the note. This obligation came due, and George, as he did on many debts at the time, found security in the form of stocks or property to secure and extend the debts. Some of the businesses that had been founded, such as the Pioneer Electric Company, had started as businesses unrelated to the church, often with Frank Cannon involved at the beginning. As many individuals were unable to make debt payments, however, George convinced Woodruff that the church would eventually profit by taking an interest and securing the debt. In this way, the church incurred $1.5 million indebtedness on behalf of Pioneer Electric. Under George's oversight, the church had spent hundreds of thousands of dollars on the Sterling gold mine in Nevada, which had not produced much income. The church had developed Saltair and built a railroad from the city to the resort at great expense and was losing money.[44]

Members of the Quorum of the Twelve such as Heber Grant, John W. Taylor, John Henry Smith, and others felt that they had not

42. GQCJ, Jan. 29, 1896; Bitton, *GQC*, 416.
43. GQCJ, Sep. 12, 1896.
44. HJGJ, Jan. 4, 1898.

been consulted much by the First Presidency or, more specifically, by George Q., on these investments and debts. They believed that Woodruff, not being sufficiently sophisticated in business affairs, had relied too heavily on Cannon, who tended to keep his own counsel. Lorenzo Snow, president of the Twelve, appeared to be just as frustrated as the other members of the quorum, though he made it clear that unity among the leaders and quorums was more important than losses. Grant, whose plural wives included a daughter of Daniel H. Wells and sister of Annie and Louie Wells, went further—he found it inappropriate that someone like John Q. Cannon, who had embezzled temple funds while in the Presiding Bishopric and had an adulterous affair, should be the editor of the *Deseret News*. A number of the apostles believed that Frank Cannon, portrayed by several as a "drunkard" and worse, should not be the principal financial and political agent of the church in the East. Some of the more financially adept members of the quorum realized that much or most of the church's financial stresses were the result of the federal government seizing the church's assets and the Panic of 1893, but George Q.'s failure to consult with them, even to "share their financial burdens with the apostles," was the worst part of it.[45]

George recognized that he was being criticized for his financial decision-making, which no doubt contributed to the sleeplessness he complained of when he felt overburdened by the crushing debt incurred by him and the church. In a moment of intense questioning, George wondered in his journal if he had been a "fool." He knew and had always known the "folly of running in debt," but over the few years before he wrote this in September 1896, he had fallen deeply into debt and had led efforts intended to save the church financially but which involved taking on substantial debt. It was almost certainly necessary, given the confiscation by the government of much of the church's real and personal property, the deep financial recession the country was going through, the perceived need to complete the Salt Lake Temple by April 6, 1896, and his close association with many businesses. With his usual sunny disposition, he believed that all would be well through the grace of God and a great deal of hard work.[46]

45. HJGJ, Jan. 4, 1898.
46. GQCJ, Sep. 22, 1896.

The beginning of the Spanish–American War in early 1898 had several effects on George's life. Cannon had seen the results of the Civil War during the time he was in Washington, DC, in the 1860s and as he crossed the country in 1864. His discussions with Thomas Kane, who was wounded in the war, only served to make him dislike war even more. Now, the Spanish–American War tested his view. Both of his two oldest sons weighed in on the war. His son Frank, a US senator, introduced a resolution in the Senate threatening Spain with war if it did not grant the independence of Cuba.[47] The *Deseret News*, which was edited by John Q., published editorials and articles both criticizing and supporting rising war fever.[48] Shortly after writing the editorials, however, John was one of the first Utahns to volunteer for service. He organized Troop I of the United States Volunteers and, as a lieutenant colonel, commanded the second regiment of "Rough Riders," a group from the Intermountain West known as "Torrey's Rough Riders." Although he and his troops languished through a hot summer in Florida and never saw action, Colonel Cannon showed the spark that many had seen in him in earlier days. Idaho US Senator George Laird Shoup, reviewing the Rough Riders, described Cannon as "one of the most striking military figures that I have ever seen and the men who followed him were well worthy of their commander."[49] More directly, George set the tone in general conference for the church's view of war, ending church ambivalence about the United States' involvement: "We should be equally willing, if it should be necessary, to lay down our lives for our country, for its institutions, for the preservation of this liberty that these glorious blessings and privileges shall be preserved to all mankind, and especially to those with whom we are immediately connected."[50]

---

47. D. Michael Quinn, "The Mormon Church and the Spanish–American War: An End to Selective Pacifism," *Dialogue* 17 (Winter 1984): 22–23.

48. "The Maine Disaster," *DN*, Feb. 17, 4; "The Age of Militarism," "The Maine Report," *DN*, Mar. 10, 1898, 4; Mar. 28, 1898, 4; Mar. 10, 1898, 4; "Latter-day Saints and War," *DN*, Mar. 31, 1898, 4; "Christianity and War," *DN*, Apr. 18, 1898, 4; Quinn, "An End of Selective Pacificism," 22, 25, 26

49. KLC, "Wives and Other Women: Love, Sex, and Marriage in the Lives of John Q. Cannon, Frank J. Cannon, and Abraham H. Cannon," *Dialogue* 43 (Winter 2010): 82; "Torrey's Rough Riders, Senator Shoup Visits the Regiment at Jacksonville, Praise for Col. Cannon," *SLT*, July 15, 1898, 2. The First Regiment of Rough Riders, was Theodore Roosevelt's.

50. Quinn, "End of Selective Pacifism," 24–25.

Woodruff's health continued to decline through the early part of 1898, though when he, one of his wives, George and Carlie, and others left for San Francisco in August, Woodruff noted that he hoped George was as well as he was. Each hoped to see his health improve by the ocean. Isaac Trumbo, with whom church leaders had recently entered into a financial settlement, offered his lovely Victorian mansion on Sutter Street and the Woodruffs, the Cannons, and others stayed at the Trumbo residence.

Woodruff seemed to be doing better physically. Trumbo took Woodruff and Cannon to the Bohemian Club for a banquet, and the church leaders met with San Francisco Latter-day Saints. The activities seemed to suggest both men were feeling better—they revisited Golden Gate Park and the Cliff House and, on August 30, even rode on "the Chutes" amusement ride, riding in a boat down a slide and into a lake. George described it as a "very novel" sensation, "especially after striking the water." Two days later, Woodruff's condition began to deteriorate quickly and specialists concluded that Woodruff's kidneys were failing. On the morning of September 2, 1898, with George Q. holding his wrist, Woodruff's pulse became increasingly weak, then "faded entirely." Cannon commented that he had known Woodruff since he was twelve years old, when he visited the Cannons' home in Liverpool, and noted that "I have loved him with great affection."[51]

On September 8, a magnificent funeral with the Tabernacle somberly decorated was held. George Q. was the last and longest speaker. The cortege to the cemetery was long and slow. Woodruff was buried in the Salt Lake Cemetery.

The Quorum of Twelve met on Tuesday, September 13. Initially attending the meeting was Frank J. Cannon to report on his recent trip east regarding financial matters. After his report, George suggested that Lorenzo Snow be appointed "Trustee-in-Trust" to carry on the business of the church, thinking it might be some time before the First Presidency was reorganized. Heber Grant and Franklin D. Richards then suggested that the First Presidency be reorganized immediately. Snow related how he had been discouraged by the

51. GQCJ, Aug. 12, 19–21, 24, 27–30, Sep. 1, 2, 1898.

"load that rested upon him" and had dressed in his temple robes and "sought the mind of the Lord." In answer to his prayer "the Lord had revealed to him that the First Presidency should be organized, and who his counselors should be." George Q. noted in his journal that he did not expect to be retained as a counselor. Snow then announced that the two counselors would be George Q. and Joseph F. Smith, the two who had served in the same positions under John Taylor and Wilford Woodruff. The announcement "met the hearty approval of all present." George "was very much overcome by emotion" and "deeply honored at the new calling." The group then went to the studio of Charles Savage for a group photograph of "14 apostles."[52]

Frank Cannon's description of what happened at the meeting or after—it is not entirely clear when—was that Snow made it clear that "he did not intend to carry out any such plan as we had suggested for the administration of the Church's finances." Snow wanted all the financial "power in the hands of the Prophet, Seer, and Revelator." To Frank, "an autocracy of financial power was confirmed to the President of the Mormon Church at a time when a renewal of prosperity among its people was about to make such power fatal to their powers."[53] One thing that Snow certainly did was to exclude Frank from further involvement with the church's finances.

John Q. Cannon, Abraham H. Cannon, and George Q. Cannon had leased the *Deseret News* from the church in 1892. The paper had not been doing well financially, and the Cannons thought they could turn it around. With Abram's death and John's military service, George was left alone. He had, no doubt, participated in the oversight of the newspaper but had not taken an active role in the day-to-day management or editorial side of the *News*. Within a few weeks of becoming president, Snow announced the church would retake control of the paper and its publishing business. He told George he wanted to make Charles Penrose the editor and, probably, Horace G. Whitney the business manager. The report in the *Salt Lake Herald* on the changes at the *Deseret News* did not mention the

52. GQCJ, Sep. 13, 1898.
53. Cannon and O'Higgins, *Under the Prophet in Utah*, 214–19.

outgoing management but did mention the new editor and business manager and that the paper had approximately $100,000 in debt.[54]

In mid-January 1899, Utah's newly-elected state legislature met to decide if Frank Cannon would be reelected to the US senate. Because of how senate seats are classified, both of Utah's senate seats in 1896 were for a short term. Frank had bolted the national Republican convention in 1897 and joined the Silver Republicans with a few other western Republicans. More important from the standpoint of reelection chances, Frank had opposed the Dingley tariff bill, which was championed by many businessmen in Utah. From the opening of the state legislature's deliberations on the election of a senator, though Frank thought he had eighteen votes (a majority was thirty-two), he never polled more than seven votes on the scores of ballots that were cast. When it was clear that Frank had no chance of being reelected, he rented out the Salt Lake Theatre and gave a grand oration he called "Senatorial Candidates and Pharisees." Those who did stand a chance of winning the election were Democrats Alfred W. McCune, a wealthy mining magnate who was accused of proposing bribes to legislators and others, William H. King, who had been elected as Utah's congressman in 1897, and Orlando W. Powers, a prominent non-Mormon lawyer and judge.[55]

Five weeks after the process began, Lorenzo Snow asked church leaders what they thought of the stalemate in the legislature. He then "slapped me [George Q.] on the knee and said, 'Here is the man that the Lord wants to go to the Senate of the United States. It is the mind and the will of the Lord that George Q. Cannon should be elected United States Senator.'" Most of the leaders happily supported George Q., and they canvassed the legislators. Snow met individually with many legislators. George was more willing to be proposed in 1899, having been told that it was God's will and with Frank having no possible chance at winning. Cannon wrote

54. GQCJ, Nov. 4, 9, 22, Dec. 9, 1898; "Deseret News Change, Arrangements Completed and It Will Take Place Jan. 1, Church Takes Control," *SLH*, Dec. 3, 1898, 1.

55. Val Holley, *Frank J. Cannon: Saint, Senator, Scoundrel* (Salt Lake City: University of Utah Press, 2020), 193–203; Stewart L. Grow, "Utah's Election of 1899: The Election that Failed," *UHQ* 39 (Winter 1971): 30–39; Cannon and O'Higgins, *Under the Prophet in Utah*, 225–33; "Senator Cannon Attacks Mormon Apostles," *SLH*, Feb. 10, 1899, 1, 2.2, 8, 9, 1899.

in his journal, "It has been manifested to me the good I could do if I were elected." At one point, George Q.'s supporters thought they had thirty-one commitments to support him. Frank, who had no chance of winning, refused to ask his sponsors to support his father, believing it would make him "guilty of the very betrayal of the people which I had publicly denounced." George never got more than twenty-three votes, and no one else received enough votes to be elected. Utah was left without a senator for the next two years.[56]

In 1899, George was called upon to make what turned out to be his last lobbying effort in Washington, DC. After statehood, the federal government needed to build a federal post office and courthouse building in Salt Lake City. There were two principal proposed locations: the "*Deseret News* corner" (the southwest corner of South Temple and Main Streets) and a lot owned by the Walker family (the southwest corner of Market and Main Streets, between 300 and 400 South). The Mormons, joined by prominent non-Mormon banker William McCornick, whose bank was on the same block, wanted the federal building to be on the north end of downtown Main Street, across from Temple Square. Most gentiles wanted the federal building on the south end of downtown Main Street, a block from the City and County Building, which had come to be the anchor of the "gentile" end of downtown. The businessmen proposing the *Deseret News* corner site promised they would pay to have the streets surrounding Temple Square paved, and the church offered to donate the site to the federal government. In discussing the issue with Snow, Cannon advised that if the federal government accepted the offer, "we will have a very fine building there. If they do not accept it, we will at least have the credit for having made the offer to the government.[57]

George Q.was designated to go to Washington "to secure the location of the building on that site." George and his friend Hiram Clawson worked together to persuade the government to construct a post office and court building across from Temple Square.

56. Holley, *Frank J. Cannon*, 193–203; Grow, "Senatorial Election of 1899," 35–39; Cannon and O'Higgins, *Under the Prophet in Utah*, 225–33; GQCJ, Feb. 23, 28, Mar. 2, 8, 9, 1899.

57. GQCJ, Jan. 27, 30, 1899.

In Washington, George and Hiram met Heber J. Grant, who also agreed to argue for the *Deseret News* corner site. The three met with the secretary of the treasury and other senior officials at the Treasury Department. The property offered by the church was by far the largest. The federal government chose the Walker site on Market and Main, causing George to muse that federal officials "dare not do anything that would give the Gentiles the least ground for saying that they favored the Mormons. ... I have had a profound desire to show the Administration that we desired as American citizens to always favor the government in every way in our power." The new post office and courthouse building was constructed soon after on Market Street on the gentile end of Main Street.[58]

At about this time, Frank Cannon convinced his father to become involved in Frank's latest get-rich-quick promotion: Charles Tripler's "liquid air" which would power automobiles, generators, and other devices. Tripler had reportedly received an offer for $2.5 million, which he had refused. A current senator and another ex-senator joined Frank in promoting the enterprise, and it was soon capitalized for $10 million. George Q. and Carlie traveled to New York to meet "Prof. Tripler," and they invested. After a brief rise in stock price, the company collapsed.[59]

One of the things that George Q. cared most about was the religious training of young people. He came home from his time as mission president in Europe convinced that young church members, particularly ones who would serve missions, needed better religious training in the scriptures and, as he called them, "first principles." He had organized a Sunday school in his home ward in 1864. The first Sunday school organization in the LDS Church after its move to Utah had been organized in 1849, and now, in October conference 1899, the church celebrated the Sunday school's 50th anniversary with a golden jubilee. Presiding over the festivities was the general superintendent of the Deseret Sunday School Union, George

58. GQCJ, Apr. 26, May 23–24, 25, 1899; "Bids Opened, Twelve Propositions for a Site for Salt Lake Federal Building," *SLT*, May 7, 1899, 1; "Dark Horse Wins Building Site, Walker Location Selected by the Government, *SLH*, May 25, 1899, 8.

59. GQCJ, Sep. 16, 19. Nov. 8, 1899; "Is Going to Europe, Senator Cannon to Leave Today in Interest in New Company," *SLH*, Sep. 23, 1899, 1; "The Tripler Liquid Air Stock," *NYT*, Sep. 2, 1901, 6.

Q. Cannon. By the time the golden jubilee program began at 7:00 p.m., the Tabernacle was filled to overflowing. Bands played, the Tabernacle Choir sang, the leaders of the Sunday school movement were honored, medals were awarded for best hymn, best musical composition (which was won by the Rev. W. Daunt Scott, a local Episcopalian minister), and the Articles of Faith were recited "polyglot," with each Article recited in a different language. Hawaiians living in Iosepa Colony in Tooele County read the fourth article of faith in Hawaiian. George Q. described the jubilee as "the grandest sight we ever had in the Tabernacle" and characterized it as "the crowning consummation of the labor of a great many years."[60]

By 1900, the *Deseret News* press was publishing books as well as the newspaper and George Q. felt uneasy having his company in open competition with a church-owned company. He was probably also tired of trying to keep the business solvent. Part of the challenge with profitability was publication of Orson F. Whitney's *History of Utah*, which took a decade to produce and was published in a handsome four-volume set with gilt-edged pages, wonderful pen and ink illustrations of many prominent Utahns, and leather binding. George offered to have the business valued and to sell it to the church. After haggling between Cannon and Snow over a few details, the business was sold, giving rise to Deseret Book and its ability to trace its pedigree to the 1860s.[61]

As George continued to liquidate assets in an attempt to escape debt before he died, he also transferred the *Juvenile Instructor*, which he founded in 1864 and edited continuously after that, to the Deseret Sunday School Union. He retained ownership of the buildings which had for decades housed the Juvenile Instructor Office (the name of his publishing house for almost thirty years; George Q. Cannon & Sons was not formally created until 1892). George noted in his journal that the business had never been truly profitable, but that there were "some things that are quite regrettable to me in going out of the printing, publishing, book-binding and book-selling business."[62]

Before he died in the summer of 1896, Abram Cannon oversaw

60. GQCJ, Oct. 8, 1899, Golden Jubilee program clipped into ibid.
61. GQCJ, July 20–21, Aug. 7, 1900.
62. GQCJ, Sep. 27, 1900.

the funding and development of a railroad from Salt Lake City to Los Angeles. Negotiations had proceeded with the Oregon Short Line railroad to purchase its rights of way over routes through southern Utah to California. Abram's death had "caused a suspension of everything connected with" the proposed railroad, and George Q. did not have the time or energy to take it on. As a result, David Eccles and Charles Nibley were assigned to pursue the possible development of this railroad. Under their guidance, the Salt Lake-Los Angeles acquired some of the Oregon Short Line's rights and worked with some eastern financiers to borrow the funds necessary to begin pursuing construction.[63] The realities of trying to develop a railroad turned out to be daunting, however. In October 1900, the entire First Presidency sat with Utah Governor Heber M. Wells, Thomas Kearns, and William A. Clark, one of the Montana copper kings, as they told the media that Clark was "fully committed" to the building of a railroad from Salt Lake City to Los Angeles, which ended Abram Cannon's dream of building his own line and George Q.'s vision of employing thousands of Mormon men to construct it. Clark's railway, known as the Salt Lake Route or the Salt Lake-Los Angeles-San Pedro Railroad, benefited when it purchased the assets of the Salt Lake-Los Angeles, on which Abram had worked so hard. The Salt Lake Route was completed in 1905.[64]

Important decisions regarding apostolic seniority in the Quorum of the Twelve were made in early April 1900. Brigham Young Jr. was ordained as an apostle in 1855 and was made a member of the Quorum of Twelve in 1868. Until 1900, Young's seniority in the Quorum was based on his ordination in 1855, which made him senior to George Q. and Joseph F. Smith. Franklin D. Richards was president of the Quorum of the Twelve when he died in December 1899. His death resulted in an examination of whether Young or George, who was made a member of the Quorum of the Twelve in 1860, was the more senior quorum member. On April 5, 1900, President Lorenzo Snow decided that seniority in the quorum would be based on when a man was admitted to the quorum, not when he was ordained an

63. GQCJ, Feb. 8–9, Mar. 29, 1897; Feb. 16, 18, Sept. 28, 1898.

64. GQCJ, Oct. 2, 1900; "Mr. Kearns on New Coast Road," *DN*, Sep. 10, 1900, 2; "The Salt Lake Route," Digital Desert, mojavedesert.net (accessed October 2021).

apostle. This meant that both George Q. and Smith were senior to Young, and that Cannon likely would have been made church president if he had outlived Lorenzo Snow. It also meant that Smith, who did outlive Snow, became church president shortly after Snow's death in October 1901 rather than Young.[65]

In April 1900, George and Carlie traveled to Houston where George attended the Trans-Mississippi Commercial Congress conference. The Utah delegation to the conference was involved, and Cannon was elected as a vice-president-at-large of the organization. From Houston, George Q. and Carlie visited Mexico City for ten days and enjoyed themselves in a different cultural environment. Later in the year, George and Joseph F. Smith were asked by Lorenzo Snow to visit Canada to meet with the Governor-General. Carlie was ill, so George Q. took their daughter, Emily, with him. There, they met the progressive Governor-General, Gilbert John Elliot-Murray-Kynynmound, the Earl of Minto, and his wife regarding disputes the church was having with the Canadian railroad. Lord and Lady Minto traveled the country widely to understand its needs. They journeyed through a horrible storm from Lethbridge, Alberta, to Stirling, a small Mormon village in southern Alberta, to meet with Cannon and other church members. George was favorably impressed by the easy manner and lack of affectation of Lord and Lady Minto.[66] In December 1900, George Q., Carlie, and three Cannon sons travelled to Hawai'i for the golden jubilee of the Hawaiian Mission.

65. Travis Q. Mecham, "Changes in Seniority to the Quorum of Twelve Apostles of The Church of Jesus Christ of Latter-day Saints" (MA thesis, Utah State University, 2009), 45–57; D. Michael Quinn, *Mormon Hierarchy: Extensions of Power* (Salt Lake City: Signature Books, 1997), 647, 718; *JH*, Apr. 5, 1900; GQCJ, Apr. 5, 1900.

66. GQCJ, Apr. 21–May 1, 1900, Sep. 11–20, 1900; "The Earl of Minto," The Governor General of Canada, gg.ca (accessed Dec. 2021). Lord Minto became Viceroy of India after serving as Governor General of Canada.

CHAPTER TEN

FINAL DAYS

"Perhaps the greatest legacy of George Q. Cannon is the astonishing success of Mormonism in the twentieth century. In a fiery crucible of bitter controversy, he was instrumental in forging the faith of modern Latter-day Saints."
—Will Bagley[1]

It was hard for George Q. to board the *S.S. Zealandia* in Honolulu on the afternoon of Saturday, January 5, 1901, to return home. He had spent a month in Hawai'i, remembering his time there fifty years earlier, and now realized he would never be back. He had been feted, honored, and celebrated. More important, the LDS presence in the islands, in which he played such a prominent role, was celebrated by thousands of Saints. He had been able to show three of his sons where he had lived, preached, and baptized for three and a half years. He spent almost a week on Maui, where his most intense Hawaiian memories were focused. He had been treated to festive dinners "with the greatest hospitality." Now he and family members who came with him were covered with leis that the throngs of well-wishers had draped around their necks. A local newspaper noted that "when the white-haired old gentleman boarded the steamer, he staggered under the weight of the leis upon him."[2]

1. Will Bagley, general editor's foreword in Roger Robin Ekins, *Defending Zion: George Q. Cannon and the California Mormon Newspaper Wars of 1856–57* (Norman, OK: Arthur H. Clark Co., 2002), 16.

2. GQCJ, Dec. 17–31, 1900, Jan. 1–5, 1901; "Mr. Cannon Departs," *Honolulu Republican*, Jan. 6, 1901, 1; "Mormon Party Left for Home," *Pacific Commercial Advertiser*, Jan. 7, 1901, 11.

The voyage took a week, and the party arrived in San Francisco on Sunday, January 13. George visited several people there. He finished the day attending an LDS meeting in a "well-filled" rented hall that evening where he spoke for forty minutes. He and his family stayed in the Palace Hotel, and the next morning he and Isaac Trumbo went to the Southern Pacific offices to retrieve passes for the train ride home in a sleeper car.[3]

The train arrived in Salt Lake City two days later at 8:30 a.m. on January 16. George was scheduled to give a speech to the Trans-Mississippi Livestock Convention at 10:00 a.m. He let the president of the convention know that he would not be able to speak. The president informed him that they needed him to speak, and they postponed his speech to 11:30 a.m. Exhausted and not feeling well, George nevertheless initially spoke for thirty-five minutes and "felt very free" in his remarks. When he finished and turned to sit down, "cries from all parts of the house" encouraged him to "go on." He did and received a "hearty" applause from the audience when he finished.[4]

Since George and his party were out of town on January 11, his seventy-fourth birthday, the annual family celebration was held on January 19. The celebration took place at Martha Telle Cannon's house and attracted many of George's children and grandchildren for the dinner and program that always made him exultant.[5]

Cannon continued to spend time in church work, creating three LDS stakes from one in Cache Valley. Having spent time researching early church documents in the preparation of books he had written, particularly *The Life of Joseph Smith the Prophet*, George obtained approval for the preparation of what the First Presidency agreed to call *The History of the Church of Jesus Christ of Latter-day Saints*, known colloquially as the *Documentary History of the Church*. It appears that George planned to compile this or to oversee the work himself, but it was eventually undertaken and completed by B. H. Roberts.[6]

In February, the First Presidency, at George's urging, decided to

3. GQCJ, Jan. 6, 13–14, 1901; "Personal Mention," *San Francisco Call*, Jan. 14, 1901, 4.
4. GQCJ, Jan. 16, 1901.
5. Bitton, *GQC*, 445.
6. JH, Jan. 31, 1901, 1, Feb. 5, 1901, 2; B. H. Roberts, ed., *Joseph Smith, History of the Church of Jesus Christ of Latter-day Saints, Period I, History of Joseph Smith, the Prophet*, 7 vols., 2nd ed. (Salt Lake City: Deseret Book Co., 1973).

open a mission in Japan. George announced it to the Quorum of the Twelve. Heber J. Grant recorded that immediately he "felt impressed that I would be called to open up this mission, and I said to myself, 'O Lord, I will make no excuses.'"[7] Grant was called; he hurriedly resolved some pressing financial issues and served for two years as mission president.[8]

George had an attack of the "grippe" (influenza) in early March, and health complications ensued just at the time that the Southern Pacific Railroad announced publicly that he was to be named to the railroad's board of directors. Cannon had a sense that he would not last much longer, so he instructed family lawyer and nephew, John M. Cannon, to prepare a last will and testament. The will provided broadly for distribution of his assets to his wives and children. It also provided that the executors were authorized to withhold distributions, in their discretion, if in their judgment any son is "improvident or is given to drinking intoxicating liquor or gaming so as to make it unwise to place said legacy at his … disposal."[9]

George's health continued to deteriorate. On March 13, 1901, he traveled to the Bay Area to see if the climate might provide some help. He, Carlie, two of their young children (Anne and Georgius), and his twenty-year-old son, Preston, with Sarah Jane, took a sleeper car to San Francisco, where they were given a suite of rooms in the hotel. That day, George Q. felt well enough to take a carriage ride through Golden Gate Park and to visit the beach. Heber Grant and nephew George Cannon Lambert were in town, and they visited and, with Preston, administered to George. Cannon decided he would be more comfortable in Monterey and began to be attended

7. Bitton, *GQC*, 446; HJGJ, Feb. 14, 1901.

8. Ronald W. Walker, "Strangers in a Strange Land: Heber J. Grant and the Opening of the Japan Mission," *BYUS* 43 (Winter 2004): 231–62.

9. "George Q. Cannon Named to Be One of the Southern Pacific Directors," *SLH*, Mar. 8, 1901, 2; "Last Will and Testament," set forth in full in Bitton, *GQC*, 465–70, at 466, paragraph e,. Frank Cannon's biographer suggests that the executors withheld distributions from Frank for, at least, "another quarter century," based on a 1905 statement in a letter to his friend Fred Dubois with no citation to a later resolution of Frank's inheritance, as well as a 1905 statement in Salt Lake City made by reformer and friend of Frank, Hannah Kent Schoff, who, in the same speech said that Frank had been disinherited and was at high risk of being assassinated. Val Holley, *Frank J. Cannon, Saint, Senator, Scoundrel* (Salt Lake City: University of Utah Press, 2020), 214–15, 217, 262.

by Dr. Frederic Clift, an LDS physician from St. George who was serving as a missionary in California. George also summoned his close friend Charles H. Wilcken, who had been a regular companion and caregiver to George for many years. On March 18, the entire party left San Francisco for Monterey, where they checked into the Hotel Del Monte, the magnificent hotel George had admired while traveling with Wilford Woodruff in 1896.[10]

Information that the world's best-known Mormon was ailing had been noted in Salt Lake City by the *Tribune* on March 10 and the *Salt Lake Herald* on March 13, with brief mentions that George was going to California to improve his health. On March 30, the *Deseret News* provided more information based on a telegraph from Wilcken. At this time, the matter seemed serious, and the *New York Times*, which had once devoted half of a front page to Cannon, began tracking him in a short front-page article stating that "George Q. Cannon, First Vice President and real head of the Mormon Church, is critically ill at the Hotel Del Monte, Monterey."[11]

Cannon was often confined to his bed but could not sleep. Carlie, Wilcken, and Preston took turns during the night reading to him. George showed his constant interest in his children when he wrote that he "was much gratified" at the news that his and Elizabeth's twenty-five-year-old daughter, Emily, was engaged to Israel E. Willey. On March 24, Dr. Clift visited and was sufficiently concerned that he remained with George. On March 27, George and his party moved to "Finch Cottage ... [which] is admirably located on a hill overlooking Monterey Bay." The next day, he felt so miserable that he telegraphed his oldest son, John Q., and lawyer-nephew, John M., to come to Monterey at once so he could talk "to them about my affairs." The two Johns also brought George's son Hugh with them. George revised his will with John M, adding his and Elizabeth's adopted daughter Rosina, his granddaughter Marba (Abram and Lillian Hamlin's daughter), brothers and sisters, and Wilcken as beneficiaries. On April 5, a specialist, Dr. Hosford, joined Dr. Clift

10. GQCJ, Mar. 12–18, 1901.

11. "Personal Mention," *SLT*, Mar. 10, 1901, 4; "Personal Mention," *SLH*, Mar. 14, 1901, 8; "A Restless Night," *DN*, Mar. 30, 1901, 1; "George Q. Cannon III," *NYT*, Mar. 29, 1901, 1.

and began working to reduce the swelling of Cannon's extremities. Frank was in Washington, DC, when he received the news of his father's illness and left immediately, arriving on April 7. Lying in his bed on this day, George took John Q., Frank, Hugh, and Wilcken each individually by the hand and gave each a special blessing. He thanked each for the "comfort and pleasure they afforded him." This was his last journal entry; he was not able to dictate further.[12]

The specialist's treatment provided George some relief, but the pain and swelling returned. Finally, at 1:20 a.m. on the morning of April 12, 1901, George Q. Cannon passed away. Carlie, sons John Q., Frank J., and Hugh J., and Wilcken accompanied the body home to Utah.[13] The train was delayed ten hours by an unrelated accident on the tracks involving a freight train. Even so, hundreds of family members and friends met the train at the station.

After a private meeting with family, church leaders, and close friends at the Cannon farm, the public funeral was held with over 11,000 people crammed into the Tabernacle, while thousands more waited outside on Temple Square. The program of the funeral represented many things that were important to George Q. Remarks were given by George Teasdale representing the Deseret Sunday School Union, Heber J. Grant representing the Young Men's Mutual Improvement Association, George Brimhall representing Brigham Young Academy, Brigham Young Jr. representing the Quorum of Twelve Apostles, and Joseph F. Smith representing the First Presidency. Church President Lorenzo Snow was too ill to attend but had his son, Le Roi, read his remarks. Joseph F. Smith noted Cannon's "great intelligence," great wisdom, and "sterling integrity," but also that "there was something about him that inspired respect and confidence and love." Smith continued, "The uppermost thought in his life seemed to be the establishment of righteousness and truth on the earth and dissemination of the gospel." All the speakers showered the deceased Cannon with praise and extolled his life and accomplishments. After the funeral, a long cortege followed South Temple Street east as 20,000 people lined the streets honoring the

12. GQCJ, Mar. 19–Apr. 7, 1901.

13. "Apostle George Q. Cannon's Body Borne to the Old Homestead," *SLH*, Apr. 16, 1901, 2.

deceased church leader. It took an hour for all the carriages in the cortege to make the two-mile journey to the Salt Lake Cemetery. George was buried next to his first wife, Elizabeth.

George Q. Cannon was an extraordinary man. His influence on the administration, policy, theology, political positions, and culture of his church were deep and lasting. He was charming, charismatic, self-confident, engaging, and positive. He had a cheerful disposition that, even when he spent sleepless nights worrying about financial matters or defending his faith or his seat in Congress, invariably showed through.

George had seemingly boundless energy—physical, mental, psychic. He attended many meetings each week: board meetings, leadership meetings, church meetings, civic meetings, and personal interviews. He was often the main speaker at public events at a time when speeches lasting an hour or longer were not artificially amplified. He attended parties, plays, museums, exhibits, and historic sites. His curiosity and interests were also broad—in 1863, he attended a reading by Charles Dickens in which the great novelist spoke in eight or nine voices depicting his own characters. George was a royals watcher and made sure he saw the Duke of York, later King George V, and his new wife, Princess Mary of Teck, in London in 1893, and he reviewed the rooms where the Prince of Wales and Princess Alexandra had been wed in the royal wedding of the century in 1863.[14]

Although he did not receive formal education beyond the age of thirteen, George educated himself through reading many newspapers, books of nonfiction, and even fiction. Through effort, he made himself into a writer and editor and edited the *Western Standard*, the *Deseret News*, and the *Juvenile Instructor*. He also wrote a number of books, long essays, and pamphlets.

He was a skilled diplomat. Upon his death, the *New York Times* said of him, "When Utah was admitted to the Union Mr. Cannon was one of the prime negotiators. It was a task that required superb diplomacy, but after five years of effort Utah became a state."[15]

Utah's first governor, Heber M. Wells, whose family harbored bad feelings toward the Cannons for some time after the John Q. Cannon–Louie Wells imbroglio, called George "a loving, indulgent

14. GQCJ, Mar. 11, 13, Sep. 28, 1863.
15. "George Q. Cannon Dead," *NYT*, Apr. 13, 1901, 9.

father and an affectionate and loyal father."[16] It is hard to believe that a polygamist with five wives and thirty-three living natural and adopted children at the time of his death could be called an affectionate and loyal father, but he was. Each wife felt that she only had a piece of him, but they all loved him and he loved all of them and worked hard to maintain a relationship with each.

Perhaps the defining characteristic of George Q. Cannon was his lack of fear. He knew every president of the United States from Abraham Lincoln through William McKinley, and was not intimidated by any of them. He sought out congressmen, senators, presidents, cabinet members, a prime minister, editors, and titans of industry and finance. When each of his elections to Congress was contested, he aggressively defended himself with zeal and persuasive arguments.

George was loyal—to family, to faith, to friends—and expected the same from others. He had little to no respect for those who attacked the church, its leaders, and him with no basis in fact. He did not like people he believed to be "apostates," ones who, having believed that the doctrines of the LDS Church were revealed truth from God at one point, turned from their faith and attacked the religion they once embraced. He defended his faith in the *Western Standard*, the *Deseret News*, and in pamphlets and essays, and in speeches in congress, the Tabernacle, and other places.

George was direct and, in most ways, scrupulously honest. When church leaders encouraged him to deny that the temple endowment included an oath that required higher loyalty to church than state, he replied that the ceremony had included such an oath when he was endowed in Nauvoo.[17]

Where George was not particularly transparent was in the secretive continued practice of plural marriage after the 1890 Manifesto. As an "ultra" polygamist, he felt a need to continue the practice after 1890 and he masterminded means of doing so until his death in 1901.

George had flaws. He once wrote, "Have I imperfections? I am full of them."[18] He could be overly protective of his children. He was sometimes difficult to deal with in connection with financial matters,

16. "Tributes to the Dead Apostle," *SLH*, Apr. 13, 1901, 1.
17. GQCJ, Dec. 6, 1889.
18. *MS*, Apr. 23, 1894, 260.

particularly if he was feeling indebted. He could be unforgiving and maintain grudges for years. He could be unpleasant in his written criticisms of others. In noting the death of his longtime friend and colleague, Brigham Young Jr. recorded in his diary: "A great man has fallen in Israel. Remarkable in his generation, thank heaven he had faults or he would not have remained among us so long."[19]

George could also be funny. While he was avoiding arrest for unlawful cohabitation (polygamy), he needed to see Hiram Clawson as soon as possible on a matter of some urgency. Cannon "disguised myself in a blue drilling jumper and pants, and with a blackened beard and a large, flapping Panama hat, [that] I might go undetected." Four separate members of the Quorum of the Twelve saw him "and said it was no disguise; they would know my face anywhere—thanks to my prominent nose and eyes."[20] In a famous penitentiary photograph, George colored his hair and beard as an inside joke to himself, remembering his unsuccessful attempts to avoid arrest by disguising himself. At a family gathering in 1894, George sang a song and recited a slightly bawdy Irish ballad, *Phaudrig Crohoore*.[21] Once, traveling through Chicago, he registered at a hotel to take a bath. The clerk asked, "What! Is this the famous Mr. Cannon of Utah?" Cannon deadpanned in response, "I am Mr. Cannon from Utah, whether I am famous or not."[22]

Younger apostles worried that George wanted to be church president and that he sometimes attempted to exercise all of the powers of the president. Cannon certainly liked to have his way and could be very persuasive. Newspapers always assumed he was the real power in the LDS Church.[23] But he always ultimately deferred to the president of the church for guidance and the final decision.

Cannon's adult life reads like a general history of the LDS Church. He was centrally involved in virtually every important event and

19. Brigham Young Jr. Diary, Apr. 16, 1901, CHL.

20. GQCJ, Sep. 15, 1885.

21. GQCJ, Apr. 13, 1894.

22. GQCJ, July 3, 1882.

23. "George Q. Cannon III," *NYT*, Mar. 30, 1901, 1; "George Q. Cannon Dead," *NYT*, Apr. 13, 1901, 9; "Condition of Apostle Cannon Is Improved," *San Francisco Chronicle*, Apr. 8, 1901, 3; "Mormon President Cannon Here," *Hawaiian Gazette*, Dec. 11, 1900, 4; "Mormon Jubilee," *Pacific Commercial Advertiser*, Dec. 12, 1900, 1.

movement and change from the mid-nineteenth century through the beginning of the new century. His imprint on that history is extraordinary. He was complex, powerful, ambitious, and driven, but he generally sought to put the interests of his church and its members before himself. He spent much of his adult life defending his faith and his people and pursuing ends that would benefit them. He sought to associate and worked well with allies and advisors who helped him defend the church and its precepts or to attain important goals such as statehood. George Q. Cannon left a legacy that continues to affect many lives today.

APPENDIX

GEORGE Q. CANNON'S WIVES AND CHILDREN

Wife, Child	Born	Married/Comment	Died
Elizabeth Hoagland	Nov. 3, 1835	Dec. 11, 1854	Jan. 25. 1882
Rosina M. Cannon	Oct. 8, 1852	Adopted*	Dec. 18, 1939
George Q. Cannon, Jr.	Jan. 29, 1856		Nov. 14, 1856
John Q. Cannon	Apr 19, 1857		Jan. 14, 1931
Abraham H. Cannon	Mar. 12, 1859		July 19, 1896
Georgiana H. Cannon	May 19, 1861		Sep. 2, 1863
George H. Cannon	May 21, 1863		Dec. 29, 1863
Elizabeth H. Cannon	Dec. 8, 1865		Apr. 26, 1867
Mary Alice Cannon	Oct. 16, 1867		Mar. 1, 1909
Lillian Ann H. Cannon	Oct. 16, 1869		Oct. 30, 1870
David H. Cannon	Apr. 14, 1871		Oct. 17, 1892
Emily H. Cannon	June 13, 1874		Dec. 13, 1955
Sylvester Q. Cannon	June 10, 1877		May 29, 1939
Sarah Jane Jenne	Sep. 11, 1839	Apr. 11, 1858	May 13, 1928
Franklin J. Cannon	Jan. 25, 1859		July 25, 1933
Angus J. Cannon	Oct. 31, 1867		Mar. 19, 1957
Hugh J. Cannon	Jan. 19, 1870		Oct. 6, 1931
Rosannah J. Cannon	June 29, 1872		Jan. 5. 1969
Joseph J. Cannon	May 22, 1877		Nov. 5, 1945
Preston J. Cannon	Apr. 12, 1881		Oct. 9, 1941
Karl Q. Cannon	Apr. 24, 1881	Adopted**	Nov. 19, 1934
Eliza L. Tenney	Feb. 9, 1845	July 29, 1865	Apr. 17, 1908
William T. Cannon	Sep. 5, 1870		May 21, 1949
Read T. Cannon	May 12, 1875		Aug. 2, 1905
Edwin Q. Cannon	Sep. 7, 1886		Aug. 3, 1971

Wife, Child	Born	Married/Comment	Died
Martha Telle	May 28, 1846	Mar. 16, 1868	Feb. 5, 1928
Hester T. Cannon	Feb. 16, 1870		Oct. 26, 1936
Amelia T. Cannon	Feb. 16, 1870		Jan. 17, 1937
Lewis T. Cannon	Apr. 22, 1872		Oct. 10, 1946
Brigham T. Cannon	Aug. 3, 1874		Nov. 9, 1954
Willard T. Cannon	June 20, 1877		Dec. 29, 1937
Grace T. Cannon	Jan. 1, 1880		Oct. 4, 1945
Radcliffe Q. Cannon	Aug. 1, 1883		Apr. 7, 1961
Espey T. Cannon	June 16, 1886		July 24, 1971
Collins T. Cannon	July 31, 1888		May 28, 1961
Emily Hoagland	Sep. 20, 1837	July 11, 1881	Nov. 15, 1906
Caroline Y. Cannon	Feb. 1, 1851	Nov. 3, 1884	July 2, 1903
Emily Ada Cannon	Aug. 13, 1870	Adopted***	Mar. 9, 1966
Caroline Y. Cannon	July 2, 1875	Adopted***	Feb. 11, 1955
Mark Y. Croxall	Oct. 4, 1877	Adopted***	Nov. 1, 1956
Tracy Y. Cannon	July 23, 1879	Adopted***	Nov. 6, 1961
Vera Y. Cannon	Oct. 13, 1881	Adopted***	Sep. 9, 1968
Clawson Y. Cannon	Oct. 27, 1885		Nov. 7, 1977
Wilford Y. Cannon	July 4, 1888		Mar. 8, 1974
Anne Y. Cannon	July 13, 1890		Oct. 1, 1937
Georgius Y. Cannon	Mar. 6, 1892		Mar. 29, 1987

* English girl adopted by George Q. and Elizabeth Hoagland Cannon.

** Illegitimate son of Frank J. Cannon; raised as a twin brother of Preston J. Cannon.

*** Children of Caroline Young Croxall and Mark Croxall, whom GQC adopted but who were not sealed to him because their biological parents had been sealed for time and eternity and the children were therefore "born under the covenant." GQCJ, Mar. 17, 1888.

ACKNOWLEDGEMENTS

I first asked for access to George Q. Cannon's journals at the archives of the Church of Jesus Christ of Latter-day Saints over forty years ago. I had to wait a long time, but was pleasantly surprised when in 1999 the church began publishing heavily annotated copies of his early mission journals. In 2016 the Church Historian's Press imprint began releasing his important later journals online. This online roll-out was completed in June 2018, not long before I was invited to write this book. Crafting an insightful biography of Cannon without access to his journals would be nigh impossible, and I deeply appreciate not only the release of the journals but the professional way in which they have been issued. It is no surprise that Davis Bitton, formerly Assistant LDS Church Historian, was permitted to review most if not all of the journals for his groundbreaking (though limited) biography of Cannon. It is a formidable task to attempt to tackle, even in small part, the detailed journals that George Q. kept for most of the time from October 1849, when he was called on his first mission as a gold miner to California at the age of twenty-two, to his death in April 1901; his books (he wrote at least seven and more, depending on how one defines "book"); the published materials related to his contested congressional elections and important legislative and legal issues; the thousands of editorials, articles, and essays in newspapers, magazines, and pamphlets; and the thousands more of sermons and speeches, a significant number of which have been published. Cannon lived a big life that was sometimes controversial. There are relatively few people to whom the *New York Times* has devoted three full front-page columns with four more columns on page 2 as it did in an article on February 13, 1895, about how Cannon had allegedly sold out Utah and much of the Intermountain West to the Republicans. The sheer volume of George Q.'s own writings and speeches and the writings about him create significant challenges to finding the essence of this gifted, energetic, complicated, faithful man. It has been my pleasure to try to introduce George Q. Cannon in an informative, sympathetic, human way.

I thank Gary James Bergera, who asked me to write a short biography of George Q. for Signature Books and who has been helpful and encouraging all along the way. Gary also significantly improved the readability and continuity of the manuscript through his edits. John Hatch further carefully edited the manuscript, forcing me to fill in some holes in the life of Cannon and further improving the flow of the book. I am grateful for John's substantial contribution. I am deeply indebted to Connie Holbrook and Geoffrey Cannon for painstakingly and critically reading two full drafts of the manuscript, challenging descriptions and conclusions and choice of narrative points and working hard to make me exercise care to provide as objective a view of the people and times in the book as possible. Their suggestions and edits were extremely helpful. Above all, I thank Ann Edwards Cannon for supporting me in my historical studies and meanderings (and everything else) for the last forty-six years and providing exceptional editorial and substantive criticism and help to my work. Any mistakes and misinterpretations are my own.

INDEX